IMAGES
of America

WILLINGTON

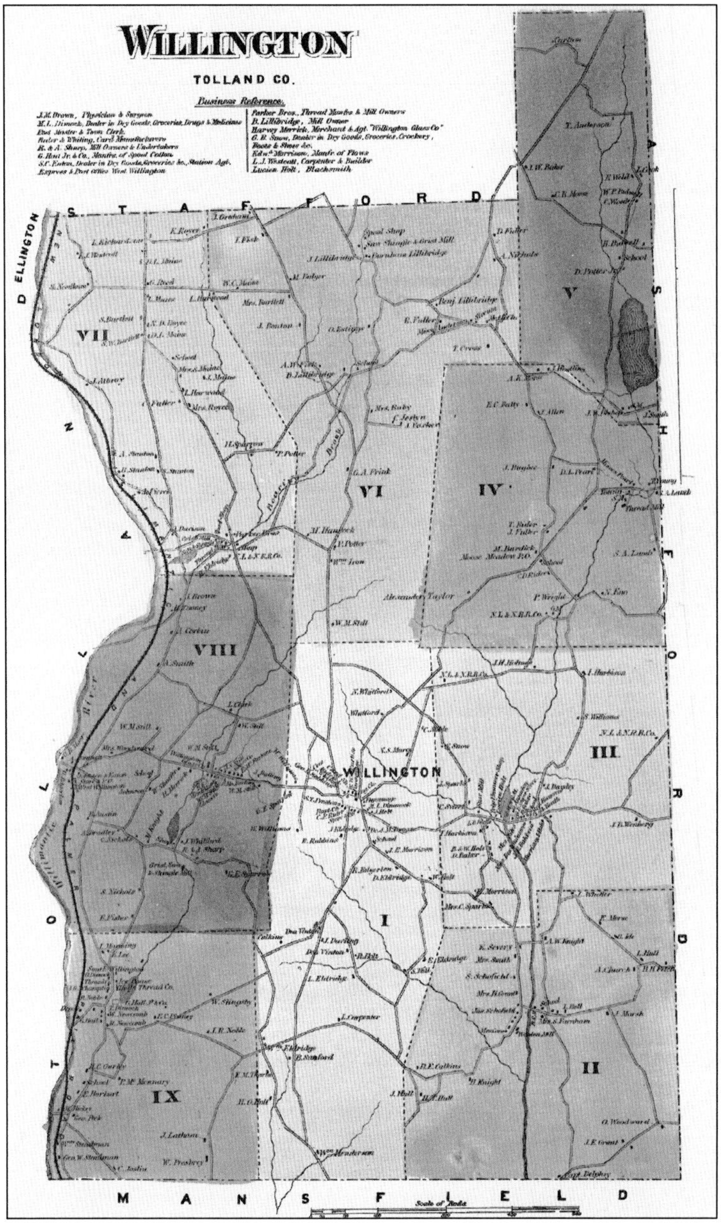

This map of Willington, estimated to be from 1869, is divided by the numbers of the school districts that once existed in the town. It is measured in rods, evidencing that it was created before the use of miles became prevalent (there are about 320 rods per mile). The map notes the names of homeowners, a railroad track, and various businesses and service providers. (Courtesy of the Willington Historical Society.)

On the Cover: The number of employees posing inside and outside of the mill for this undated photograph of the Hall Thread Company in South Willington speaks volumes about the importance of this industry to Willington's economy. Gardiner Hall Jr. persevered despite challenges caused by the Civil War, fire, and lightning. The company provided employment for many residents from 1860 through its 1954 closing. (Courtesy of the Willington Historical Society.)

IMAGES
of America

WILLINGTON

Joe and Trish Froehlich for the
Willington Historical Society

ARCADIA
PUBLISHING

ISBN 978-1-4671-2107-1

Published by Arcadia Publishing
Charleston, South Carolina

Printed in the United States of America

Library of Congress Control Number: 2013945887

For all general information, please contact Arcadia Publishing:
Telephone 843-853-2070
Fax 843-853-0044
E-mail sales@arcadiapublishing.com
For customer service and orders:
Toll-Free 1-888-313-2665

Visit us on the Internet at www.arcadiapublishing.com

This book is dedicated to the memory of Isabel Weigold.
Without her research, the authors could not have completed this project.

Contents

ACKNOWLEDGMENTS

Before moving to Willington in 2002, the authors knew nothing about the town or the Willington Historical Society. Their first exposure came during the 2002 flea market on the town green. Isabel Weigold and Betty Robertson staffed the historical society's booth, wearing old-fashioned, floor-length dresses and bonnets. Their warm welcome quickly persuaded the authors to buy a book and a map of old Willington and become members of the historical society. Careers, family, hobbies, and a new home, however, prevented the authors from doing anything more than framing the map for display in their home office until 2012, when Joe Froehlich was appointed town historian and they truly began exploring Willington's history. The authors are in awe of and appreciate the extensive research that Isabel Weigold conducted, and they regret that, other than that chance meeting, they never had the opportunity to speak with her again. It is the work of Isabel Weigold, Ronald Demers, and Marion Doran that forms the foundation of this project.

Much appreciation goes to the Willington Historical Society's president, Robert Shabot; the society's membership; and the many Willington residents, past and present, who have shared their time, memories, and photographs, especially centenarian Esther Phelps. Unless otherwise noted, all images appear courtesy of the Willington Historical Society.

The authors are especially grateful to town clerk Donna Hardie; assistant town clerk Maureen Gantick; first selectman Christina B. Mailhos; her administrative assistant, Robin B. Campbell; Wilbur Gangaway, president of the Willington Senior Center; and Isabel Wiegold's son Paul, who carries on his mother's mission of preserving and documenting Willington's history.

The authors would like to thank the members of the Federated Church of Willington, not only for their assistance in providing historical data but also for their weekly encouragement of this project. Dawn Yedziniak's willingness to share details about the Czechoslovak Society of America and its bungalow was instrumental to the authors. It was the Saturday morning that Brenda LaFemina-Weber spent sharing her memories and photographs that sparked the authors' combined energies and ignited their commitment to documenting Willington's history of fellowship with this book.

Introduction

Willington, once known as Wellington, is approximately 20 miles northeast of Hartford, Connecticut's capital, which allows residents of this rural community easy access to the government functions, insurance industry, and entertainment venues that Hartford offers. Many choose, however, to remain in town and avoid the congestion and traffic of the city. Willington was established in 1727, and the Connecticut General Assembly based its decision to allow incorporation on the size of its population. There were 592 inhabitants at that time; today, there are closer to 6,000 people living in Willington. Roger Wolcott, one of Willington's original landowners, later became the governor of Connecticut.

Although Connecticut no longer has county government, Willington is located in Tolland County. Its 33.5 square miles are bordered to the north by the towns of Stafford and Union, to the west by the towns of Tolland and Ellington, to the south by the town of Mansfield, and to the east by the town of Ashford. Willington is separated from Tolland by the Willimantic River. The Fenton River flows from the northeast corner of Willington into Bissonnette Pond and then southwest through town into Mansfield. Quintessential country roads are dotted with homes dating to the 18th and 19th centuries. The names on current street signs spring to life when one makes even a cursory review of Willington history and sees the same names on class pictures, minutes of town meetings, and programs from local events. Potter, Eldredge, Fermier, Bidwell, Balazs, Schofield, and Ruby Roads are examples of these family names.

The town common is at the intersection of what are currently known as Routes 74 and 320 and Jared Sparks and Common Roads. There is some indication that the Underground Railroad during the Civil War passed through this section of Willington. Route 74 was once known as Route 44; today, the two roads intersect in neighboring Ashford. The common is framed by the old town hall, which was originally the Congregational church; the new Congregational church, built in 1829, which is now known as the Hill Church; private homes; and the Daniel Glazier Tavern, which the Willington Historical Society is restoring for use as its museum. There are no shops, restaurants, businesses, or parking lots. It remains a traditional New England gathering space for community events, minus the small businesses that dotted the green in the 1700s. The common is part of the town's historic district and has been in the National Register of Historic Places since December 18, 1990.

In some ways, the Willington of yesteryear was more developed than it is today. At one time, there were post offices in the East Willington, Moose Meadow, South Willington, West Willington, and Willington Hill sections of town; today, residents are hopeful that the one post office in town will remain open. It had a police constable, whereas now there is no organized police department. The Connecticut State Police from Troop C in nearby Tolland regularly patrol the area and respond to calls for emergency assistance. Willington once had the benefit of passenger rail and stagecoach service, but passenger trains no longer service Willington, nor is there commercial bus service. The rest area on Interstate 84 and the large truck stop are convenient for those traveling through Connecticut to or from New York and Massachusetts and beyond.

Willington's current residents take pride in its forests and work to preserve the land; one resident has even noted that Willington is home because there are more trees than people. The current interest in preservation is so strong that many citizens recently opposed the erection of a cellular telephone tower that will be visible from the town green. Undeterred by the reality that signs of modern technology will eventually be visible from the green, the historical society requested that the owner of the tower at least cloak the upper portion in greenery so that it does not detract from the peacefulness of the historical district in which the green is located.

Willington's early industry included the manufacture of thread, buttons, and glass. Rare bottles from the West Willington Glassworks (1814–1872) are featured in the Museum of Connecticut Glass, located in nearby Coventry. Willington currently has no chain stores or strip malls. There is a large ground-shipping center. The recent proposal to add another truck stop on the westbound side of Interstate 84 created controversy among some residents. There is a small shopping plaza, and the award-winning Willington Pizza House features a photograph of the historical building and its original owner on the cover of its menu and is known throughout the state. The former West Willington railroad depot served as a bank in the 1970s and is now home to David Wright Jewelers. The surrounding property is home to the popular Track Nine Diner, which was once a post office and general store. The former home of postmaster Hans Hanson and the birthplace of centenarian Esther Hanson Phelps is now the All in All Pastime and Curiosity Shop.

Many residents are direct descendants of the town's forefathers, some of whom participate in the Willington Historical Society and some of whom worship at the Clara Hall Elliott Memorial Church, named in honor of a member of one of Willington's earliest manufacturing families. One woman proudly announces that she is a Hall, while another smiles shyly as she acknowledges that she is an Eldredge and that her family came to "the colonies" on the second voyage of the *Mayflower*. Another woman shares that her grandmother was sent off to live in New York City when, as a young, unwed woman, she became pregnant, which was scandalous in 1930 but is a commonplace and acceptable choice for young women in this 21st century.

Willington became home to many citizens of Czechoslovakia, and the hardworking immigrants formed their own clubhouse, which was used for weddings and parties and as an entertainment venue. The current owners of the former Czechoslovak Society of America's clubhouse have lovingly preserved the ticket booth in what is now their home. They have also maintained the raised stage, the trap door to the basement, and the membership plaques that adorned the walls of the clubhouse entrance.

This work is not intended to be an in-depth study of Willington's geography, its citizens, or its political, religious, or social history. Instead, it is a pictorial invitation to whet the reader's appetite; to honor the talents, energy, and determination that created and maintain this New England community. Variations in the spellings of names and places result from differences in handwritten records from the 1700s and 1800s. Individual perceptions and memories of events and personalities differ, and opinions regarding the impact of business and economy throughout the years vary. This book is a collection of those perceptions and memories and a celebration of the people who have given Willington its vitality.

One

Center School District

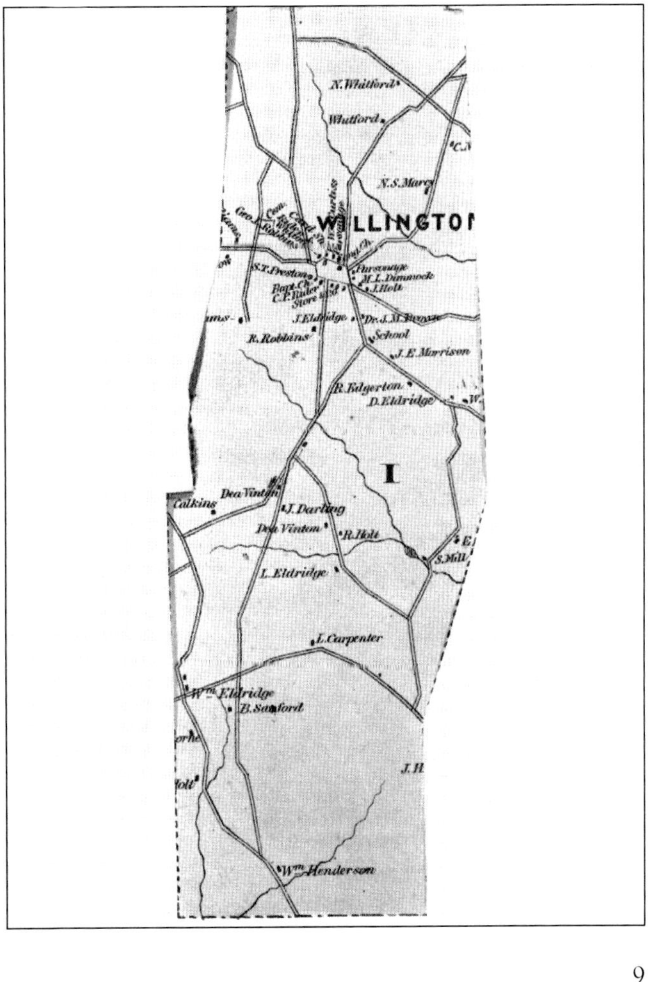

Willington's town common, or town green, is located almost centrally between Willington's west and east borders and slightly south of center between its north and south borders. The homes that currently surround the green date to the 1700s and 1800s, including one that is known as the oldest house in Willington. The Willington Historical Society's future home, at the western end of the green, was once the Daniel Glazier Tavern.

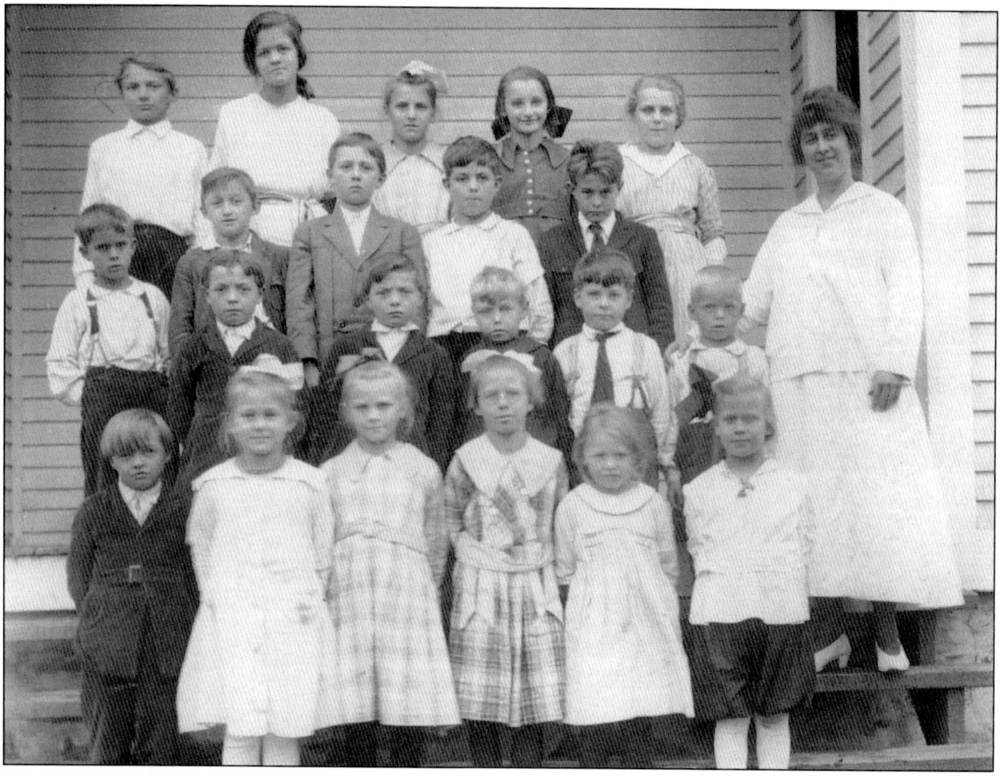

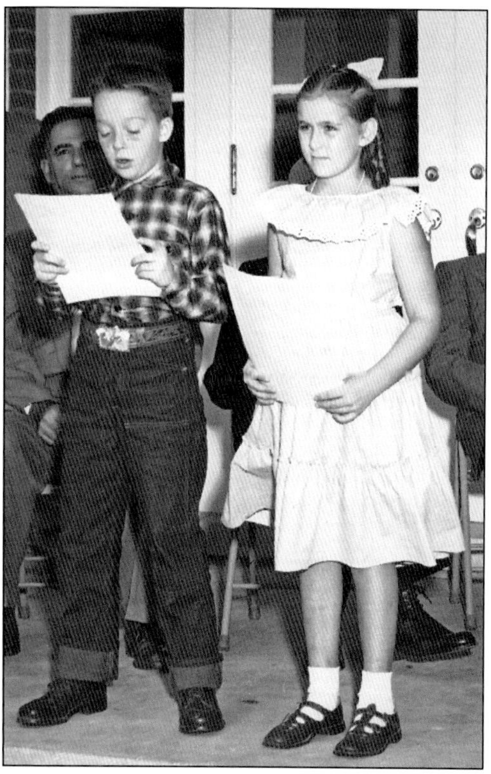

The 1919 Center School class included, from left to right, (first row) Joe Cavar, ? Pokorny, Carrie Pelican, Susie Cavar, Carrie Zizka, and Ethel Wraight; (second row) John Cavar, Mike Cavar, Teddy Krivanec, Joe Fliegel, Oliver Davis, and teacher Mrs. Gahan; (third row) Frank Davis, Frank Parizek, Otto Vonasek, Harvey Davis, and Clarke Ruby; (fourth row) Frank Felix, Ruth Davis, Rose Pelican, Emily Burns, and Caroline Mirtl.

The Center School was originally built in 1791 on Old Farms Road, where St. Jude's Church is currently located. In about 1910, that building was moved on logs to what is now Route 74. Here, Robert Lee and Pamela Moss participate in the dedication of the new Center School, once again on Old Farms Road, in September 1953.

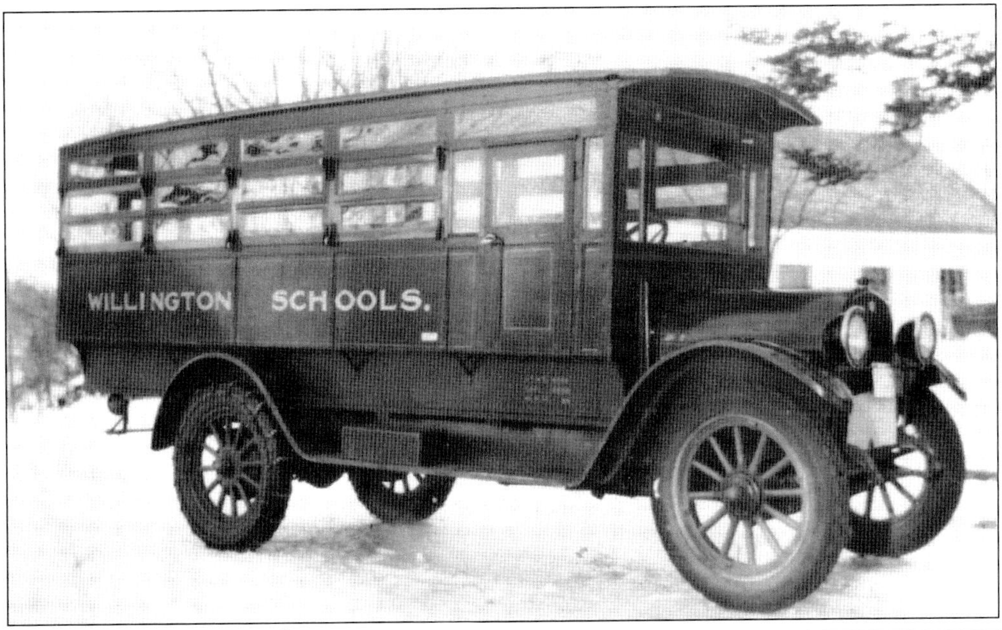

The school year began with excitement in 1923 when Willington showcased its first town-owned bus for student transportation. None of the other area towns owned school buses. The bus must have eased the burden for students who were used to walking miles to and from their homes to their one-room schoolhouses despite the weather.

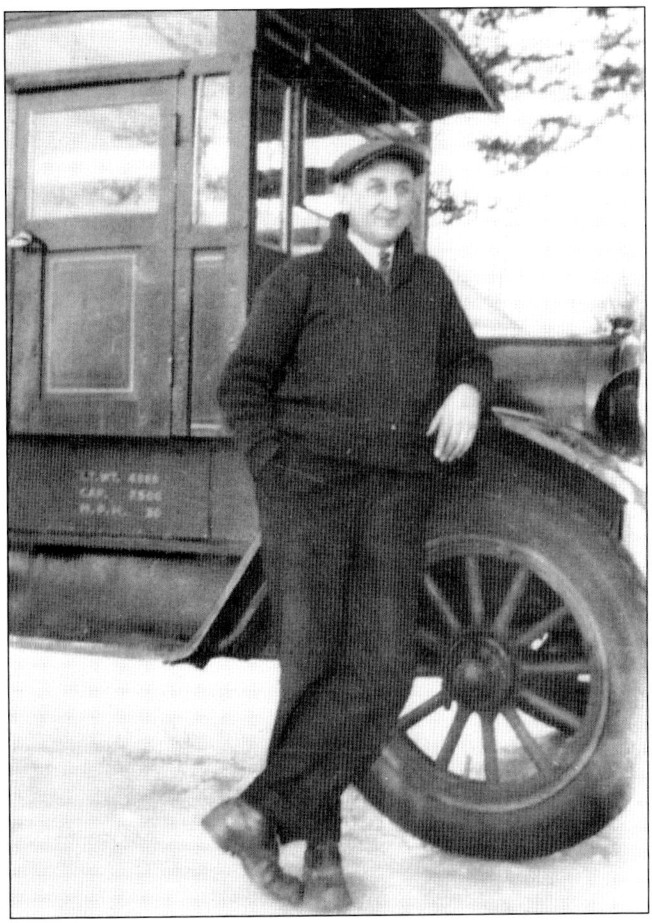

Arthur Devereaux, Willington's first bus driver, appears to be pleased with his new job as the only town-employed school bus driver in the area. In March 1923, it was decided that the seventh- and eighth-grade students from the various one-room schools would be combined in a new school in South Willington. Devereaux's routes during the 1923–1924 school year included trips to and from Hall Memorial School.

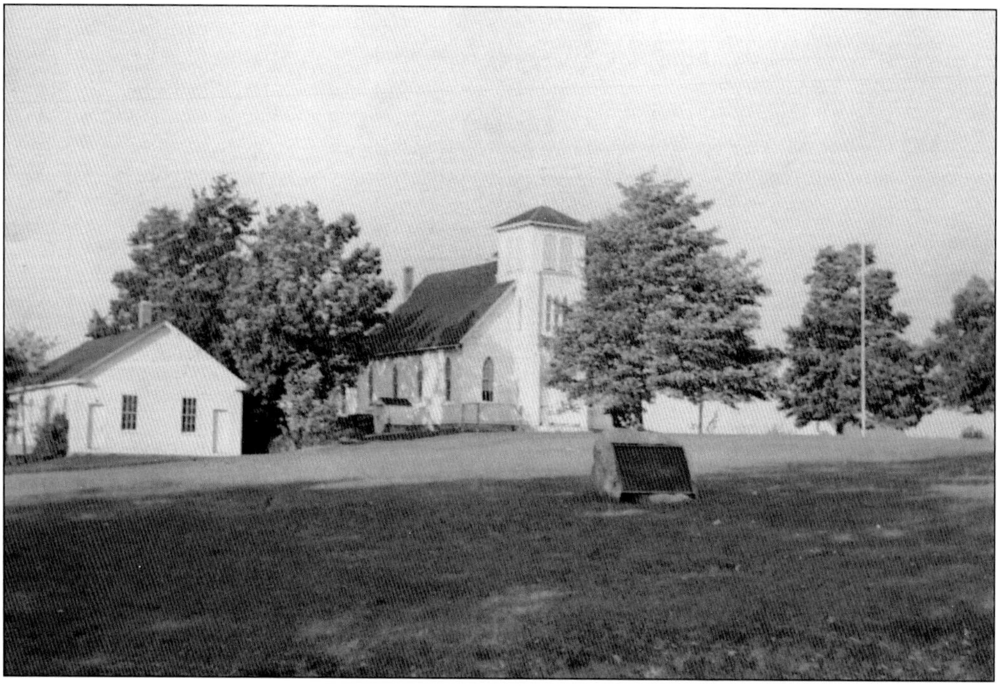

The small building on the left, built in 1876 and seen here in a 1944 view of the town green, was once the town hall. In 1925, it was renovated so that children could use it as a place to socialize and play games. The Boy Scouts, which first formed in Willington in 1919, began using the building in 1926 and still meet there once a week.

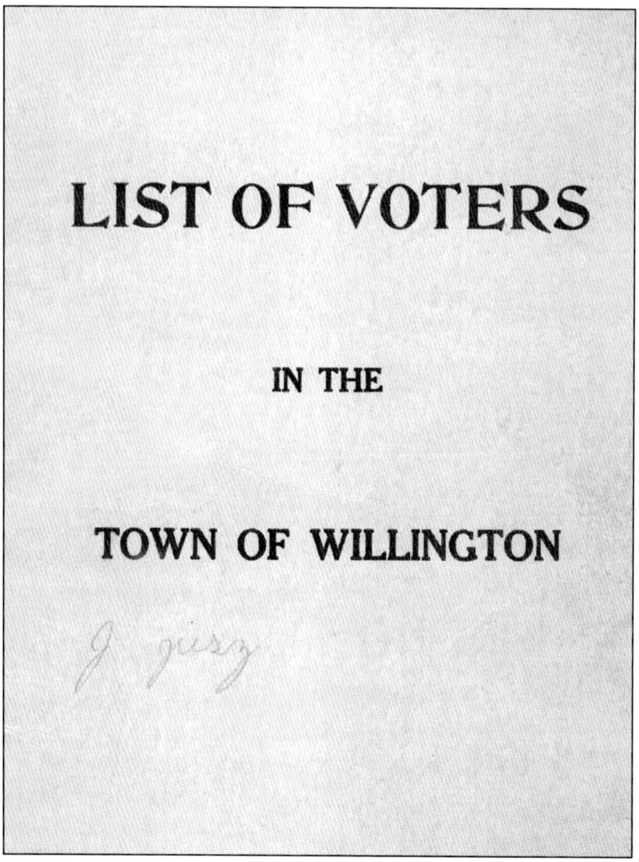

LIST OF VOTERS

IN THE

TOWN OF WILLINGTON

The 19th Amendment to the US Constitution changed the face of America's voters: after its 1920 ratification, women were allowed to vote. This November 1, 1928, alphabetical list of voters is separated in columns titled "male" and "female." Of the 457 voters, 191 were women exercising their recent right to vote, including teachers Lillia I. Fenton and Caroline Mirtl and farmer Mary Hipsky.

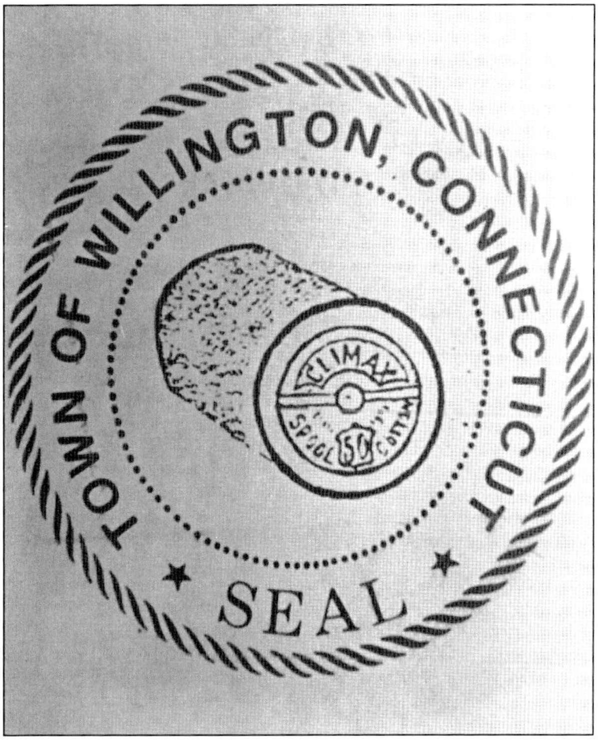

On December 22, 1919, Willington residents unanimously voted to create a corporate seal to commemorate the making of the first spool of thread in the United States and the home of America's thread industry. The seal has been used on public documents since January 1, 1920, when Willington joined other unique Connecticut towns that had created a seal of historical significance. (Courtesy of the Town of Willington.)

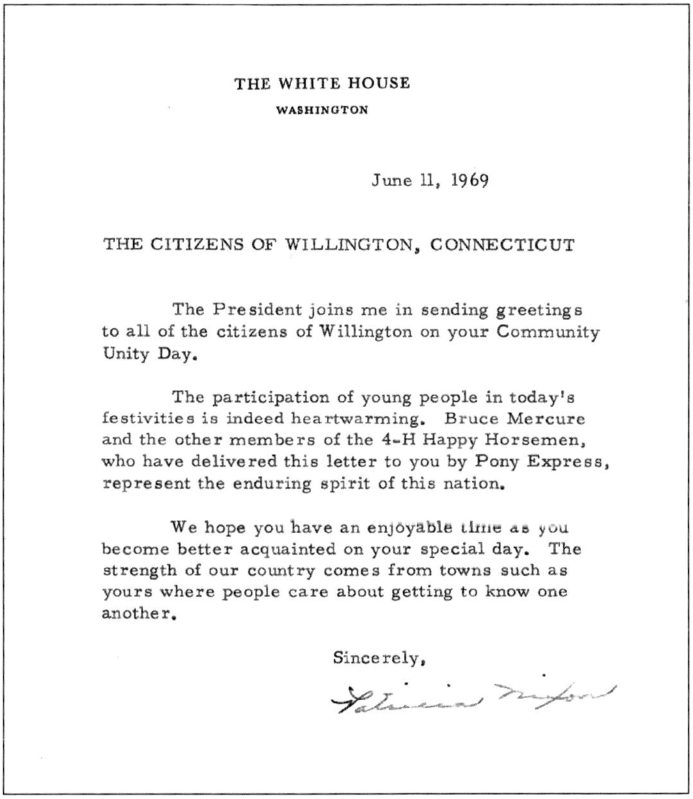

THE WHITE HOUSE
WASHINGTON

June 11, 1969

THE CITIZENS OF WILLINGTON, CONNECTICUT

The President joins me in sending greetings to all of the citizens of Willington on your Community Unity Day.

The participation of young people in today's festivities is indeed heartwarming. Bruce Mercure and the other members of the 4-H Happy Horsemen, who have delivered this letter to you by Pony Express, represent the enduring spirit of this nation.

We hope you have an enjoyable time as you become better acquainted on your special day. The strength of our country comes from towns such as yours where people care about getting to know one another.

Sincerely,

Patricia Nixon

Frances Daly organized Willington's first 4-H Club in 1946. Creative 4-H'ers Beverly and Carol Amidon, Julie Glendhill, Brenda and Holly Hatch, Patty Kelley, and Bruce Mercure participated in a 1969 version of the Pony Express, riding from Route 32 to Pinney Hill, Navratil, and South Willington Roads and on to Route 320, to the firehouse on Old Farms Road, where they delivered First Lady Patricia Nixon's letter to first selectman Alphonse DeCicco.

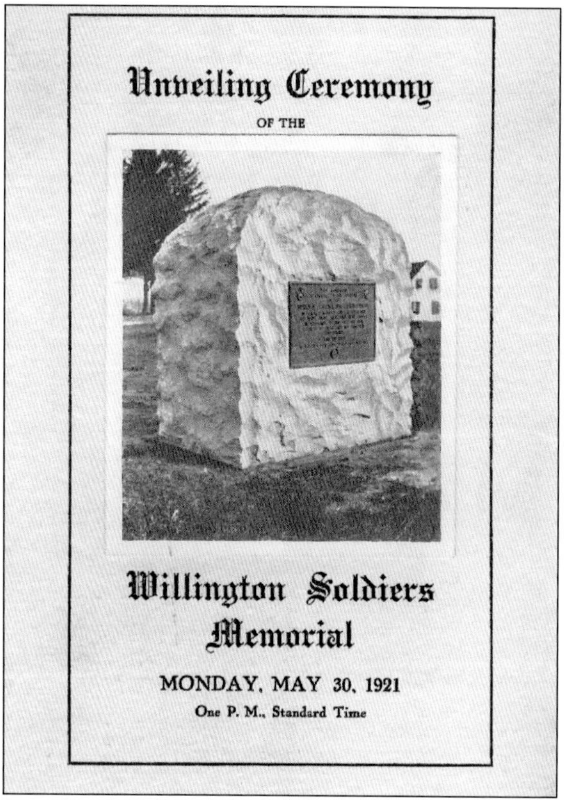
Unveiling Ceremony

OF THE

Willington Soldiers Memorial

MONDAY, MAY 30, 1921

One P. M., Standard Time

In December 1919, Willington's town officials agreed to dedicate $1,000 toward the cost of a Soldiers and Sailors Memorial monument to recognize those residents who had served in World War I. An additional $1,000 came from donations. The 1921 dedication ceremony consisted of prayers, music including the "Star-Spangled Banner," and Gov. Everett J. Lake's formal address. The monument remains on the town green today.

The rear of the Soldiers and Sailors Memorial is seen on the left in this 1962 photograph of the town green. Wilbur Roy Frankfort was born in Willington on January 27, 1894, and was lost at sea during World War I. Henry Toberman was born in South Willington on November 22, 1896, and died on November 7, 1918, as the result of wounds received in action during the war.

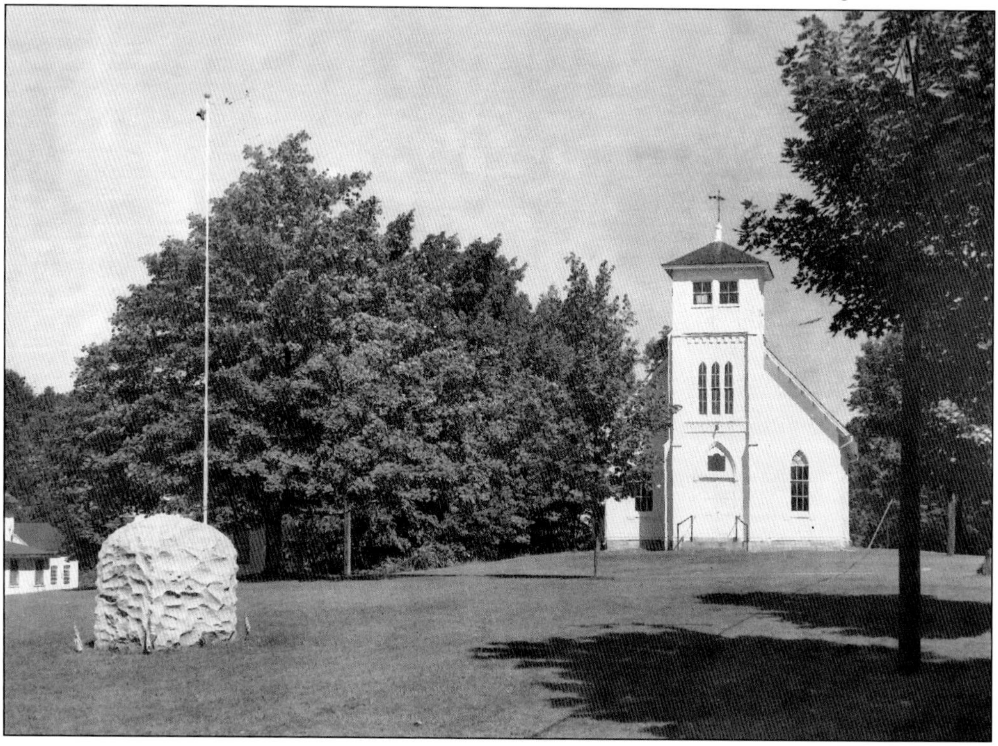

In 2013, at age 100, Esther Phelps recalled the World War II civil defense practice of having residents man the bell tower of the town hall at night to search for enemy aircraft. The walls of the bell tower were marked north, south, east, and west so that those on duty could alert others as to the direction from which the aircraft was coming or going. Someone wrote his shifts—"4/20/13," "12/15/43," "1/27/44," "3/1/44," and "4/6/44"—in pencil on the wall. There is also a note that says, "Italy surrenders on 9/8/43," along with anti-Hitler and Mussolini slogans and the ever-patriotic reference to the "land of the free, home of the brave." The severely tattered American flag, with stars representing the 48 states, gives the bell tower a slightly chilling aura even on a warm, sunlit day.

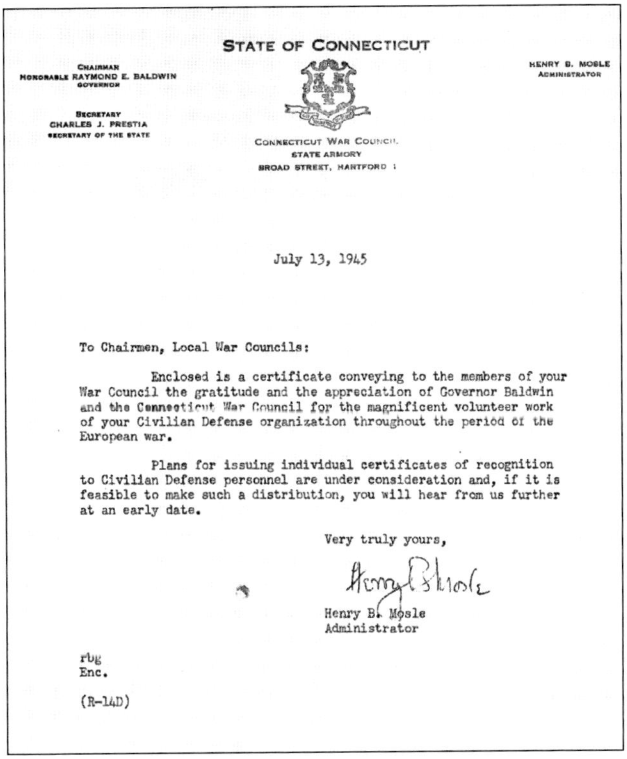

STATE OF CONNECTICUT

CHAIRMAN
HONORABLE RAYMOND E. BALDWIN
GOVERNOR

SECRETARY
CHARLES J. PRESTIA
SECRETARY OF THE STATE

HENRY B. MOSLE
ADMINISTRATOR

CONNECTICUT WAR COUNCIL
STATE ARMORY
BROAD STREET, HARTFORD 1

July 13, 1945

To Chairmen, Local War Councils:

Enclosed is a certificate conveying to the members of your War Council the gratitude and the appreciation of Governor Baldwin and the Connecticut War Council for the magnificent volunteer work of your Civilian Defense organization throughout the period of the European war.

Plans for issuing individual certificates of recognition to Civilian Defense personnel are under consideration and, if it is feasible to make such a distribution, you will hear from us further at an early date.

Very truly yours,

Henry B. Mosle
Henry B. Mosle
Administrator

rbg
Enc.

(R-14D)

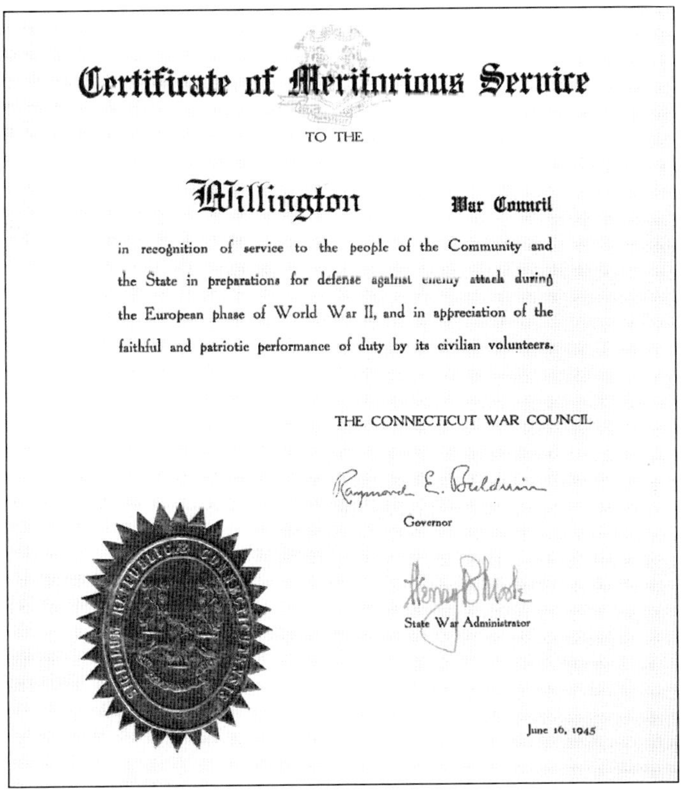

Certificate of Meritorious Service

TO THE

Willington War Council

in recognition of service to the people of the Community and the State in preparations for defense against enemy attack during the European phase of World War II, and in appreciation of the faithful and patriotic performance of duty by its civilian volunteers.

THE CONNECTICUT WAR COUNCIL

Raymond E. Baldwin
Governor

Henry B. Mosle
State War Administrator

June 16, 1945

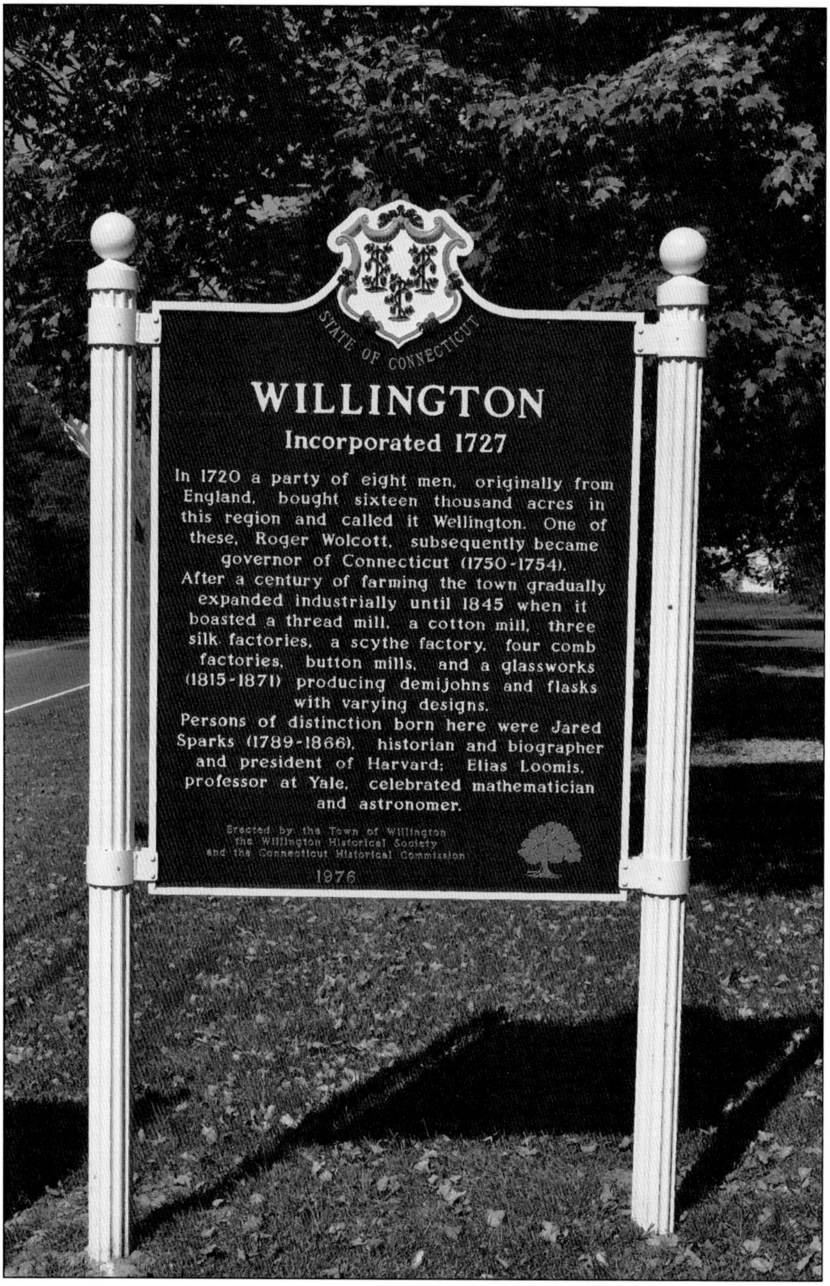

The Town of Willington, together with the Willington Historical Society and the Connecticut Historical Commission, commemorated Willington's history with this sign, erected on the town green in 1976. It is not merely a warm welcome to the town's center, it is also an opportunity for residents and visitors to pause for just a moment and enjoy a brief introduction to Willington's history. New Englanders refer to the grassy area of town often surrounded by businesses, churches, and homes as either the common or the green, sometimes depending on the specific area from which they hail. Willington's town common offers an opportunity to laze in the sun, read a book while awaiting piano lessons at a nearby home, toss a ball, or enjoy refreshments at the annual flea market or car show, both held in September. (Courtesy of Marion Cullimore.)

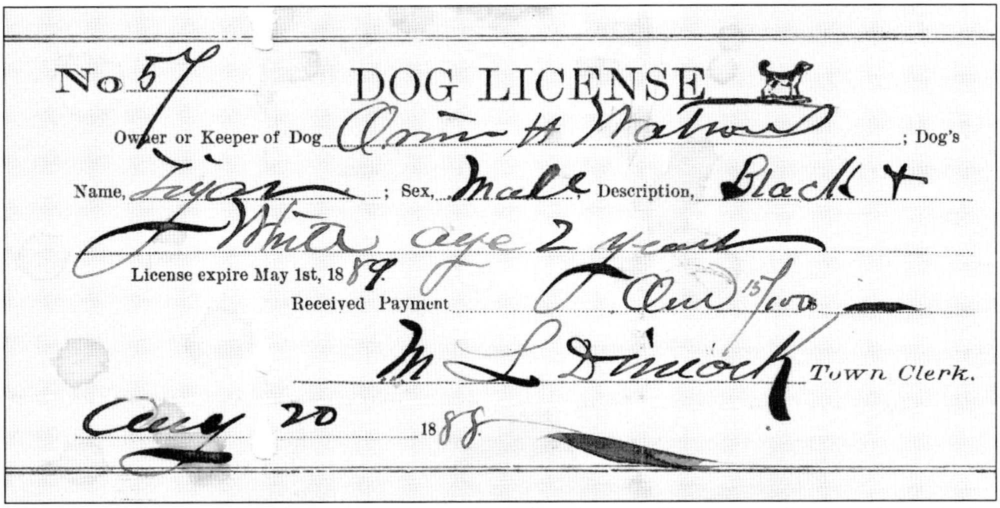

No 57 DOG LICENSE

Owner or Keeper of Dog Orrin H Watson; Dog's Name, [illegible]; Sex, Male Description, Black & White age 2 years

License expire May 1st, 1889

Received Payment One 15/100

M L Dimock Town Clerk.

Aug 20 1888

Many of Willington's early photographs include family pets. From its early days through the present, Willington has required that dogs be licensed. The proud owner of this two-year-old male encased his 1888 license in glass. Joseph Dobrowsvosky donated it to the Willington Historical Society after finding it in the rafters of an attic in a house on Ruby Road.

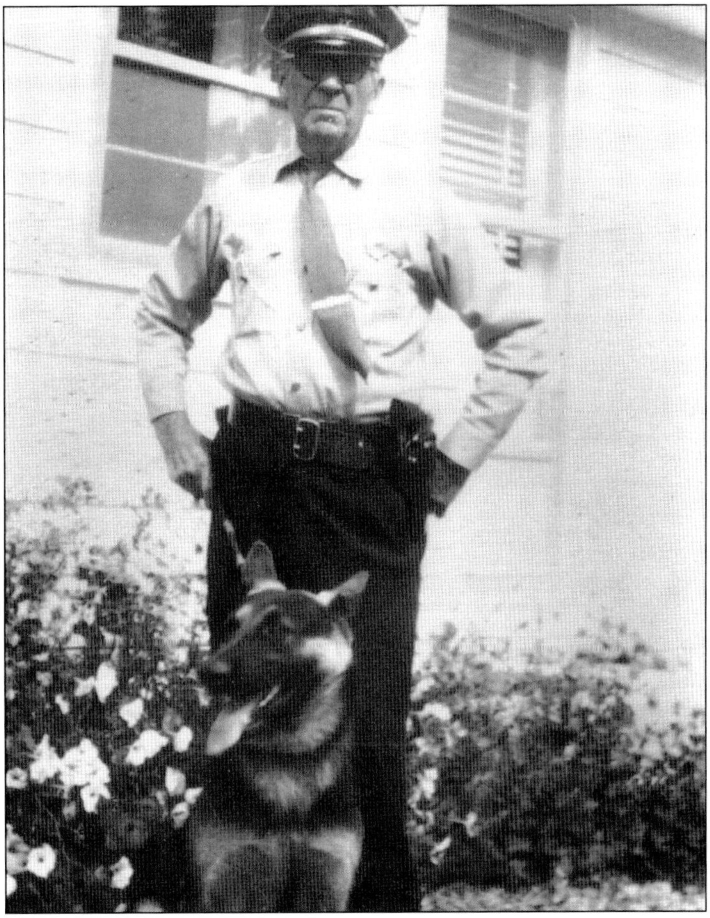

Willington has never had its own police department. Connecticut law, however, allows town officials to appoint constables to serve for a specified term to preserve the peace. Joseph Williams, seen in this undated photograph with his unidentified canine partner, was one such constable who assisted residents. (Courtesy of Dale Dyer.)

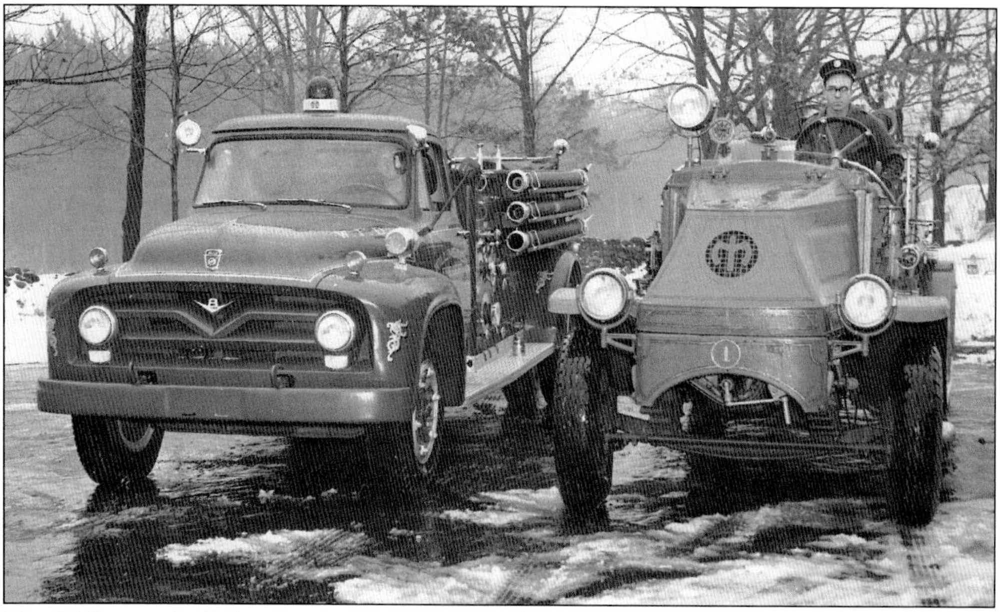

The Willington Hill Fire Department was formed on May 20, 1952, and incorporated on June 27, 1952. It was originally known as Willington Fire Department No. 2, but the name was later changed to the Willington Hill Fire Department Inc. David Booth, seen on the right in this 1955 photograph, was an experienced firefighter, having served in another town's department before moving to Willington. (Courtesy of Roger Wilson.)

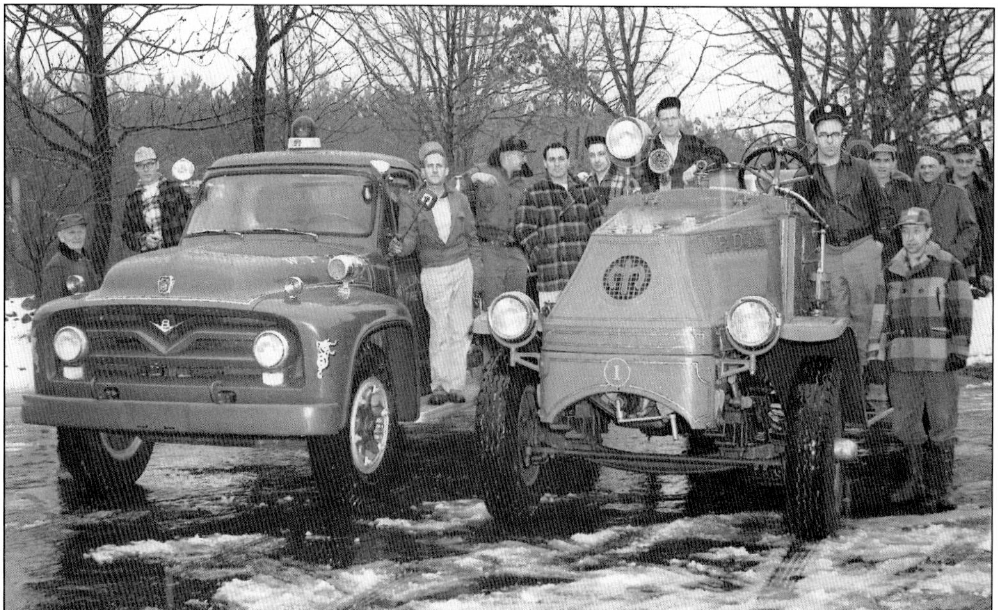

This 1955 photograph shows the Willington Hill Fire Department's brand-new truck (left), delivered on March 5, 1955, and the original fire truck (right). The fire department members are, from left to right, Ernie ?, Ralph Pratt, fire chief Mike DaRose, ? Carbino, Ronald Cushman, Andy Hanson, unidentified, David Booth, John Blessington, unidentified, Henry Farra, and (front) Harold Cushman. (Courtesy of Linda Myhaver.)

The cornerstone for the original Congregational church was laid in 1876. The building was dedicated in September of that year and cost $5,256 to build. Members of the congregation donated $3,735 toward the price of construction. Donors from New Haven and Bristol provided an organ, a chandelier, and lamps. On October 5, 1876, church members purchased a bell from the First Church of Stafford. It weighed 1,250 pounds, cost $300, and is currently mounted on a pedestal outside the building. The Congregational church was across the town common from the Baptist church, with which it became federated in 1911. After the federation, the Congregationalists relocated to the Baptist church. In 1926, the town bought the old Congregational church for $1 for use as the town hall.

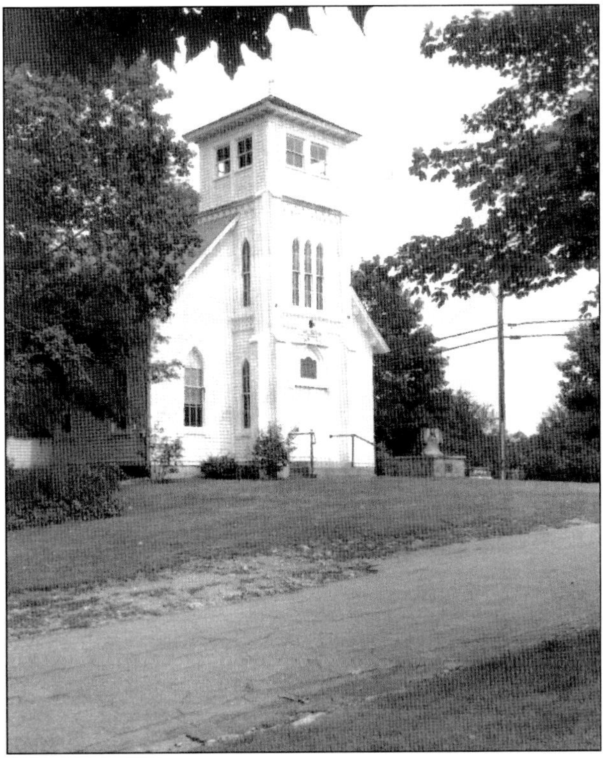

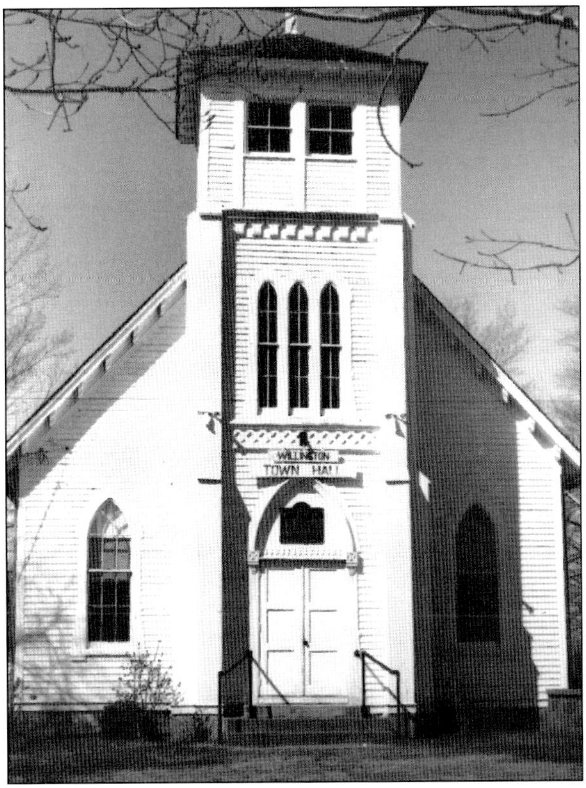

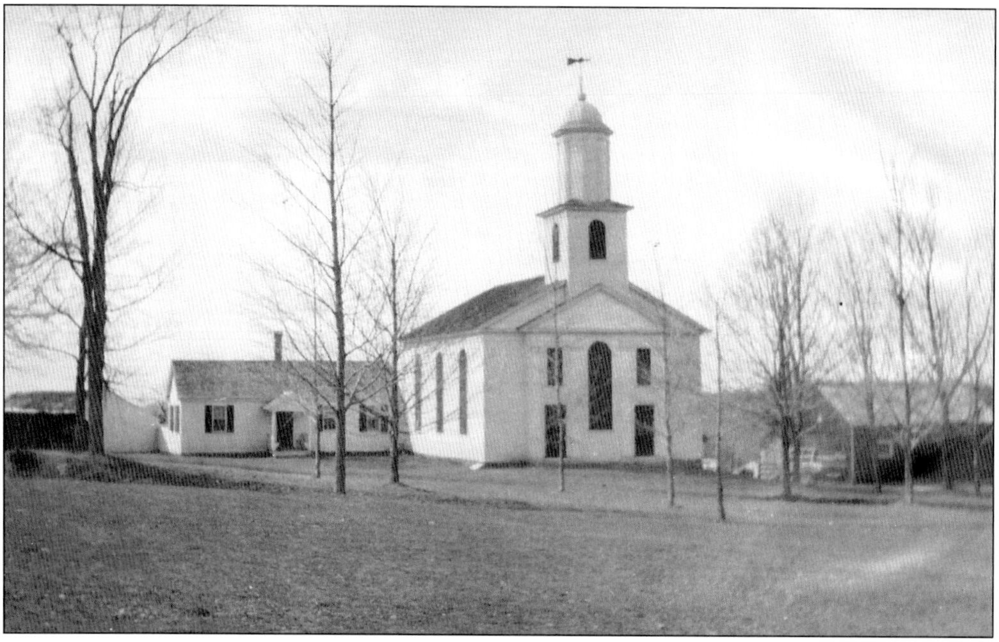

This undated photograph of the Hill Church, at which members of the Federated Church of Willington worship during the summer, shows a wagon shed on the far left that no longer exists. The addition to the right of the wagon shed is now a nursery school. Ushers still ring the bell shortly before the start of services each Sunday at 10:00 a.m.

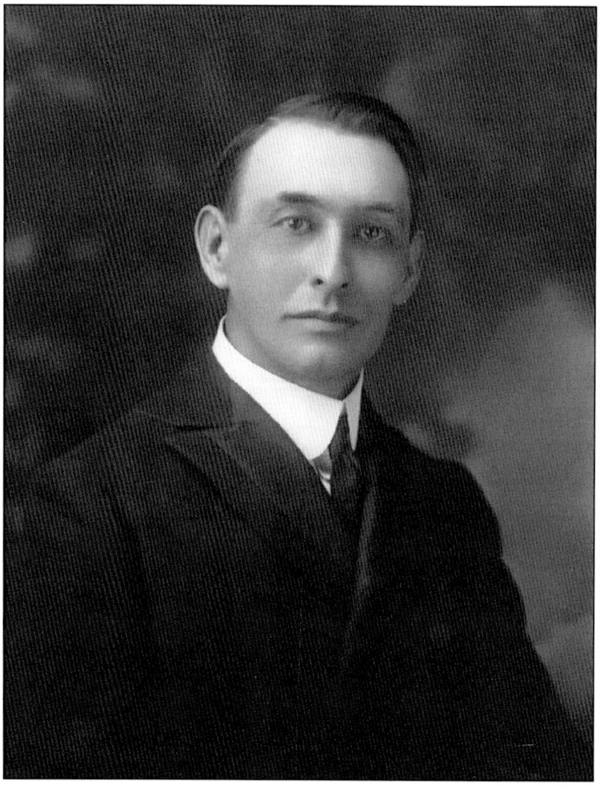

Born in 1878, Rev. Earle W. Darrow served in Willington from 1908 through 1915. He was pastor when the Baptist and Congregational churches entered into a formal agreement known as the Articles of Federation in 1911, which led to the dedication of the Hall Memorial Church that same year. Today, services are held at the Hall Church from mid-September through April and at the Congregational church from May through early September.

Rev. Edwin Sundt became minister of the Federated Church of Willington in 1924, just 13 years after the Congregational and Baptist churches merged. He remained until 1929, during which time he organized vacation church schools, fellowship suppers, a Boy Scout troop, and a Young People's Society. He was also a historian who studied the Willington Baptist Church.

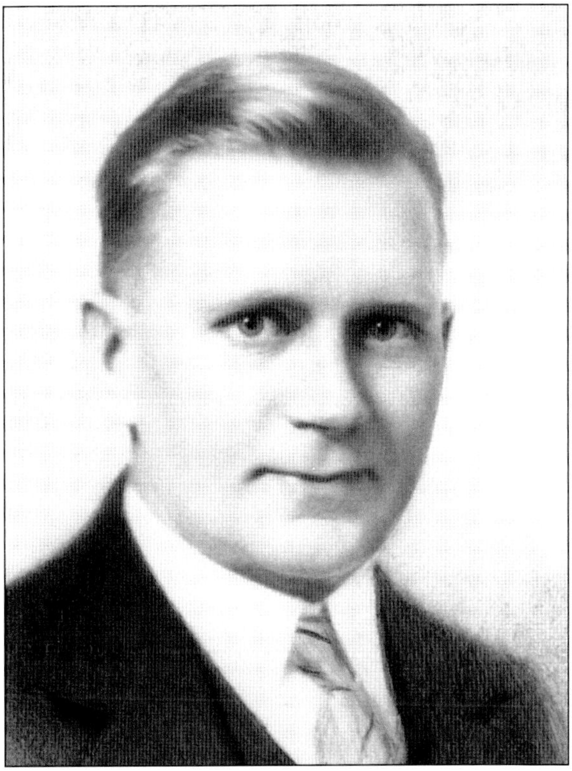

The Federated Church of Willington has hosted a flea market on the town green on the Saturday after Labor Day each year since 1962. Vendors offer everything from crafts to furniture, and the church booths offer pie, chowders, burgers, hot dogs, and white elephant items. Below, shoppers peruse local produce at the flea market on September 12, 1987. (Courtesy of the Federated Church of Willington.)

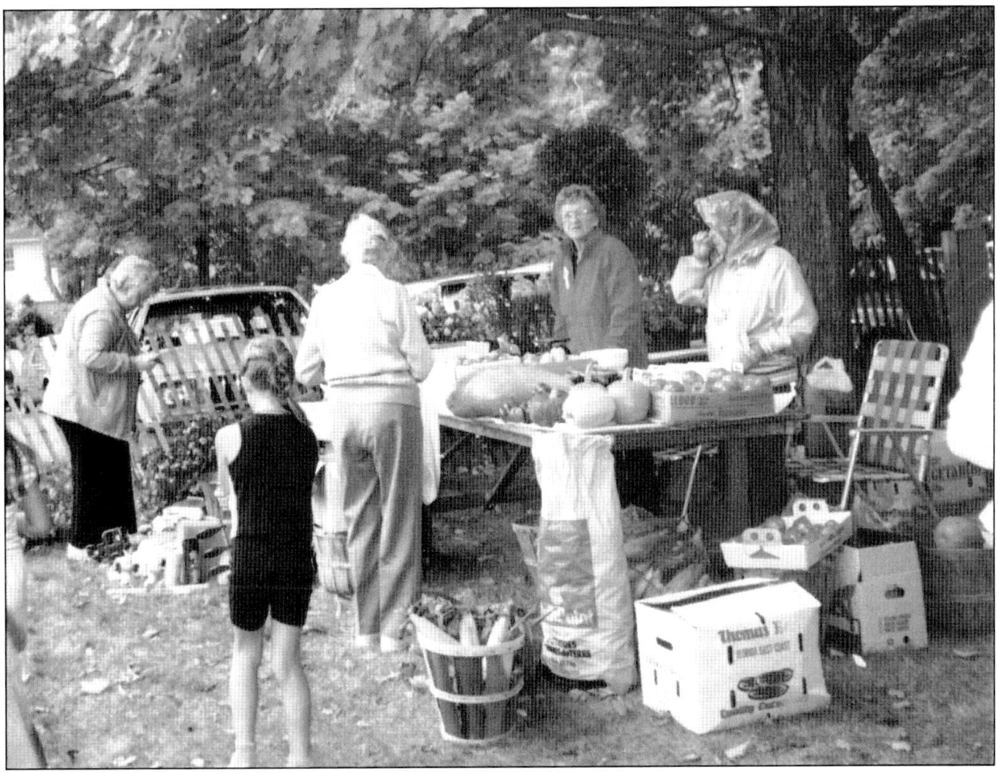

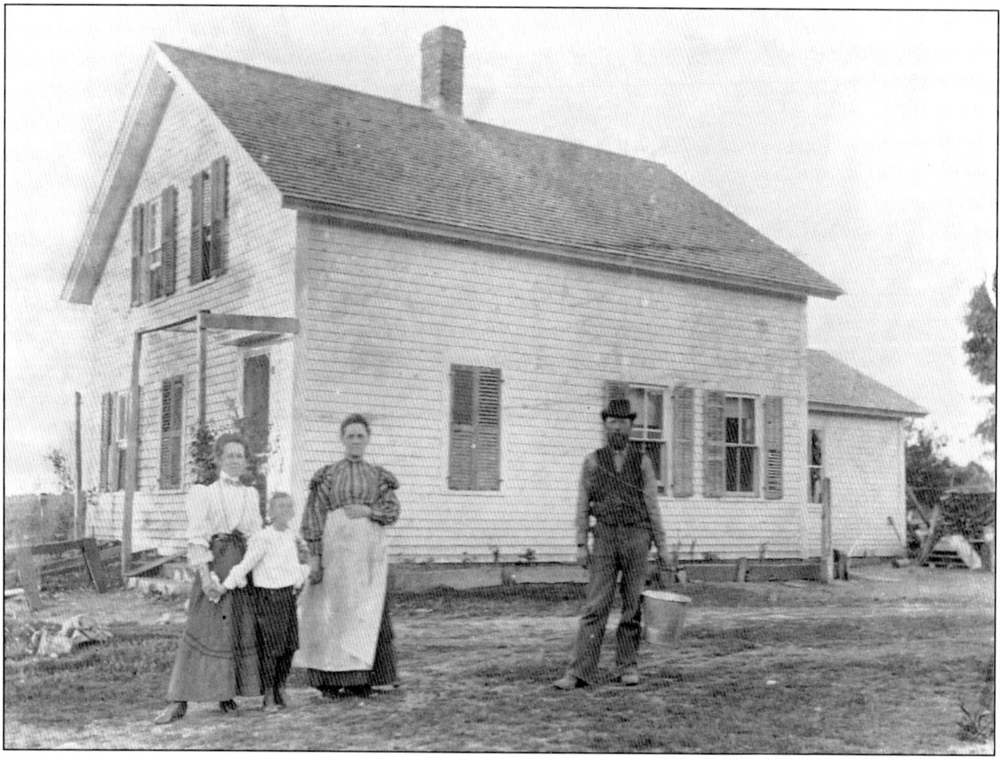

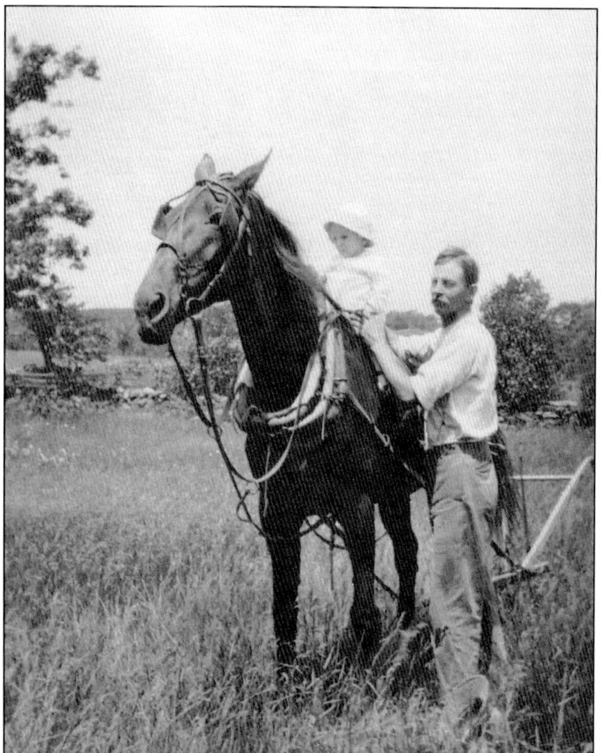

Pictured around 1900 are, from left to right, unidentified, William Jeremiah Latham, Cynthia Richardson Latham, and Charles Latham. Cynthia Richardson married Charles Latham on November 14, 1874, in Willington. Their son William Jeremiah "Jerry" Latham was born on February 19, 1891, in Willington. (Courtesy of Claudia D'Agata.)

Clarence Eldredge treats his son Claude, born in 1917, to a ride on the horse. Despite the fact that a year earlier there were automobiles passing through Willington and that a Ford dealership opened in Willington in 1916, it was still more common when this photograph was taken, on July 1, 1917, to use a horse to pull the plow through the fields. (Courtesy of Claudia D'Agata.)

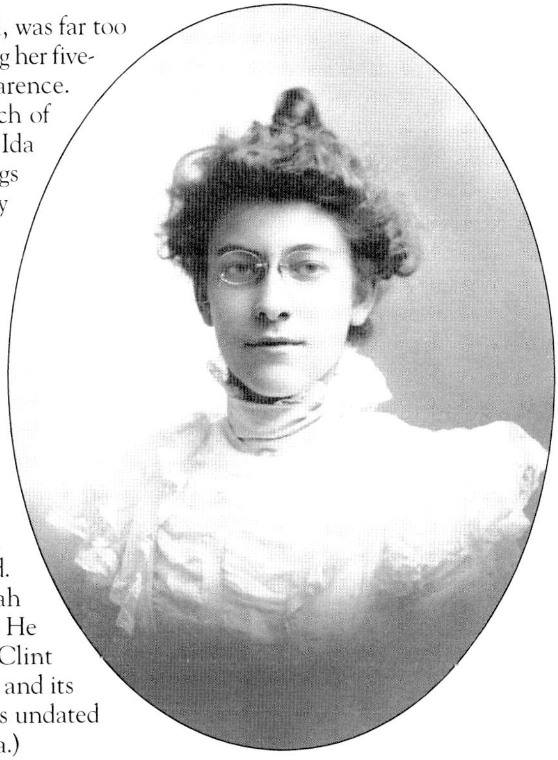

Ida Allen Eldredge, born on April 24, 1881, was far too young when she died in October 1921, leaving her five-year-old son Claude and her husband, Clarence. She was a member of the Federated Church of Willington. Just the day before she died, Ida went to the fair in nearby Stafford Springs with her husband and little boy. (Courtesy of Claudia D'Agata.)

Elijah Eldredge, born in Willington on March 20, 1770, married Bethia Chapman on March 17, 1791, in neighboring Ashford. The marriage produced 10 children. Elijah built the large home pictured here in 1834. He died nine years after building it. Driving Clint Eldredge Road today shows that the home and its outbuildings look much as they did in this undated photograph. (Courtesy of Claudia D'Agata.)

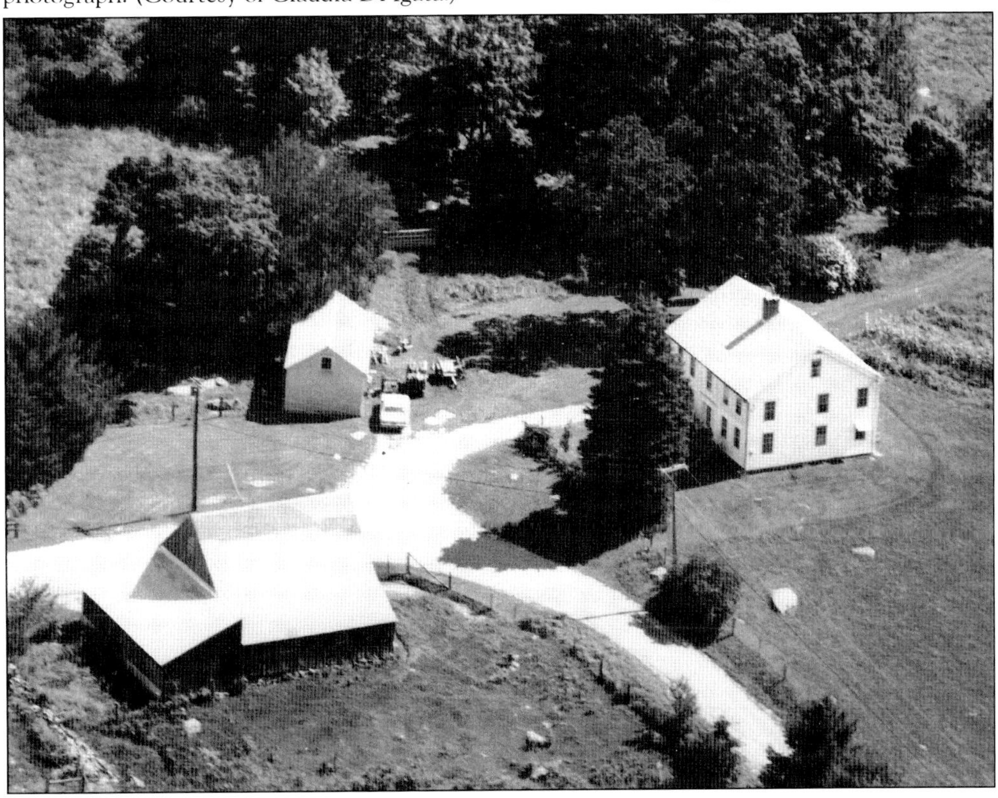

1727 *OFFICIAL PROGRAM* *1927*

Bi-Centennial Celebration

Town of Willington, Connecticut

July 2-4, 1927

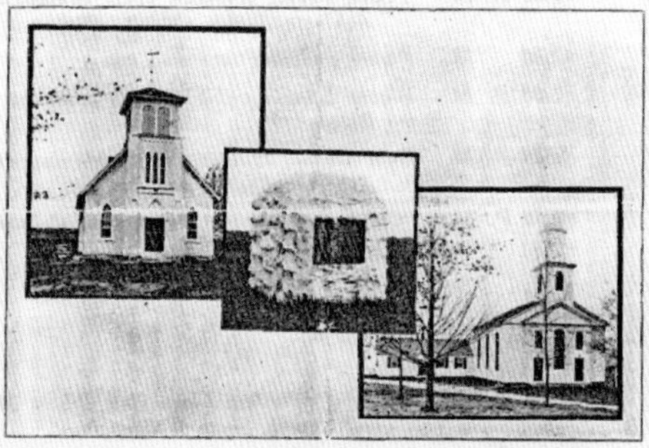

CELEBRATING

Bi-Centennial of the Town of Willington

Bi-Centennial of the Congregational Church

Centennial of the Baptist Church

Willington residents celebrated their town's bicentennial on Fourth of July weekend in 1927. During the three-day event, there were picnics, religious services, fireworks, musical performances, and family reunions. Athletic events included a track meet and a ball game. There were also water sports and a swimming contest at Lake Beauty, now known as Hall's Pond. The program also included a pageant describing Willington's chronology.

1727--Bi-Centennial Celebration--1927
Town of Willington
Connecticut
July 2 - 4, 1927

PROGRAM FOR MONDAY, JULY 4th

10:00 A. M.—Band Concert, B. P. O. E. Band of Willimantic
CHARLES N. C. WHEELER, Director
Town Common, Willington Hill

1 March .... "National Emblem"
2 Overture .... Lustspiel"
3 Selection .... "Memories of the War"
4 Overture .... "Gypsie Queen"
5 March .... "Old Circus Band"

10:30 A. M. The Children's Pageant
At "The Old Tavern," Willington Hill
REMEMBERED PICTURES OF OLD DAYS IN OUR TOWN
1757 — 1857
Arranged and Directed by Mrs. George V. Smith
Assisted by Mrs. H. M. Hansen and all the Teachers

The Spirit of Memory .... Barbara Amidon
Aids to Memory
Sight .... Thelma Cushman
Sound .... Marian Krivenac
Fragrance .... Lucy Wraight

EPISODE ONE—"A Strange Honeymoon"
By Moose Meadow School, Athena Bowler, Teacher

Rachel .... Emma Zugeber
Aunt Charity .... Ethel Lustig
Grandmother .... Amelia Hipsky
Grandfather .... George Mrocskowski
Judge John Fuller .... Fred Fermier
Rev. Daniel Fuller .... Bernice Mrocskowski
Sheriff from Tolland .... George Mrocskowski
Deacon .... John Brager
1st Witness .... Amelia Drobney
2nd Witness .... Wilma Hipsky
Susannah .... Ethel Lustig
Thomas .... Joseph Hipsky

EPISODE TWO—"Gideon Noble and Abram Weston Go to War"
By Village Hill School, Katherine Balazs, Teacher

Rev. Gideon Noble .... Edward Murphy
Mrs. Gideon Noble .... Beatrice Fisher
Nancy Crocker .... Esther Murphy
Mrs. Merrick .... Alice Bradnon
Dorcas Fenton .... Annie Balazs
Captain Parker .... George Palacho
His Orderly .... Joe Kreydatus
A Soldier .... Wilfred Fisher
Gideon Noble .... Bertha Banning
Abraham Weston .... Richard Fisher

Students from each of the one-room schoolhouses acted out scenes from Willington history written by their teachers during the July 4, 1927, bicentennial program. Robert Preston of the Willington Hill School portrayed Jared Sparks. The program included a slideshow depicting the development of industries from lumbering to spinning to spooling and glassblowing. The 11-hour celebration culminated with fireworks that could be seen from the South Willington athletic field.

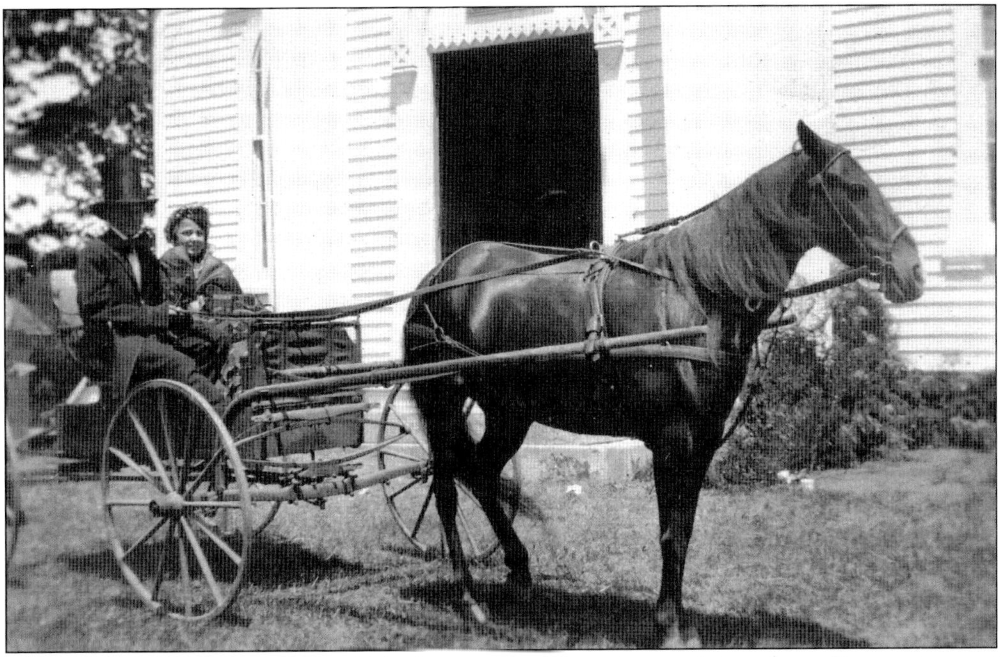

Earl Eldredge, age 13, and Carolyn Eldredge, age 11, are seen here with their horse Topsy in front of the former Congregational church on July 4, 1927. The church was sold to the town in 1924 for $1 with the understanding that if it was not used for public meetings, it would revert back to the church. Public meetings are still occasionally held at the old town hall. (Courtesy of Claudia D'Agata.)

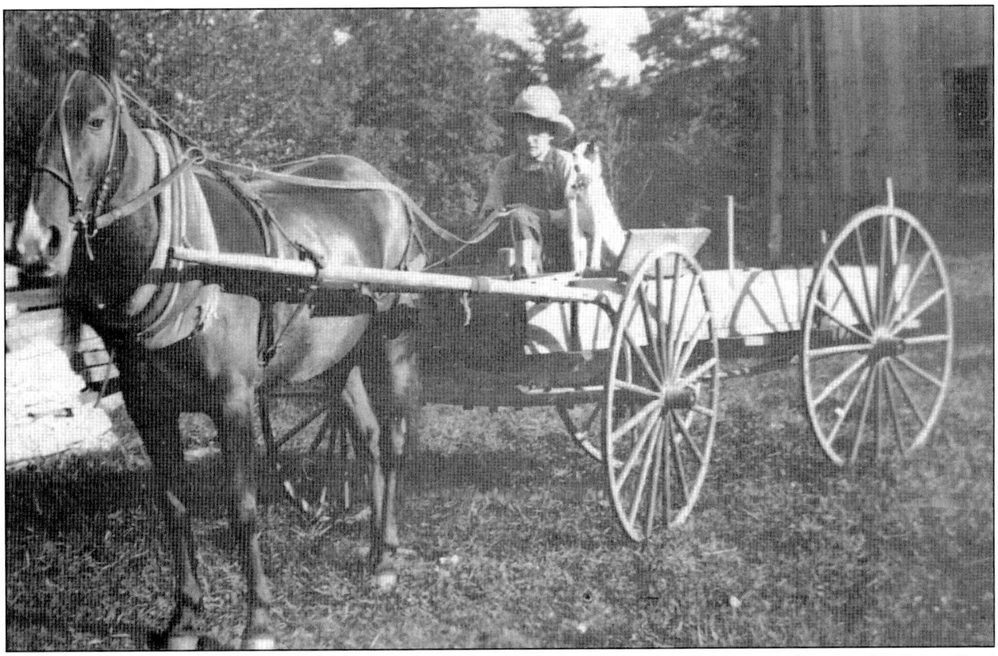

Claude Eldredge, age 10, is accompanied by his dog Buster as he drives a farm vehicle pulled by his horse Topsy in 1927. Members of the Eldredge family came to the United States on the second voyage of the *Mayflower*, and there are references to members of the Eldredge family in Willington as early as 1722. (Courtesy of Claudia D'Agata.)

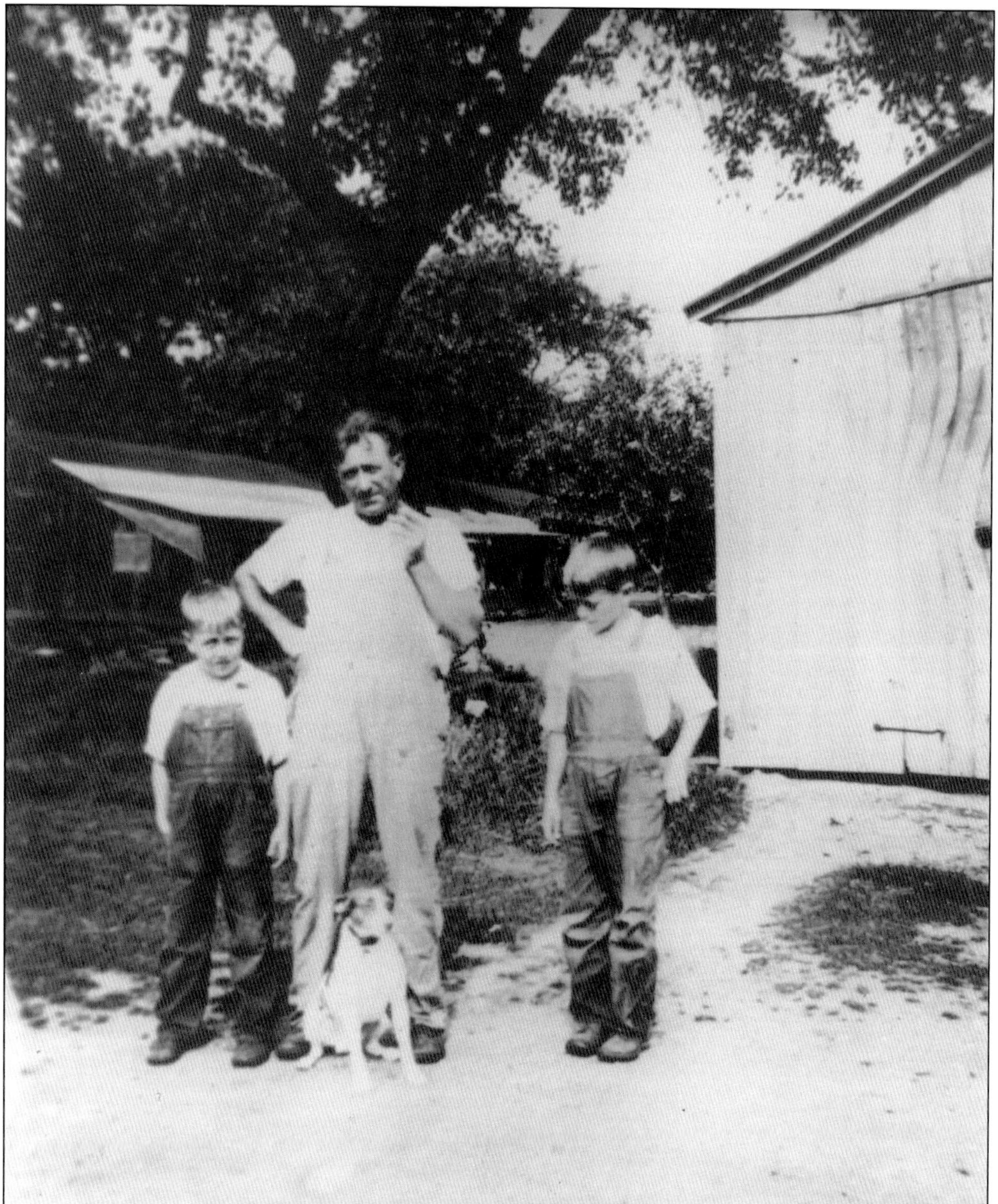

The male members of the Wraight family are seen here in 1928 at Cozy Croft Farm on Common Road. They are, from left to right, Frank E. Wraight, George H. Wraight, and Nelson G. Wraight. George died just two years after this photograph was taken, leaving his wife, Lucy, to operate the chicken farm, which she did until 1954. (Courtesy of Jeffrey Wraight.)

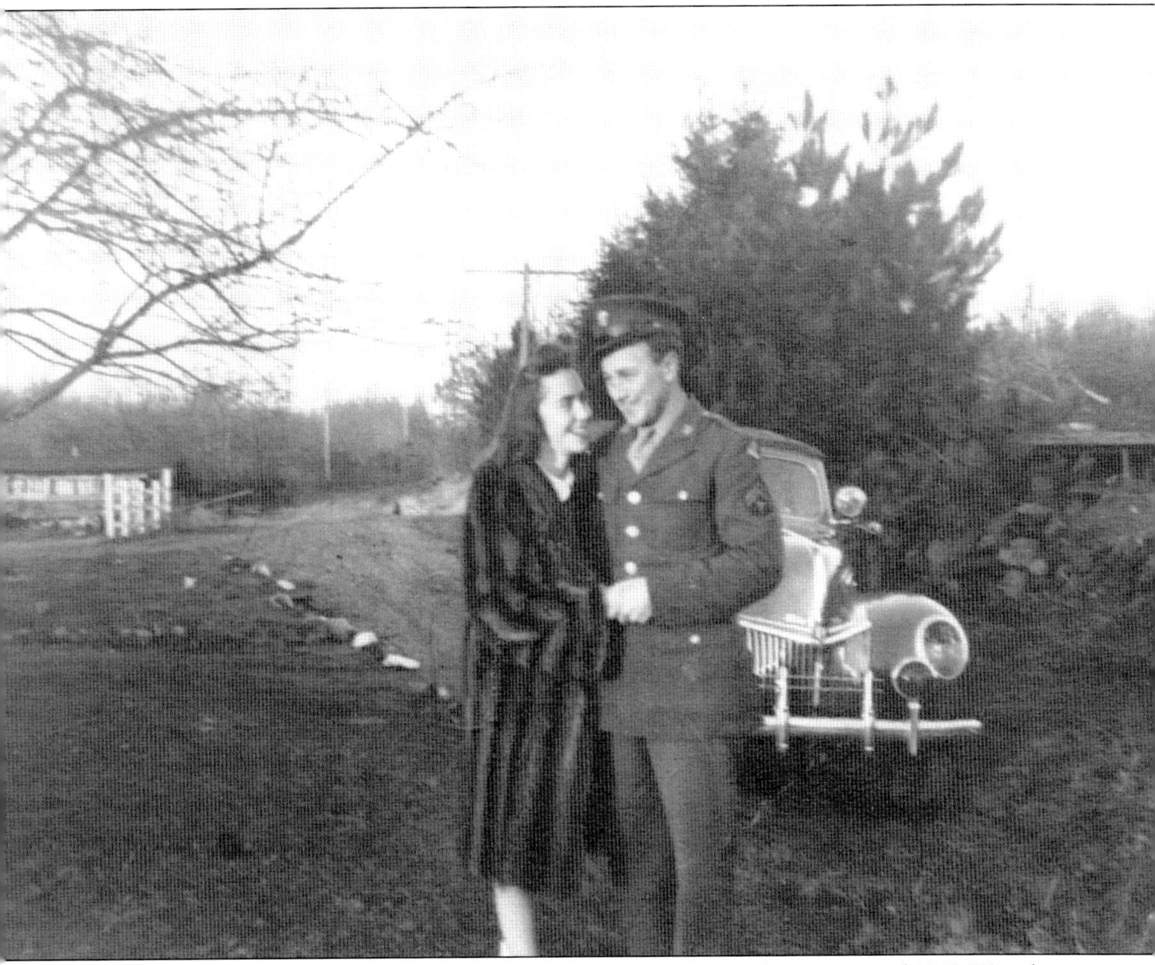

Maureen Lintner enjoys a moment with Frank E. Wraight at Cozy Croft Farm around 1945. Wraight joined the Army as a young man and served in World War II, becoming a staff sergeant. His Ford convertible is seen in the background. The two later married. (Courtesy of Jeffrey Wraight.)

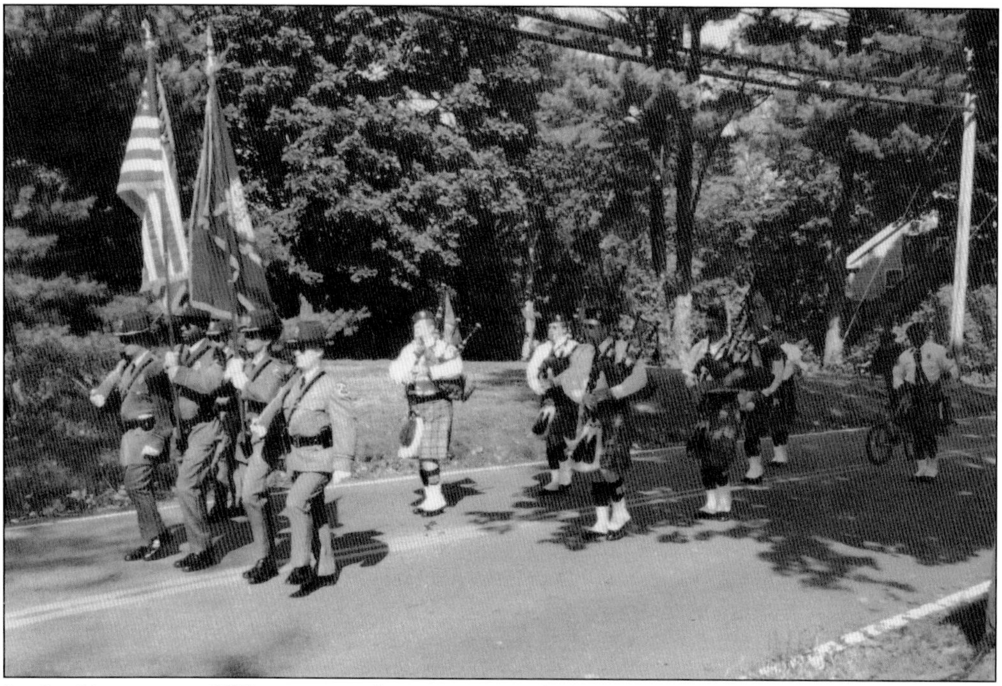

In the 21st century, Willington residents continue the long history of honoring and celebrating the anniversary of the town's founding. The October 5, 2002, parade in these photographs was in honor of the 275th anniversary, in which participants executed a formal parade march. Above, the American and Connecticut flags show the loyalty residents have to both their country and their state. Below, resident Wilbur Gangaway's tractor and parade float capture some of Willington's agricultural history and expresses freedom of religion. Based on this history of celebrations, it is anticipated that the town's recognition of its tricentennial will be extensive. (Both courtesy of Roseanne and Jerry Parizek.)

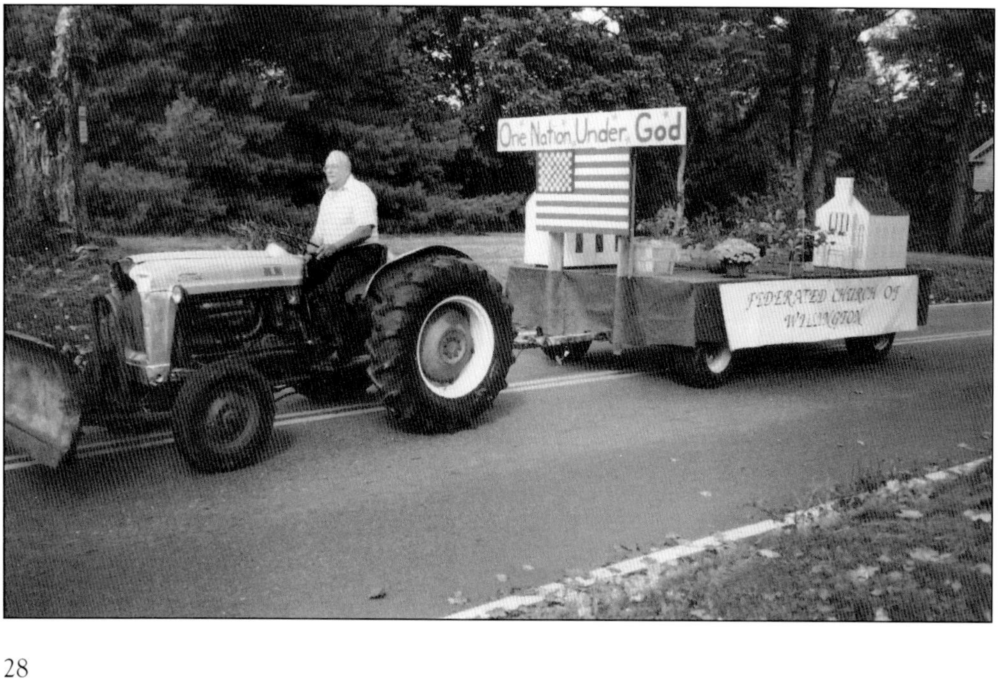

Two

Daleville (Topliff) School District

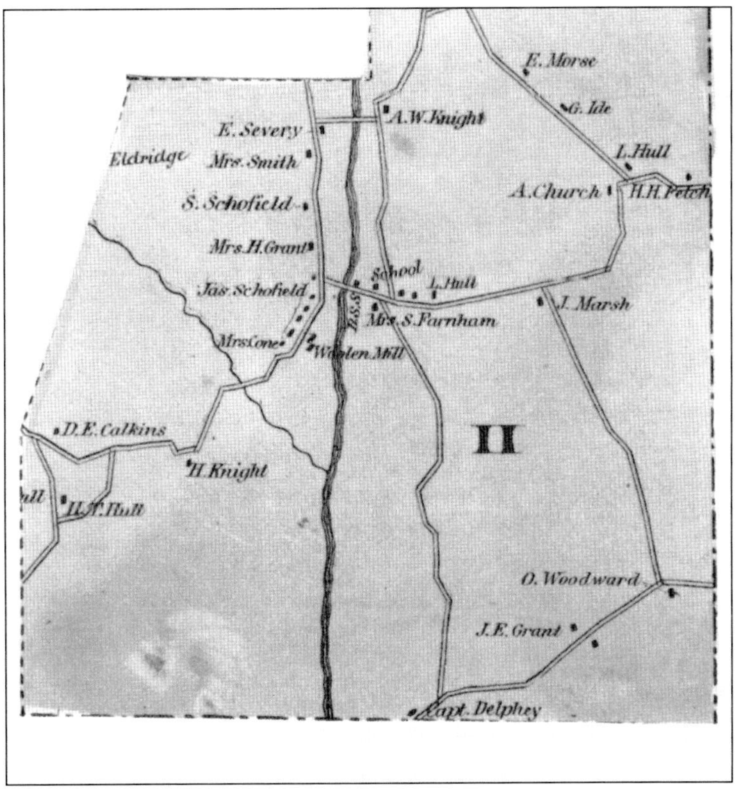

Clement Topliff created a variety of businesses in Willington's southeastern corner in the early 1800s, leading settlers to call this section of town Topliff. On April 6, 1840, Willington's selectmen admitted Englishman Thomas Dale to their community. Although the silk mill he operated did not survive the economic difficulties of the Civil War, the area and its school were renamed in his honor.

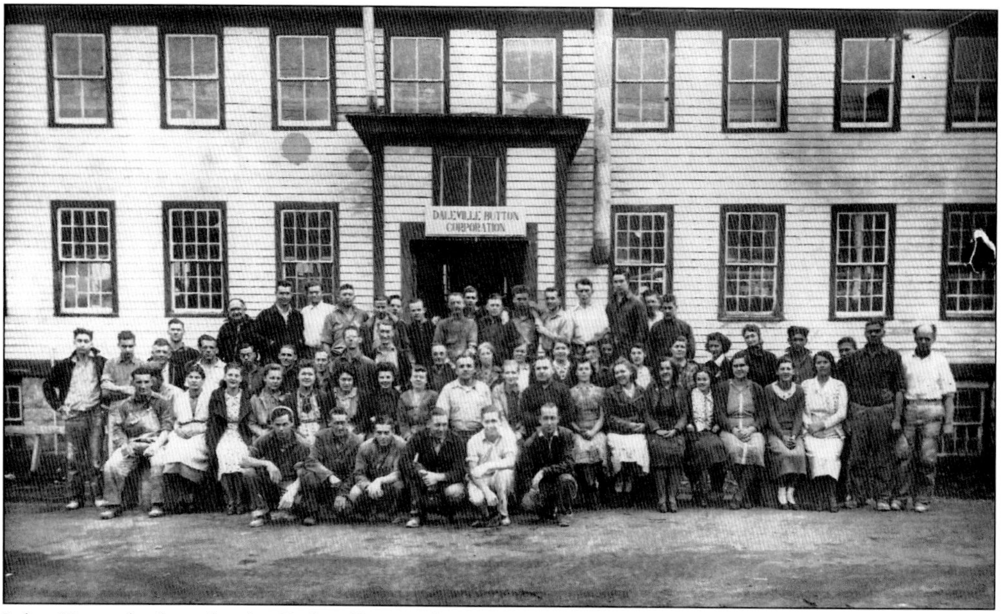

John Divorsky bought the Daleville Woolen Mill from Commercial Farmers Bank and opened the Daleville Button Shop in 1907. In 1912, Anton Hack, a pearl button manufacturer, bought the mill from Divorsky. The button shop operated under various owners but was still in business when employees posed for this group photograph in 1934 or 1935.

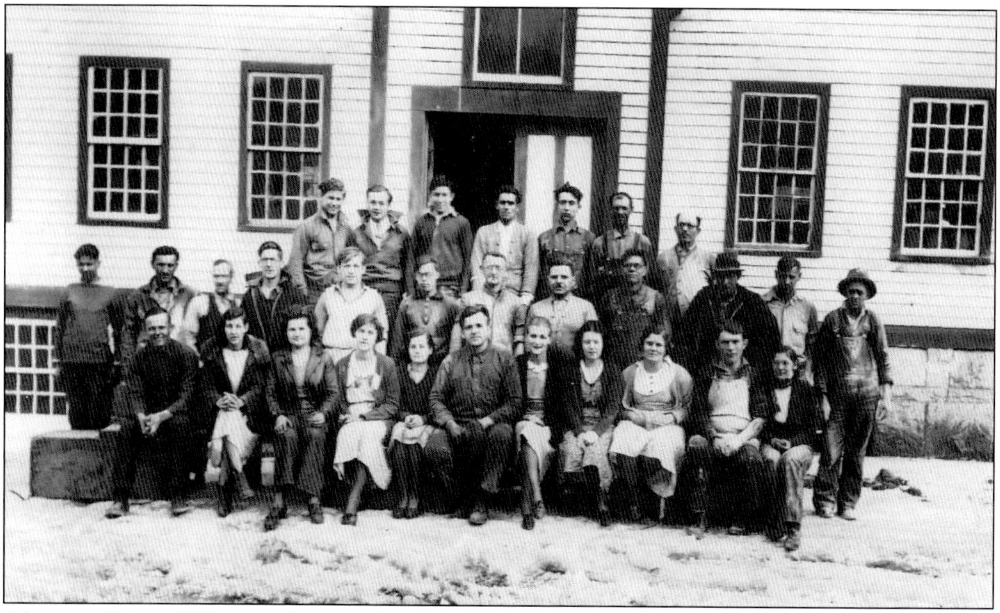

Also in 1934 or 1935, these button shop employees are, from left to right, (first row) John Toth, Louise Dreisch, Wanda Litvincyk, Mary Cushman, unidentified, Jerry Parizek, Frances Rifkin, Camella Hackenschmidt, Esther Davis, Bill Cisar, and Sophie Maichuk; (second row) Blazey Duhanskey, Frank Kotrba, Joseph "Red" Bennett, Ralph Pratt, Henry Kuchla, Tootsie Woodworth, Charles Tranka, Ned Rifkin, William Marco, George Bidwell, William Janiak, and John Gracie; (third row) Alex Janek, Eddie Hughes, Robert Hackenschmidt, Clifford Mirriam, Harold Cushman, ? Mitchell, and William Cisar.

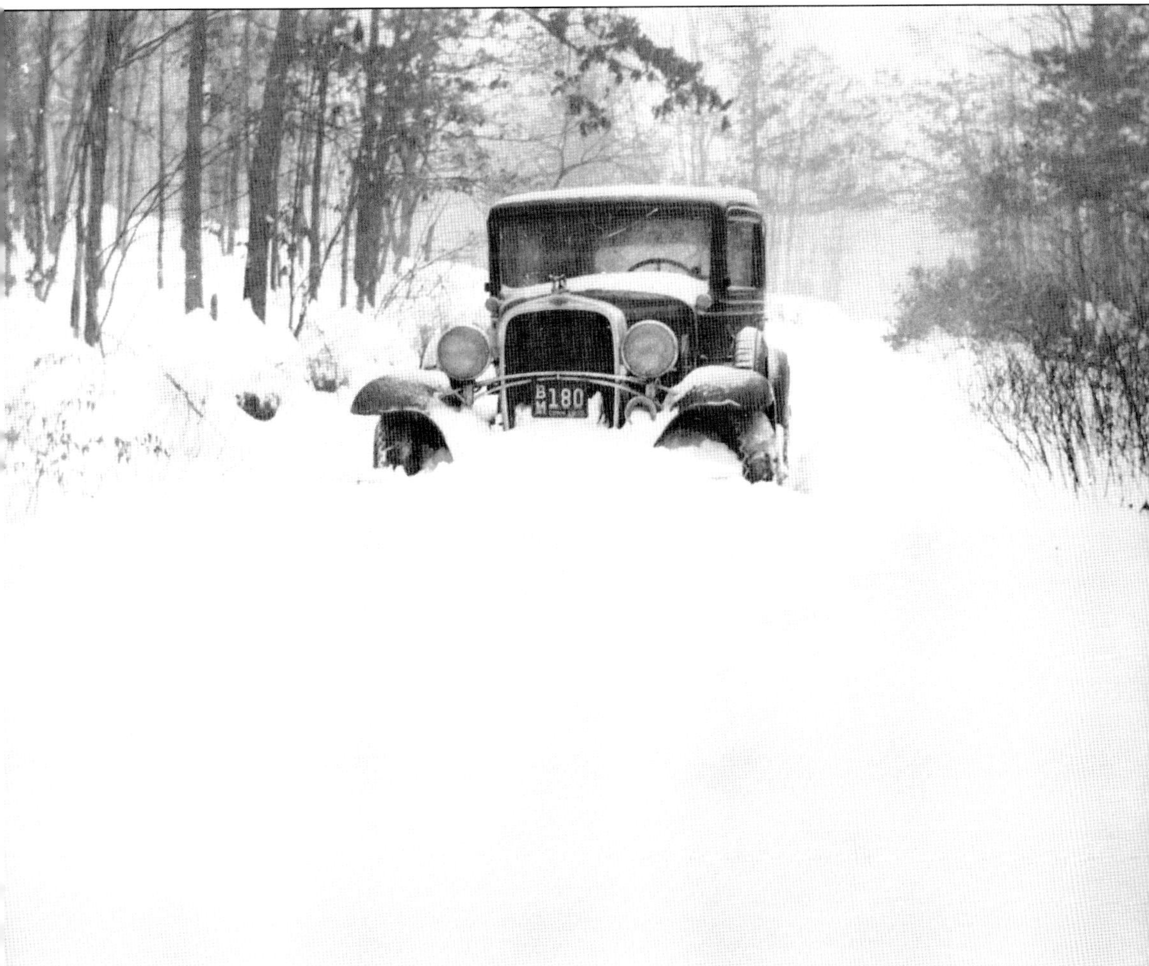

In 1900, Willington officials submitted the necessary application to the US Postal Service so that residents could get rural free delivery. After five years, they met the Postal Service requirements, meaning that residents no longer had to pick up their mail at the post offices but would instead receive it at their homes. In 1905, Charles Lyon was hired as the first mail carrier. He was known for his determination and had a reputation for delivering the mail to his patrons even when the roads seemed impassable. His determination brought to life the oft-quoted phrase about "neither snow nor rain" prohibiting postal carriers from delivering the mail. Lyon was traveling east out of Daleville in this 1931 photograph. He served as the mail carrier in Willington until retiring in 1954.

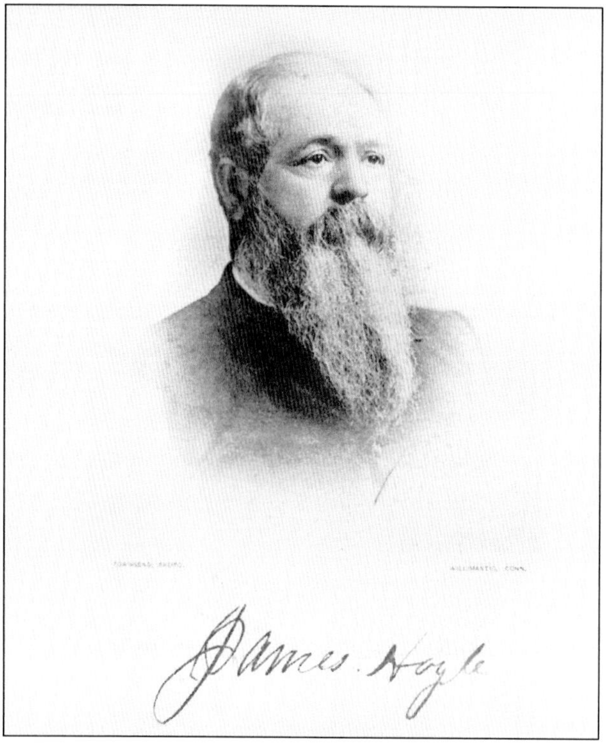

James Hoyle, a native of England, purchased a one-half interest in the floundering Willington Silk Mill in 1873, repairing it and converting it into a woolen factory. He successfully managed the mill until his death in 1902. The mill closed two years later and was destroyed in a 1940s fire after having been used as a chicken coop for some time.

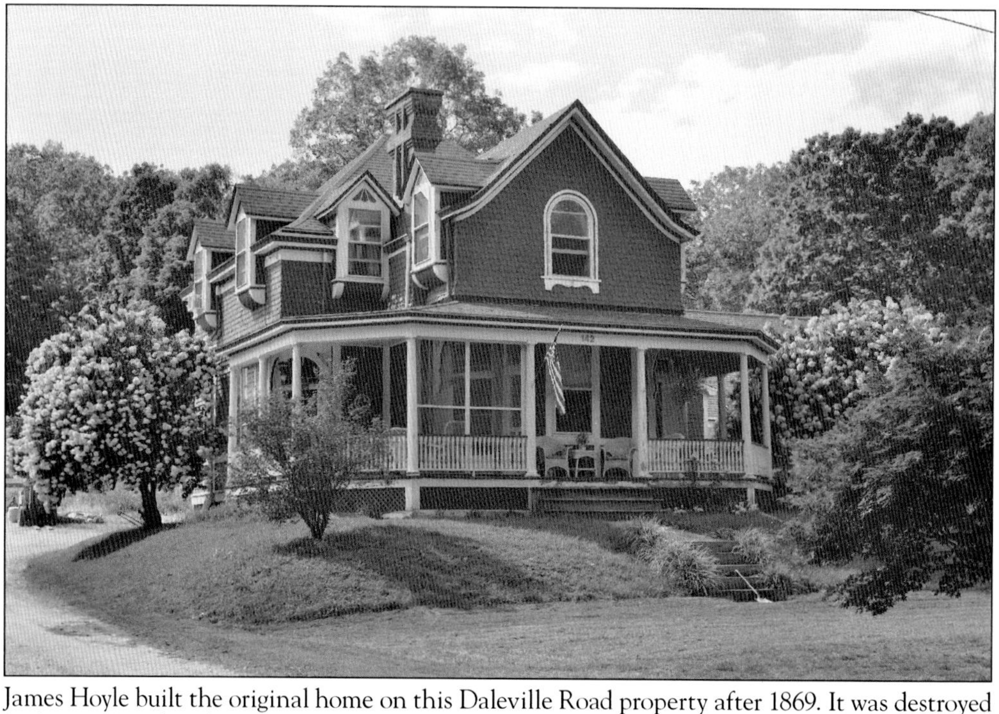

James Hoyle built the original home on this Daleville Road property after 1869. It was destroyed by fire in 1882, but the second home was modeled after the first. The Fenton River flows near the house, so the original owners created a manmade knoll to prevent flooding. The existing house includes a 1973 addition. (Courtesy of Marion Cullimore.)

Three

East Willington School District

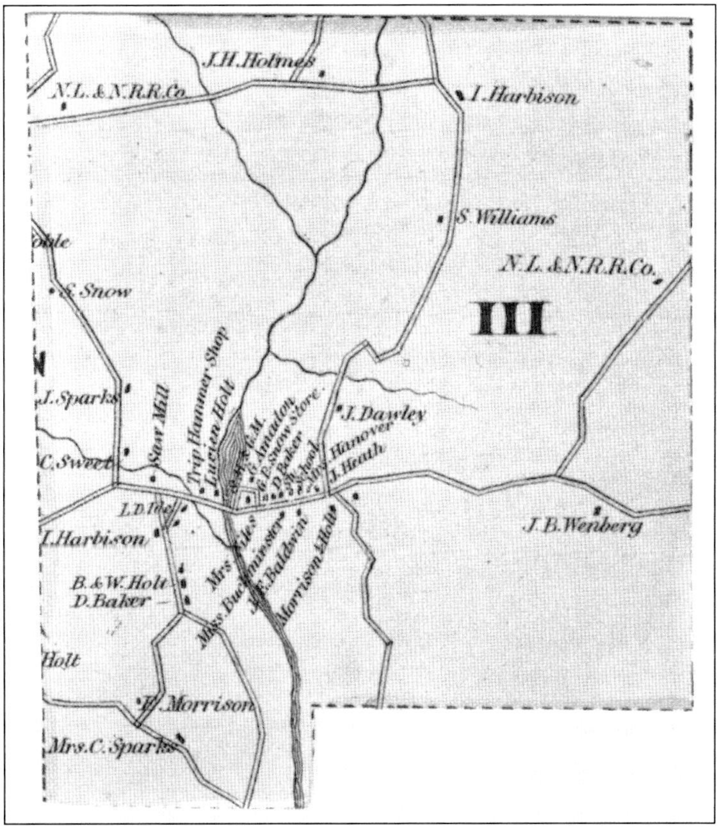

Early residents referred to East Willington as the Hollow. This now-rural section on the eastern side of Willington was once known as a city because of the multitude of businesses in the area. With the tannery and wagon shops now long gone, the area is now home to the Moose Meadow Campground, which sits on a section of the scenic Fenton River.

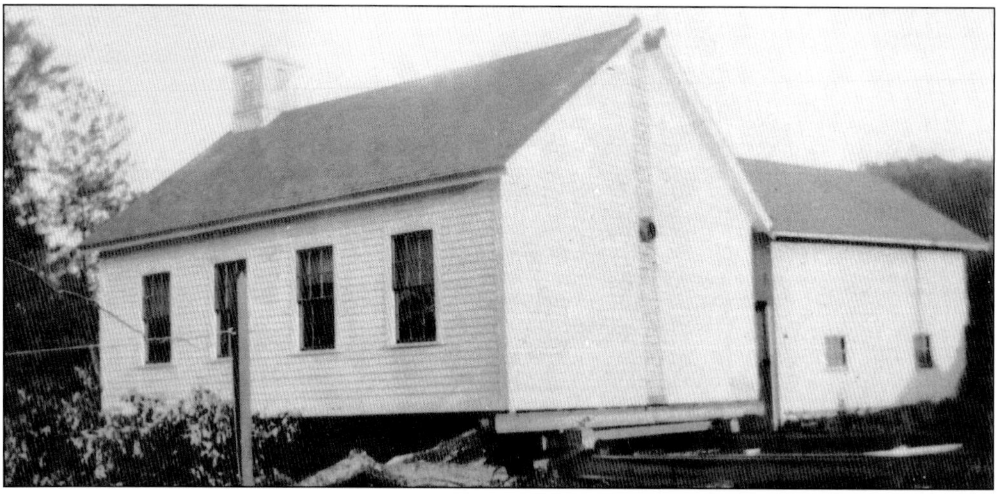

East Willington was once considered a city. Its multiple small businesses included a tannery, a shoe factory, a furniture factory, factories in which animals' hooves and horns were boiled and shaped into combs, tin and paint shops, and photography studios, then known as daguerreotype rooms. The 1856 East Willington School was eventually moved to Moose Meadow Road. Since 1936, it has housed Veterans of Foreign Wars Post 938, near the current Baywood Kennel.

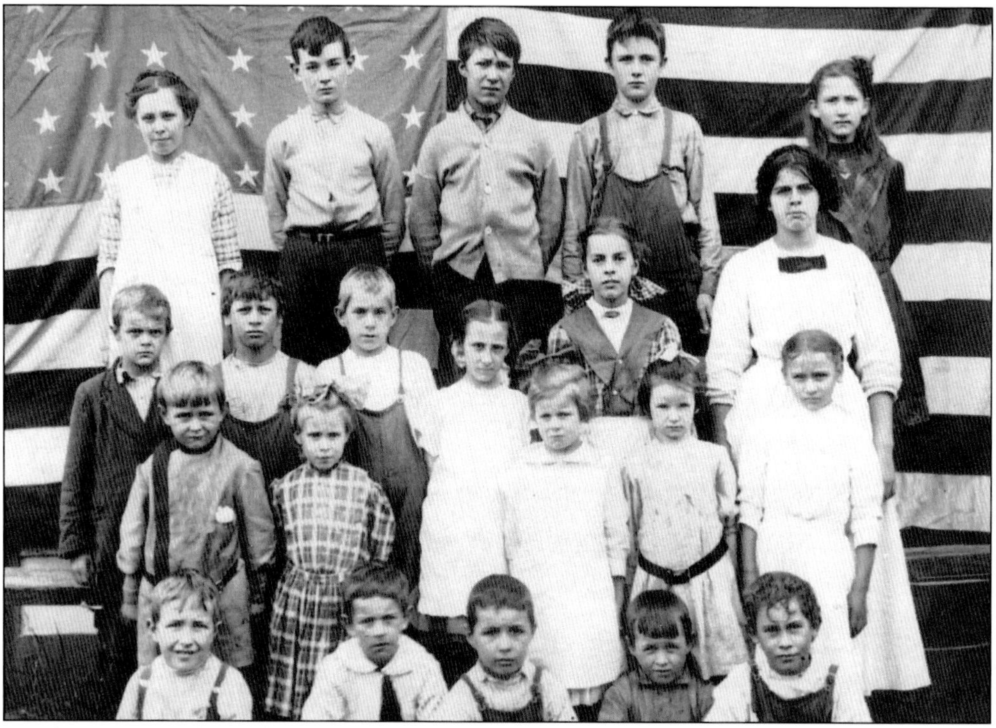

Hazel MacCormack and her pupils at the East Willington School are seen here between 1914 and 1916. From left to right are (first row) Harold Cushman, Rudolph Amidon, Steve Choma, Mike Choma, and John Hochla; (second row) Rudy Kalbac, Dorothy Wilson, Hazel Amidon, Caroline Jensen, and Mamie Hochla; (third row) Lawrence Amidon, Netro Hochla, unidentified, Doris Amidon, unidentified, and teacher Hazel MacCormack; (fourth row) Florence Wilson, John Choma, Leroy Wilson, Irving Barry, and unidentified.

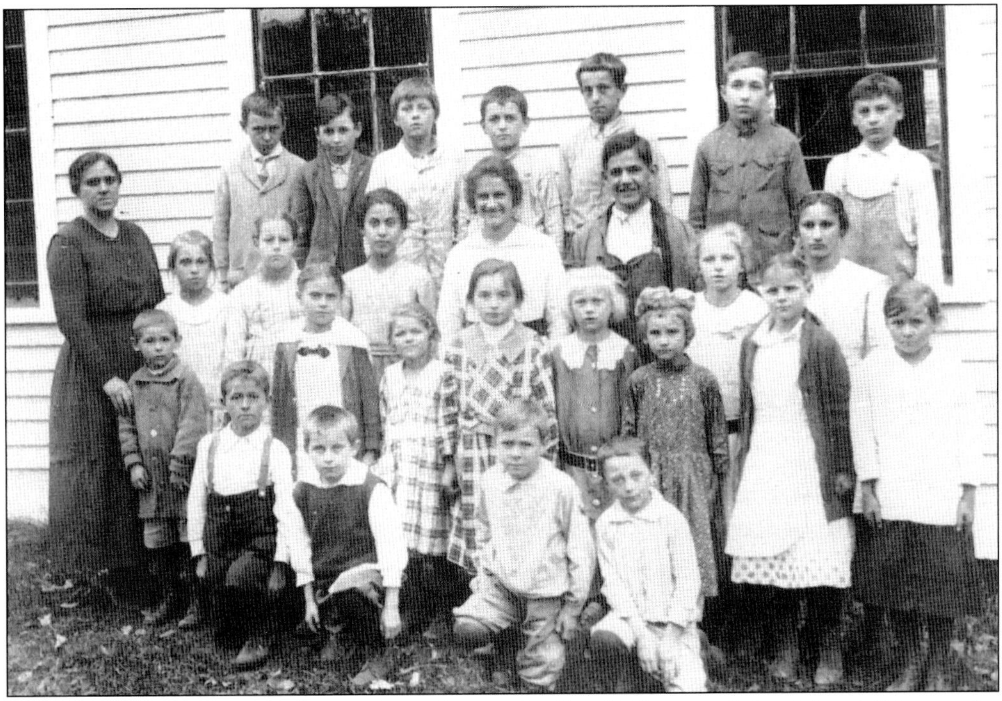

In 1922, Alice Downes taught this large class at the East Willington School. In addition to the families who sent their children to the school between 1914 and 1916, this class included children from the Vlk, Lowry, Sekar, Mrockowski, Slotick, and Kasper families. The school was built after a vote in November 1856 appropriated $400 to construct a new schoolhouse.

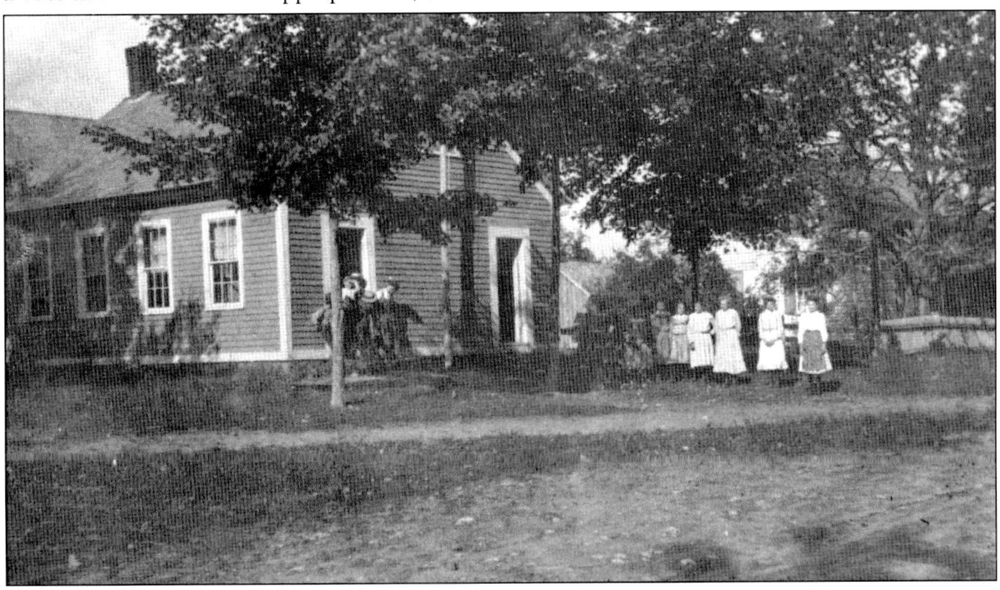

By the time this photograph of the East Willington School was taken in 1922, residents had long abandoned their early efforts to have the area, once known as the Hollow, made part of the neighboring town of Ashford so they would not have to travel to the Willington common for church services and town meetings. It is unknown why these unidentified women gathered for the photograph.

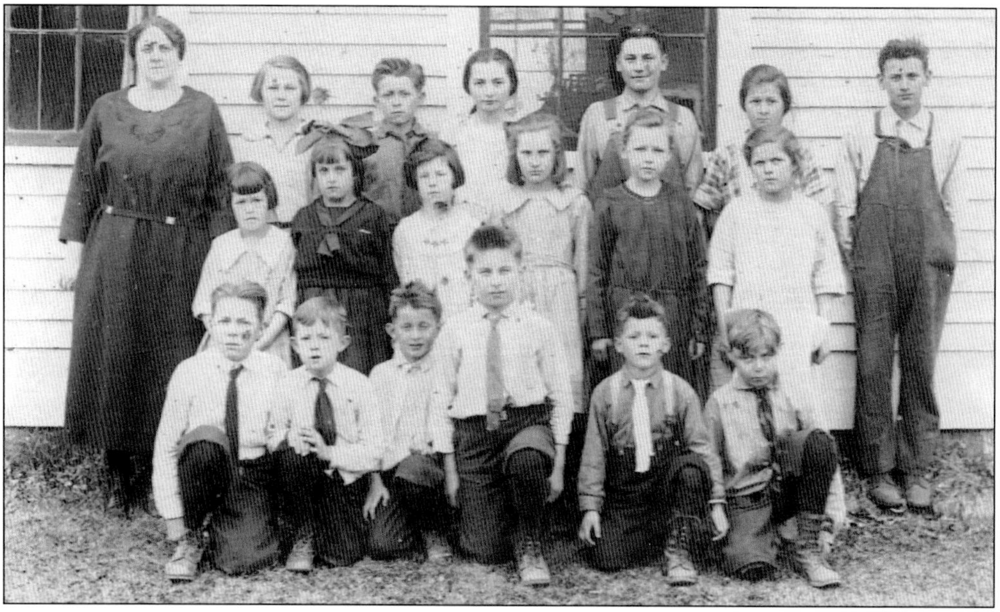

Alice Downes was still teaching at the East Willington School when this photograph was taken in 1926 or 1927. Her pupils were, from left to right, (first row) Merrill Wilson, Henry Walton, Stanley Kasper, Walter Kasper, John Vlk, and Teddy Krivanec; (second row) Sylvia Cushman, Barbara Amidon, Alice Walton, Mamie Hockla, Carrie Krivanec, and Rose Vlk; (third row) Alice Downes, Georgiana Pokorny, William Vlk, Margaret Choma, Steve Hockla, Lillian Vlk, and Paul Hockla.

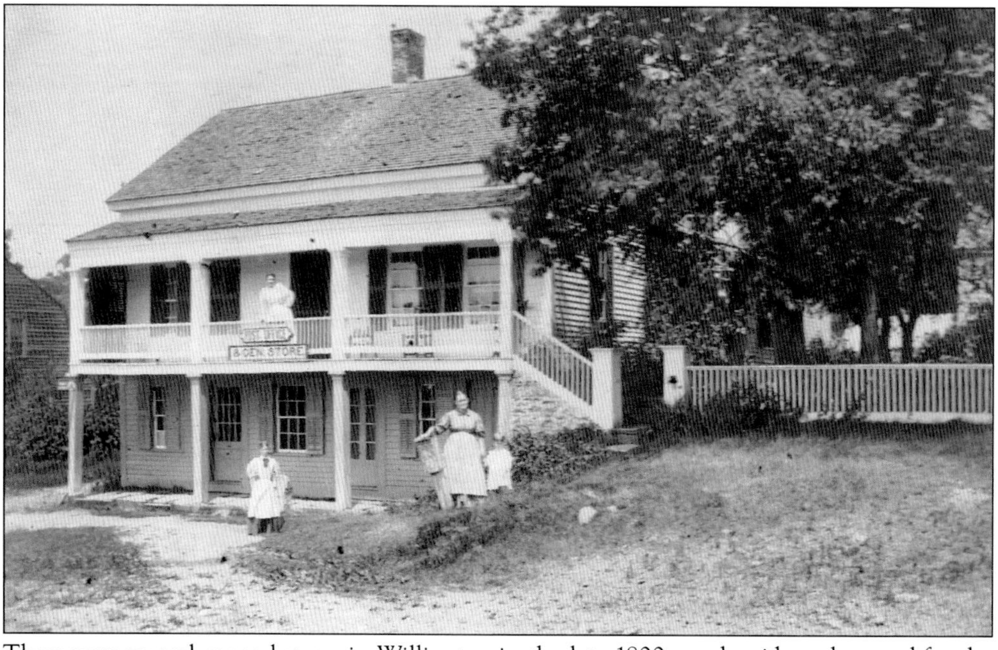

There were several general stores in Willington in the late 1800s, and residents bartered for the products the shopkeepers offered. The Charles Rider store, seen here around 1880 and located in East Willington, also served as the post office. The current residents' desire to preserve Willington as a rural community means that there are no chain stores and only one convenience store in town.

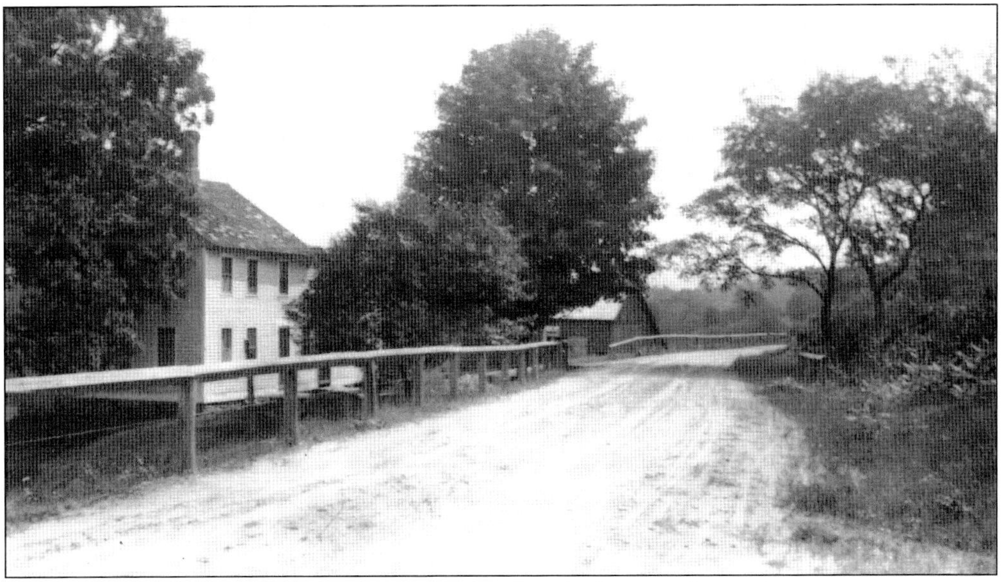

Because early residents of the East Willington section had to travel great distances to participate in life on the Willington village green, they tried to join with nearby Ashford. This photograph of East Willington was taken from a glass slide, not from film; it is estimated to have been taken before the 1880s.

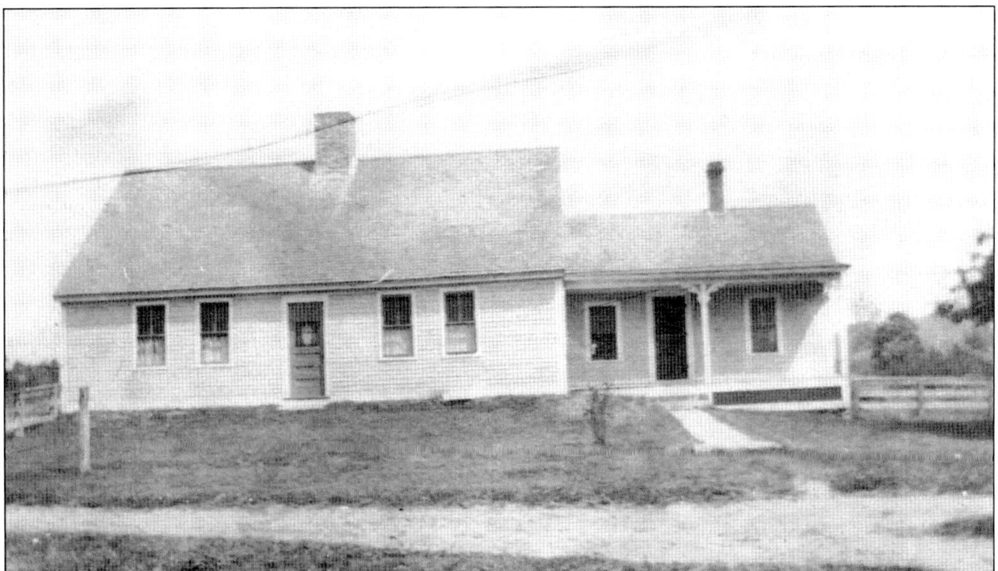

First selectwoman Christina Beebe Mailhos readily identified the house in this 1900 photograph as being on Route 74, also known as the Tolland Turnpike. It is located next to the termite and pest control business originally owned by her father and presently owned by her brother Eric. It is speculated that the house was built as early as 1815. (Courtesy of Evelyne A. Parizek.)

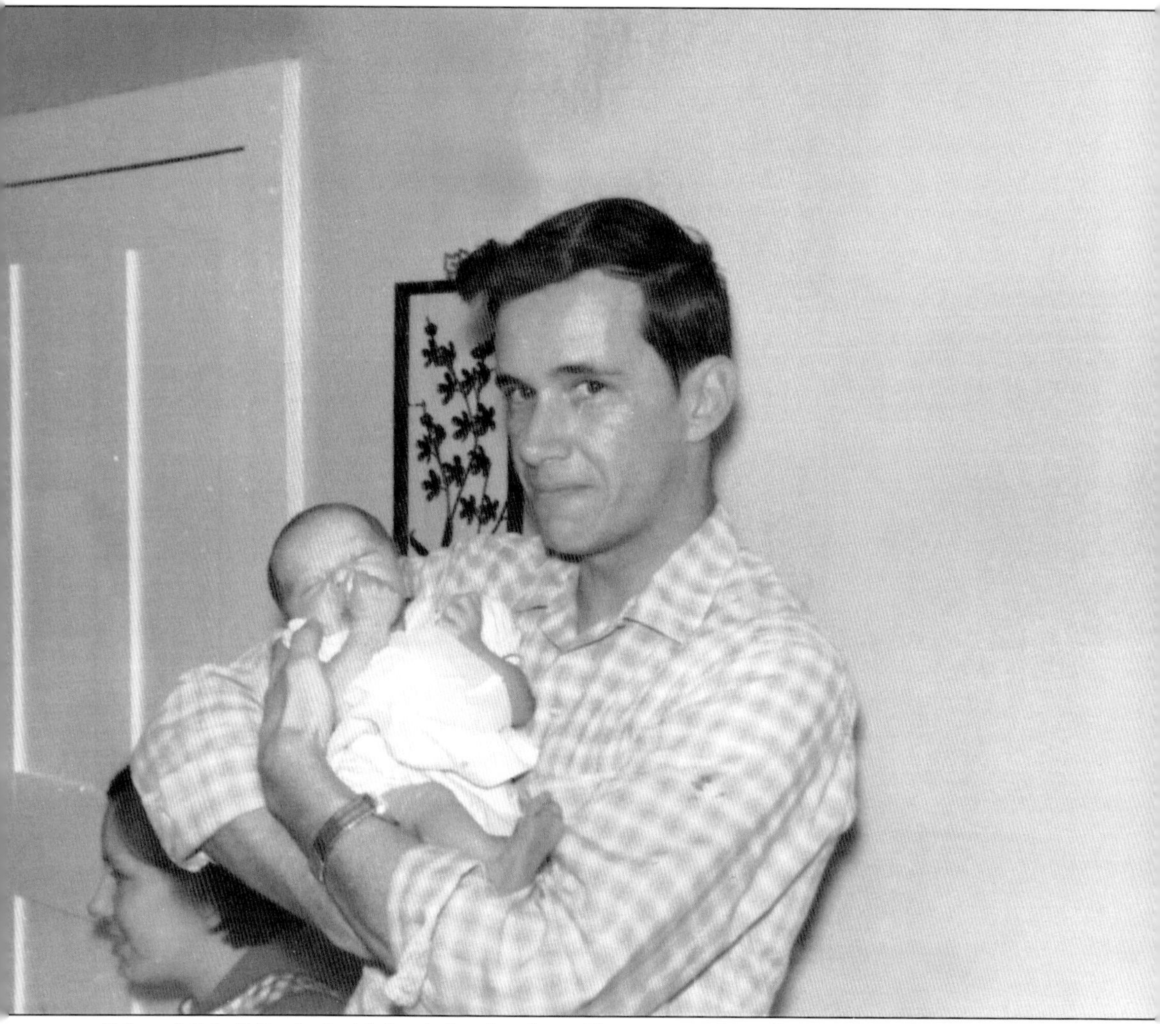

Edward "Ned" Beebe holds his baby daughter Christina on March 29, 1970. Christina was born shortly after her father and mother, Lena, moved to Willington from New London. Ned served in the Navy from 1961 to 1965, including a tour of duty on the USS *John A. Boyle* during the Vietnam War. Ned started his business, Willington Termite and Pest Control, in 1978. He was the commander of the Willington Veterans of Foreign Wars post and the president of the Willington Hill Fire Department. One of Willington's unique characteristics is that in addition to Democrats and Republicans, there is a third political party, known as the Sentinels, which Ned was one of the founding members of in 1995. Christina Beebe married Richard Mailhos and became Willington's first selectwoman in 2009. (Courtesy of Christina Beebe Mailhos.)

Four

Moose Meadow (Rider) School District

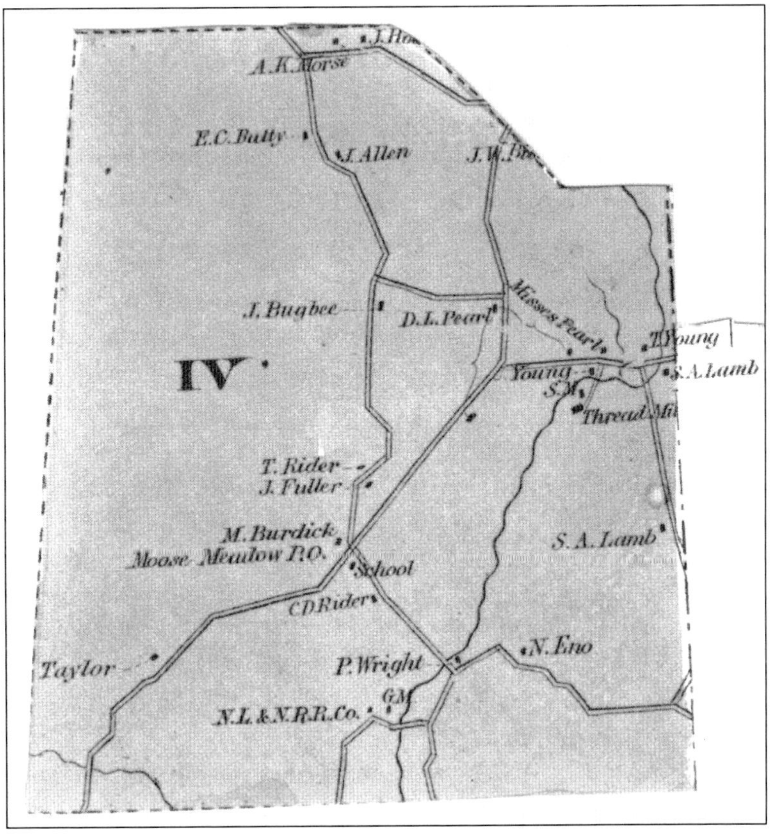

This eastern section of town was once part of neighboring Ashford. It currently consists of far more homes than businesses. Deer, coyote, fisher cats, and foxes frequent its many fields and meadows. The area is home to Fenton Ruby Park and Wildlife Preserve, a quiet destination for hiking, snowshoeing, and wandering along the Fenton River.

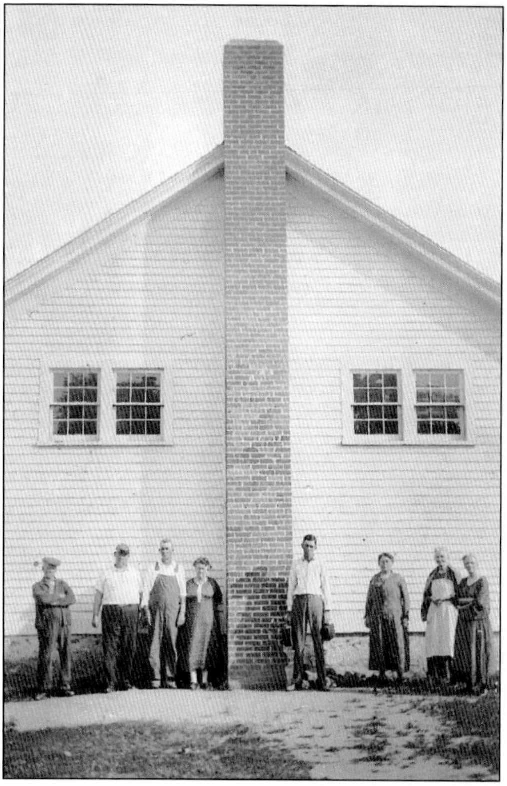

There were originally 11 one-room schoolhouses in Willington; nine, including Moose Meadow, survived the consolidation of August 2, 1869. The Moose Meadow School District was originally named after Hiram Rider, who served as a state legislator, county sheriff, state treasurer, and Tolland County Court judge. The unidentified people in this undated photograph stand in front of the newer, more modern Moose Meadow School, which was built in 1910.

This undated interior photograph of the Moose Meadow School shows the woodstove that was used to heat the building throughout the cold New England winters. A multitude of American flags show the efforts to Americanize children of foreign-born parents. It is also possible that a teacher used one of the switches that were so prevalent at the time to chastise the child who carved his initials into the desk in the right foreground.

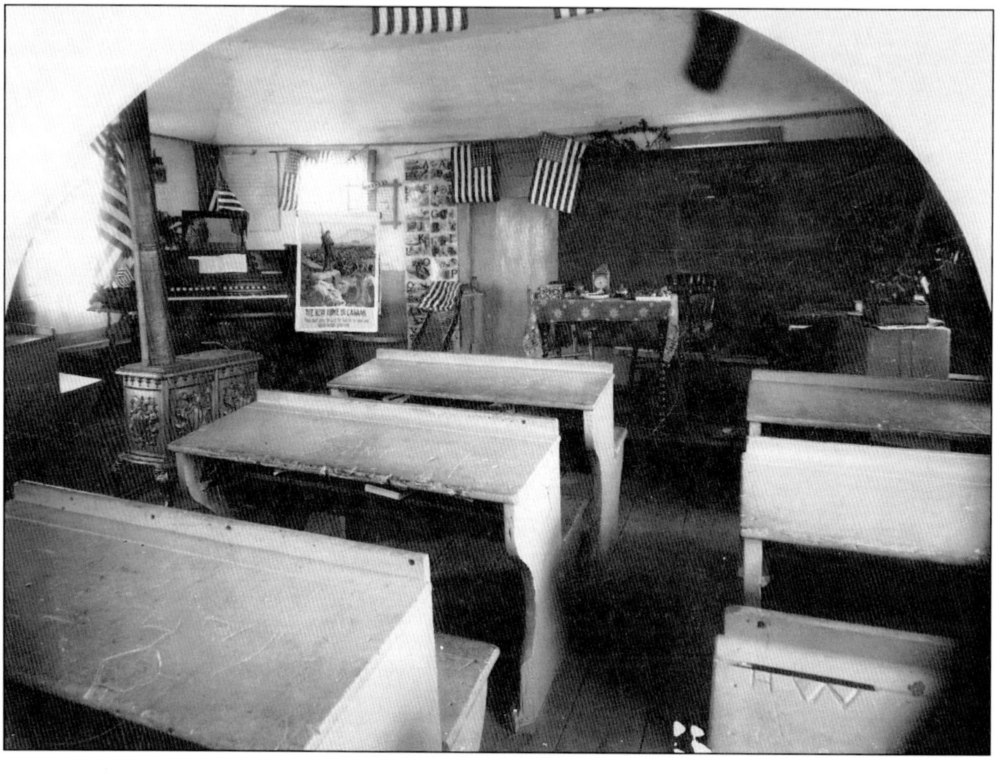

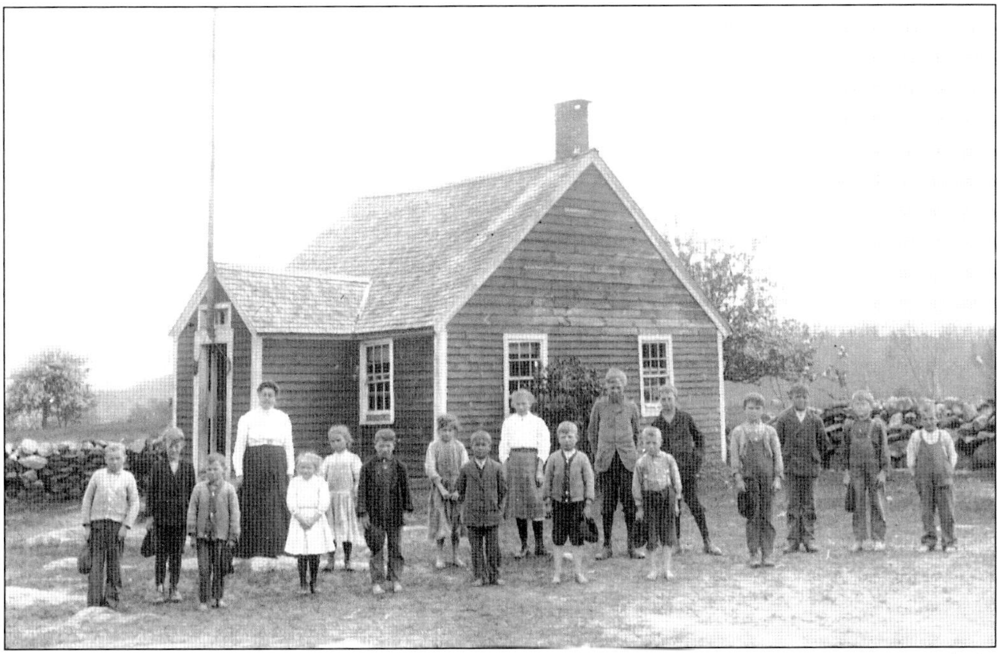

Teacher Lillia Fenton posed at the original Moose Meadow School for this undated postcard. As the new Moose Meadow schoolhouse was built in 1910, this photograph was taken before then. During the 1911–1912 school year, Lillia earned $360 for 180 days of teaching, or $2 per day.

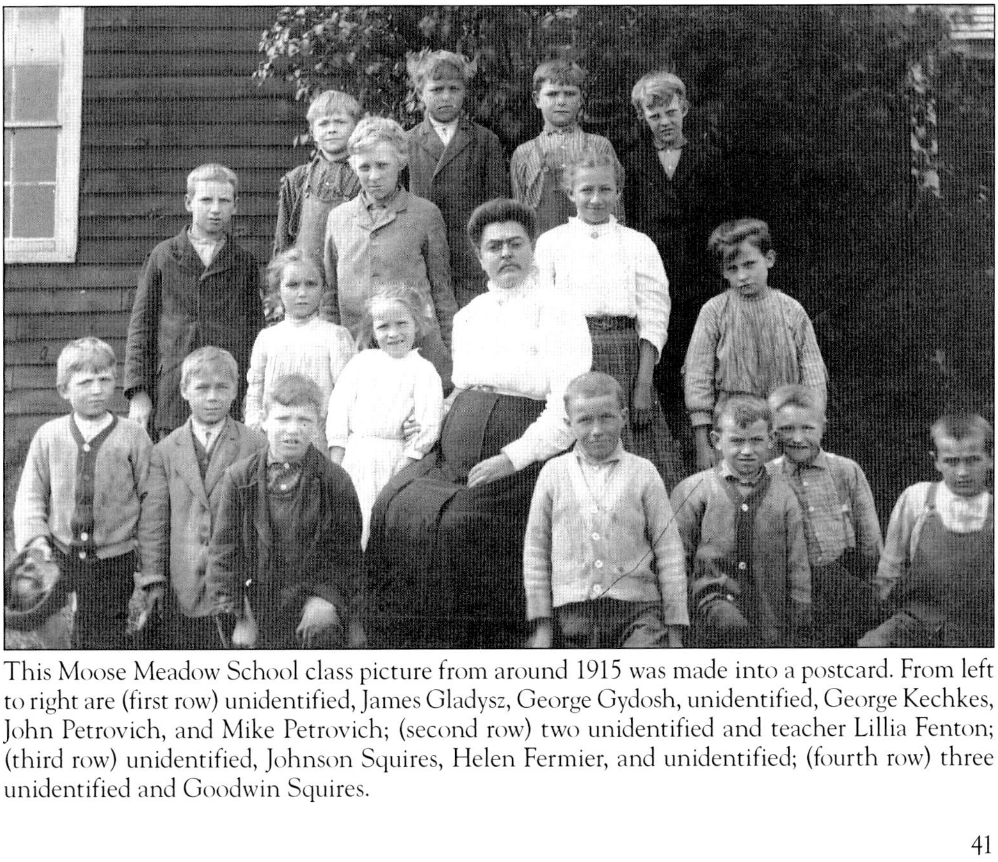

This Moose Meadow School class picture from around 1915 was made into a postcard. From left to right are (first row) unidentified, James Gladysz, George Gydosh, unidentified, George Kechkes, John Petrovich, and Mike Petrovich; (second row) two unidentified and teacher Lillia Fenton; (third row) unidentified, Johnson Squires, Helen Fermier, and unidentified; (fourth row) three unidentified and Goodwin Squires.

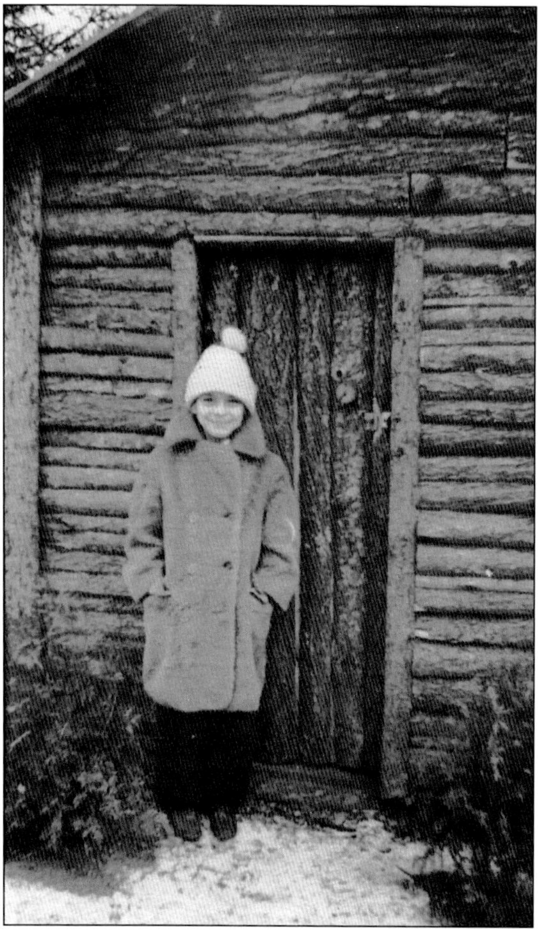

For the students at the Moose Meadow School in the mid-1900s, it was more than just "reading, writing, and 'rithmetic." Moose Meadow students not only cleaned the building and started the fire, they also learned to build. This log cabin they built near their school is an example of the broad education the students received under the guidance of their creative teacher. (Courtesy of Brenda LaFemina-Weber.)

The Methodist Episcopal church was built in 1834. The plastering and papering of the interior was completed in 1889. At the celebration of its 50th anniversary, pastor F.C. Newell shared Methodism's history in Willington and noted that the first pastor was Rev. William Wolcott. This photograph, developed on August 30, 1935, shows the demolition of the church on Moose Meadow Road just over 100 years after its construction.

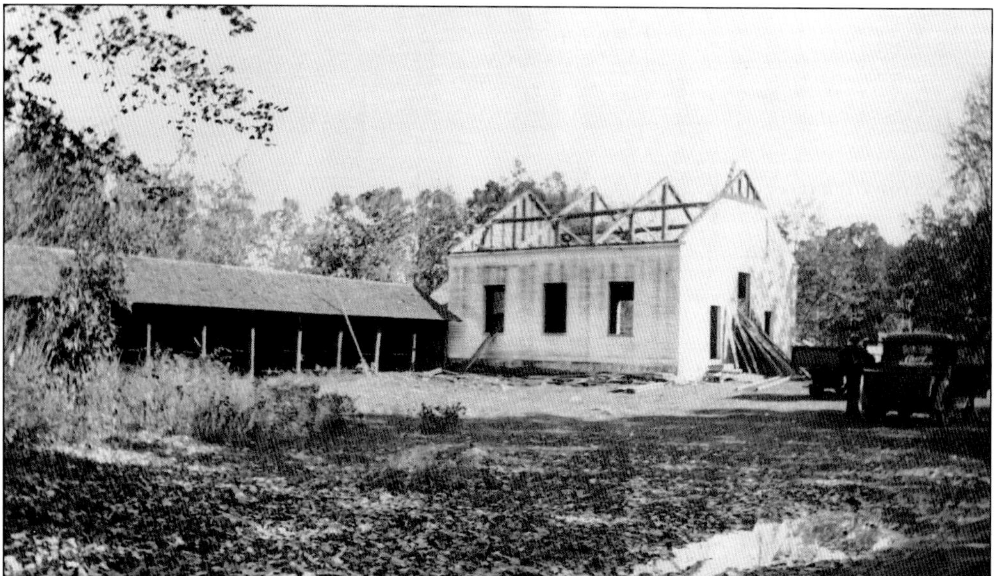

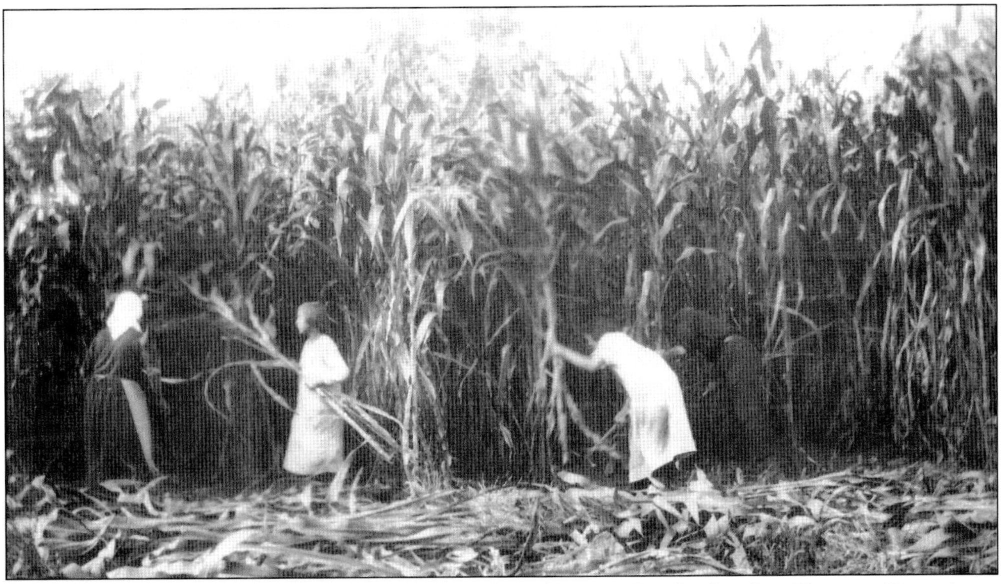

Born on November 20, 1875, in Krupina, in what later became Czechoslovakia, Katarina Ruznakova married Jan Hipsky on February 4, 1894. They later came to the United States, where Katarina became known as Katrin. Two of their ten children were born in the United States. When Jan died on November 14, 1937, Katrin (left) continued to tend the farm, including harvesting the corn, as seen here with unidentified helpers. This photograph was developed on March 20, 1946. (Courtesy of Brenda LaFemina-Weber.)

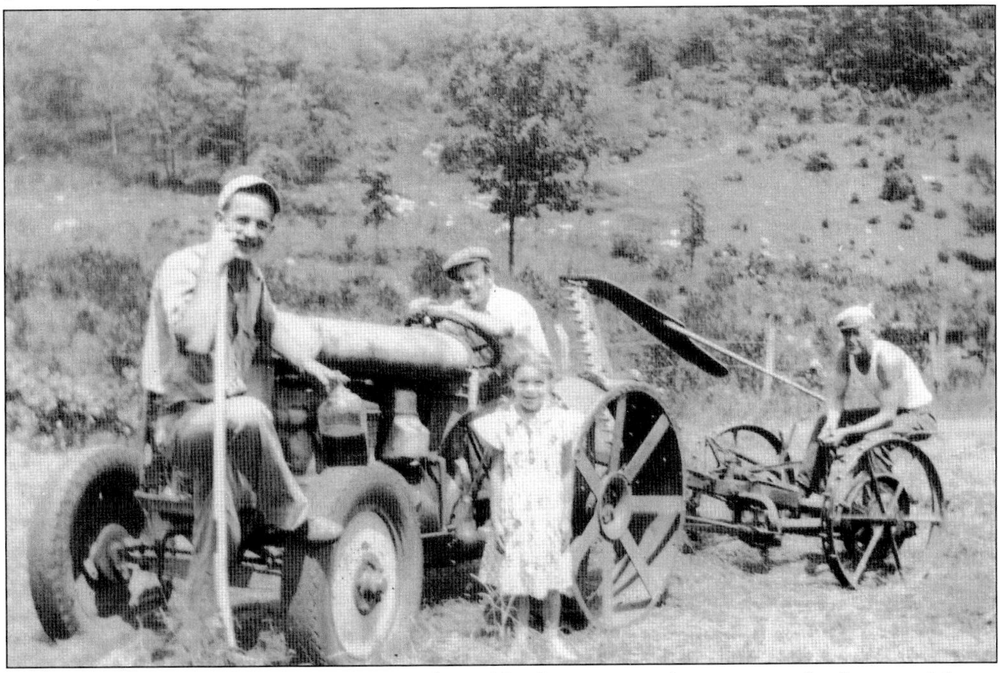

After her husband's death, Katrin Ruznakova Hipsky continued to operate the farm on Moose Meadow Road. She and her daughter Mary and Mary's daughter Lillian made and sold butter, cheese, milk, and eggs. Seen here on July 4, 1938, are, from left to right, Matthew Holda, Lillian Hipsky, and two unidentified workers. (Courtesy of Brenda LaFemina-Weber.)

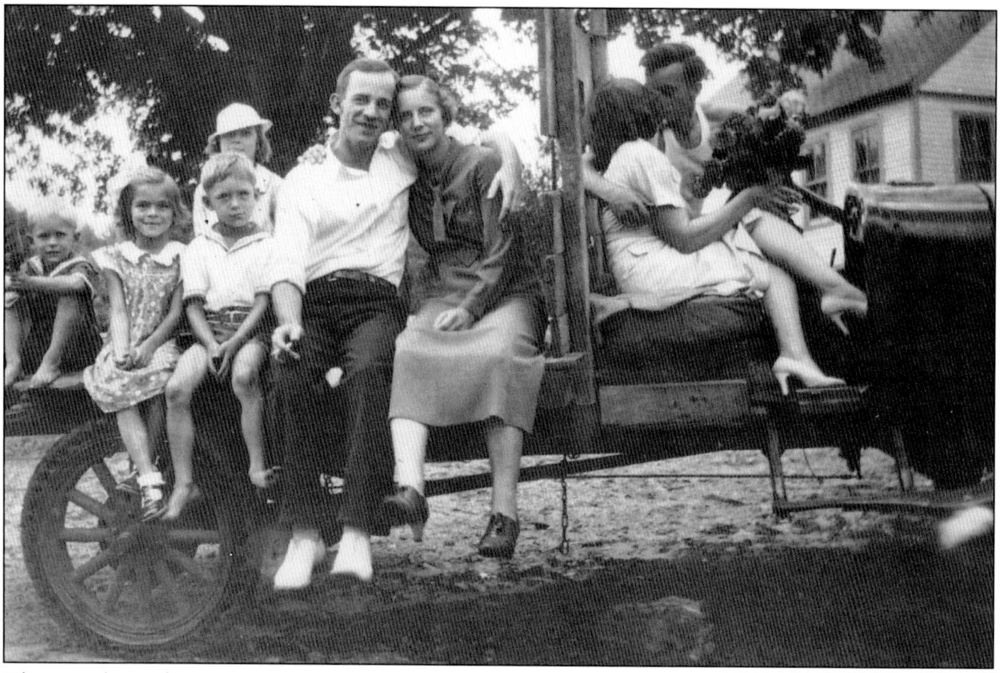

The people in this undated photograph are, from left to right, unidentified, Lillian Hipsky, two unidentified, Matthew Holda, Katie Hipsky, Sophie ?, and Joseph Hipsky. Joseph was the eighth of Katrin and Jan Hipsky's children. He married Sophie on June 5, 1937. (Courtesy of Brenda LaFemina-Weber.)

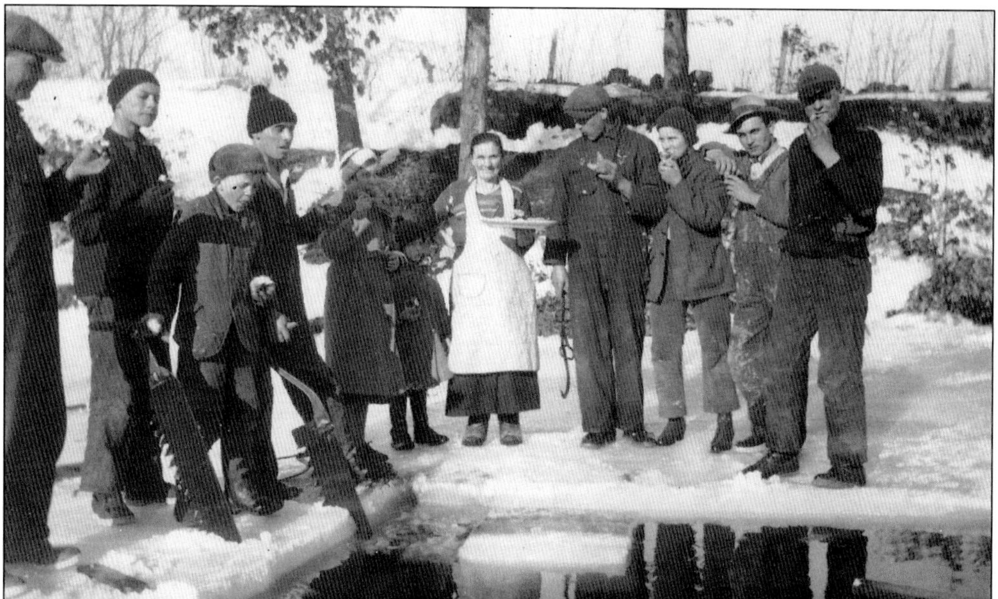

Katrin Ruznakova Hipsky is in the center of this undated photograph with her young granddaughter Lillian and a group of unidentified people who seem happy to help cut ice from the pond in exchange for Katrin's homemade doughnuts. Sawdust was used to preserve the ice in an icehouse located near the Hipsky farm on Moose Meadow Road. (Courtesy of Brenda LaFemina-Weber.)

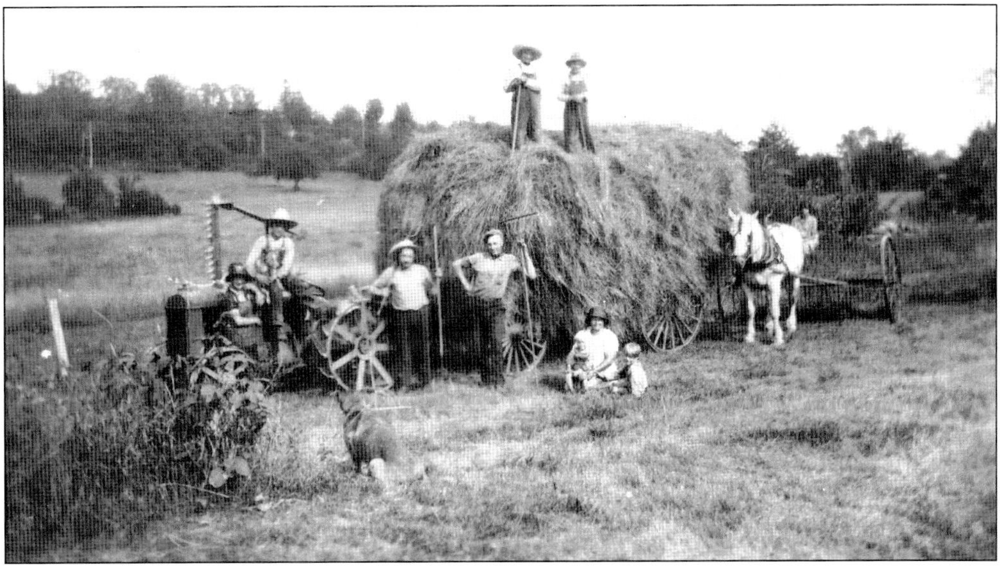

The herculean task of loading hay on Katrin Hipsky's farm on Moose Meadow Road required the assistance of family and friends, unidentified in this photograph but of immeasurable assistance to the matriarchal farm where Katrin lived with her daughter Mary and granddaughter Lillian. This photograph was developed on March 26, 1946, meaning it likely took place in the summer or fall of 1945. (Courtesy of Brenda LaFemina-Weber.)

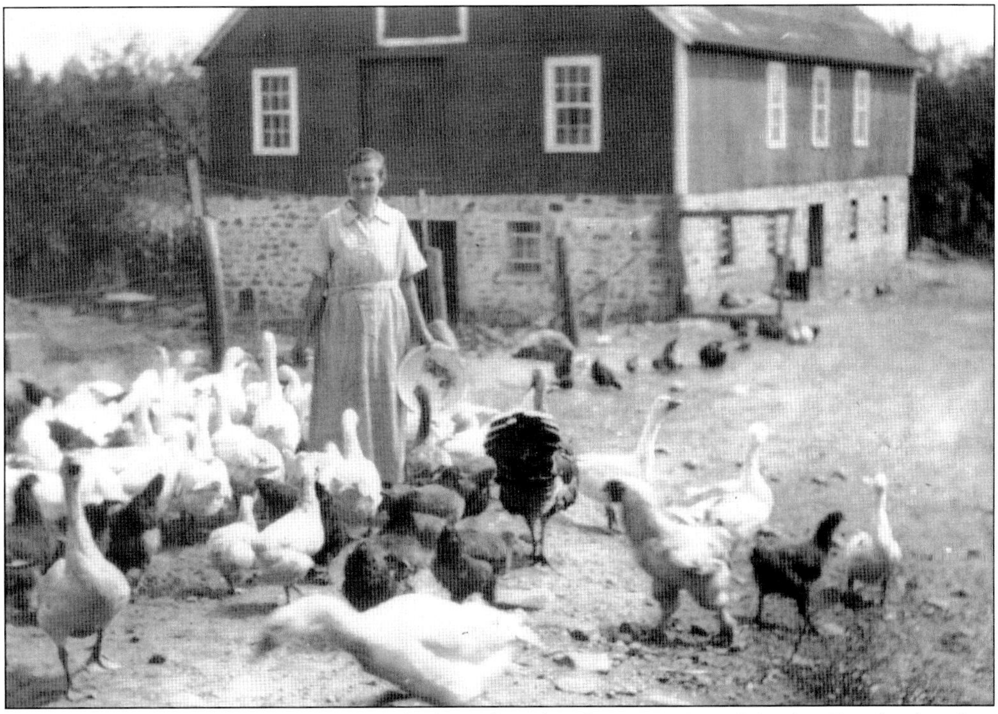

In 1945, Katrin Hipsky sent geese and chickens from her farm on Moose Meadow Road to butcher shops in New York City, where they were sometimes hung in a window as advertisements. This barn still stands on Moose Meadow Road and is currently used by Hipsky's grandson-in-law Ralph LeFemina as the R&R Tire Shop. (Courtesy of Brenda LaFemina-Weber.)

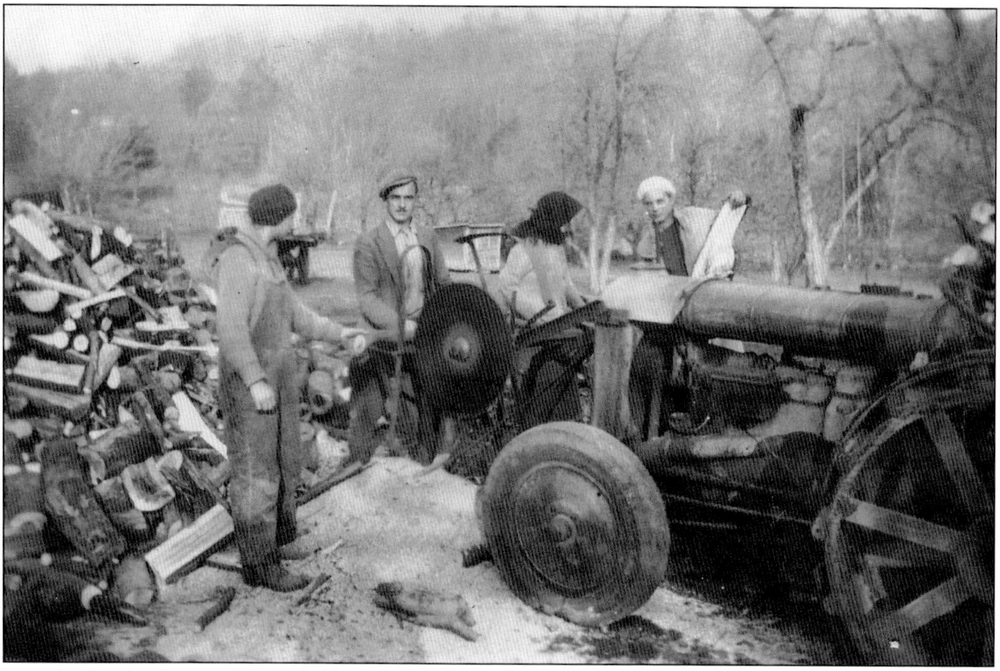

Joseph Hipsky (second from left) is seen here with unidentified workers on his mother's Moose Meadow Road farm. Joseph, Katrin's youngest son, was born on December 13, 1911, before the family came to Willington. After leaving Czechoslovakia, the family lived in Canada before coming to the United States. (Courtesy of Brenda LaFemina-Weber.)

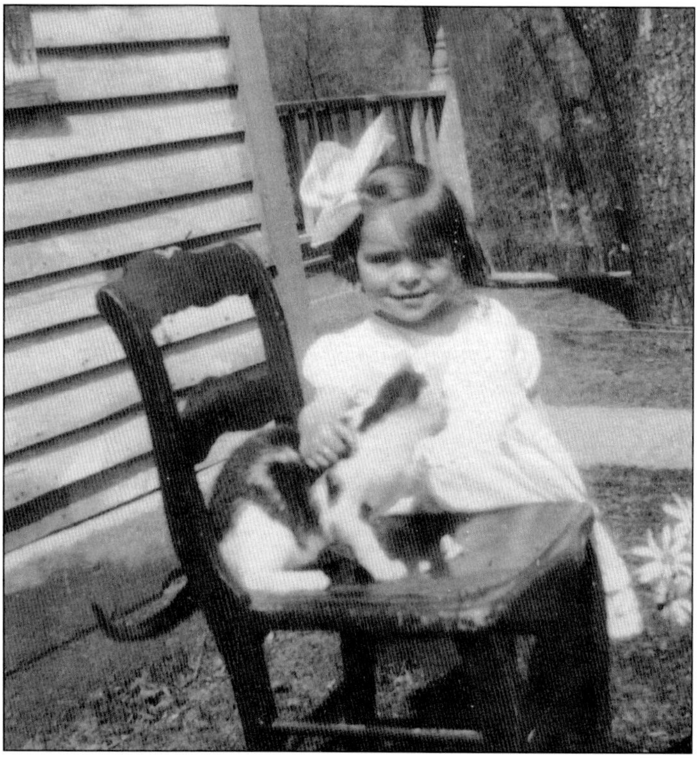

Lillian Hipsky grew up on the family farm on Moose Meadow Road, where she learned by example from her mother and grandmother the values required to successfully manage a farm: discipline, determination, responsibility, and resilience. In this undated photograph, she takes advantage of an opportunity to pause with one of the many cats the family had throughout her life. (Courtesy of Brenda LaFemina-Weber.)

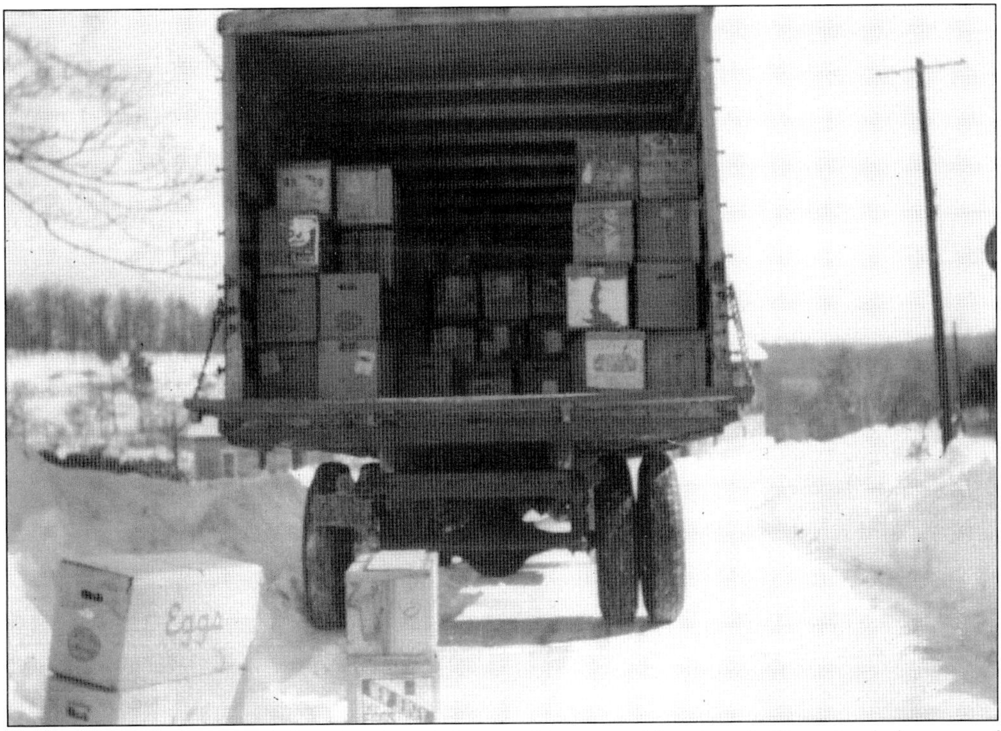

Katrin Hipsky, along with her daughter Mary and her granddaughter Lillian, loaded crates of poultry, eggs, and milk from their farm on Moose Meadow Road to be sold at markets as far away as New York City. The truck in this undated photograph is being loaded for travel on the snow-covered roads. (Courtesy of Brenda LaFemina-Weber.)

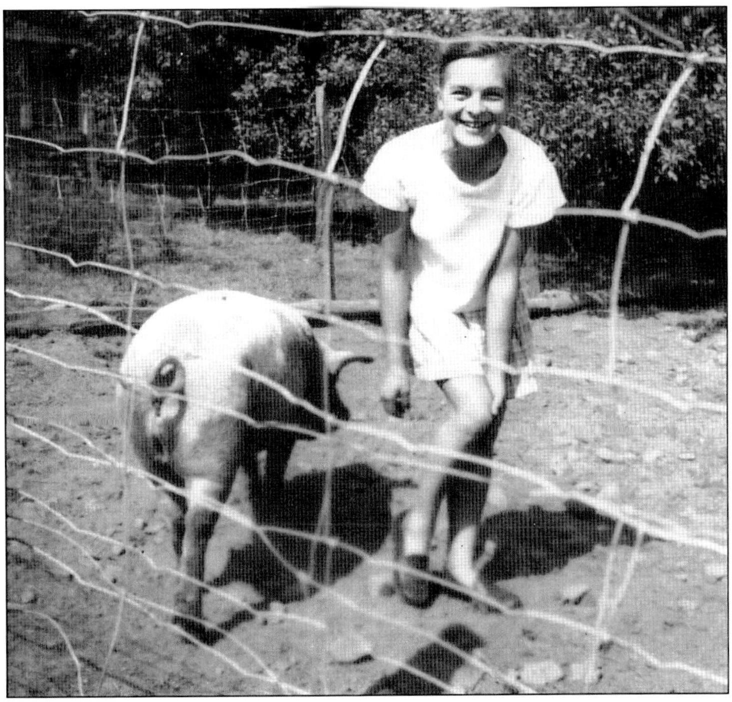

This undated photograph of Lillian Hipsky reveals her enthusiasm for tending to the animals on her grandmother's farm on Moose Meadow Road. She was 79 years old when she died in the farmhouse she had lived in her entire life. She was remembered as being hardworking and industrious, maintaining a farm while simultaneously running a household and making cottage cheese from the milk of her own cows. (Courtesy of Brenda LaFemina-Weber.)

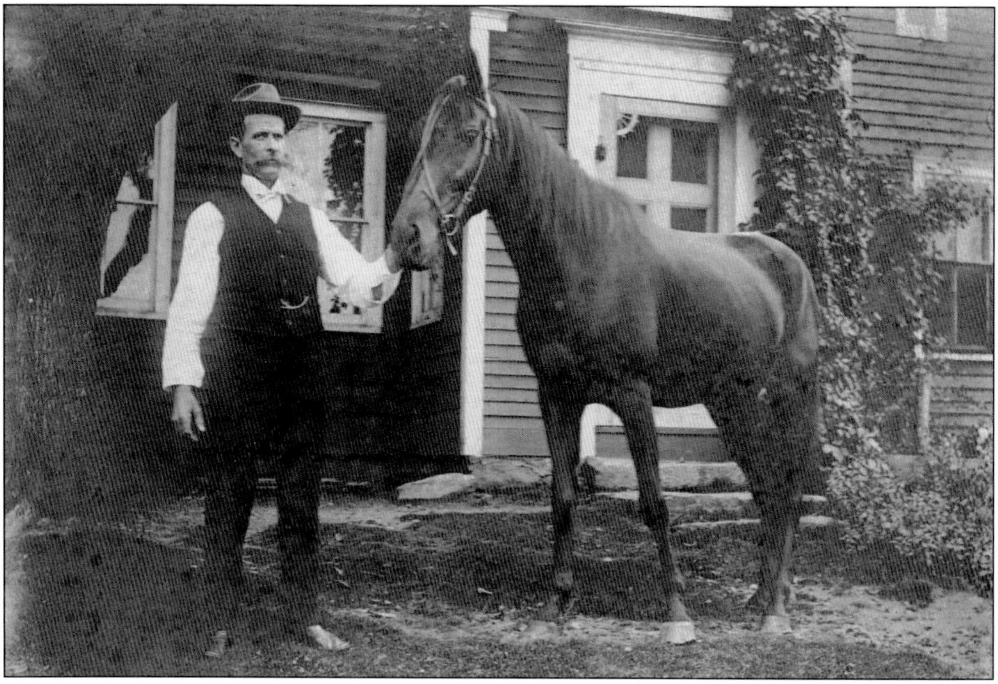

In April 1840, residents of the Moose Meadow section benefited from the establishment of a post office at the corner of Moose Meadow and Jared Sparks Roads. Benjamin Lillibridge was the first postmaster. There are no longer district post offices in Willington. This post office later became the home of Edward Burdick. The man in this undated photograph is unidentified. The house is still occupied today.

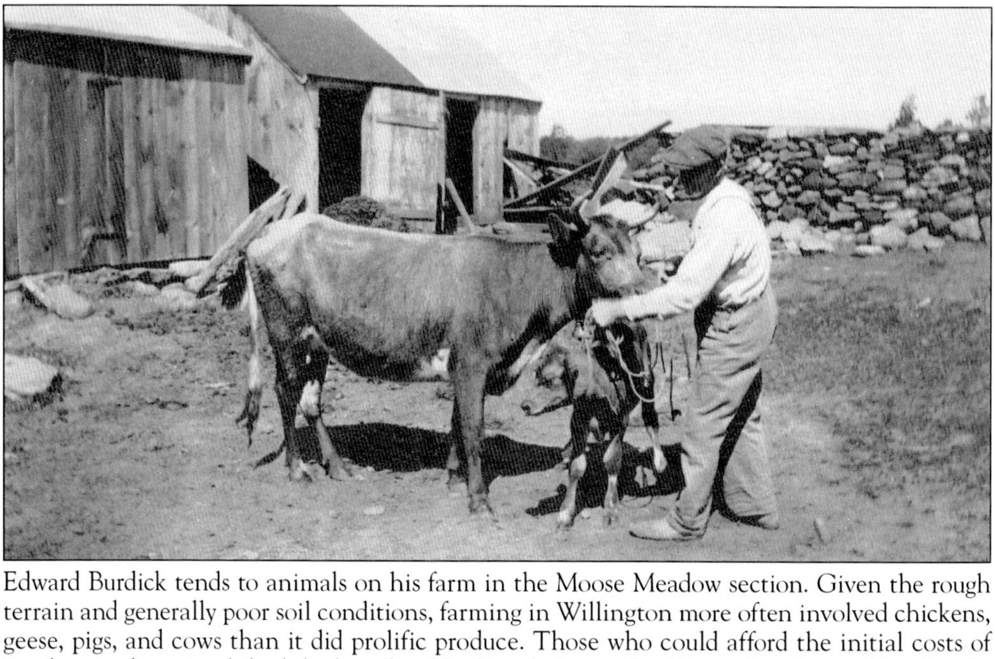

Edward Burdick tends to animals on his farm in the Moose Meadow section. Given the rough terrain and generally poor soil conditions, farming in Willington more often involved chickens, geese, pigs, and cows than it did prolific produce. Those who could afford the initial costs of purchasing the animals had the benefit of feeding their own families and perhaps selling locally or to the larger marketplaces outside Willington.

Five

Potter School District

This remote section of town is located far from the mills, shops, and stagecoach and railroad stations of early Willington. There were no industries located in this district. Today, Interstate 84, also known as the Wilbur Cross Highway, travels through the area, although there is no access to or from the highway. Instead, an area that was once acres of farmland is now heavily forested and still sparsely populated.

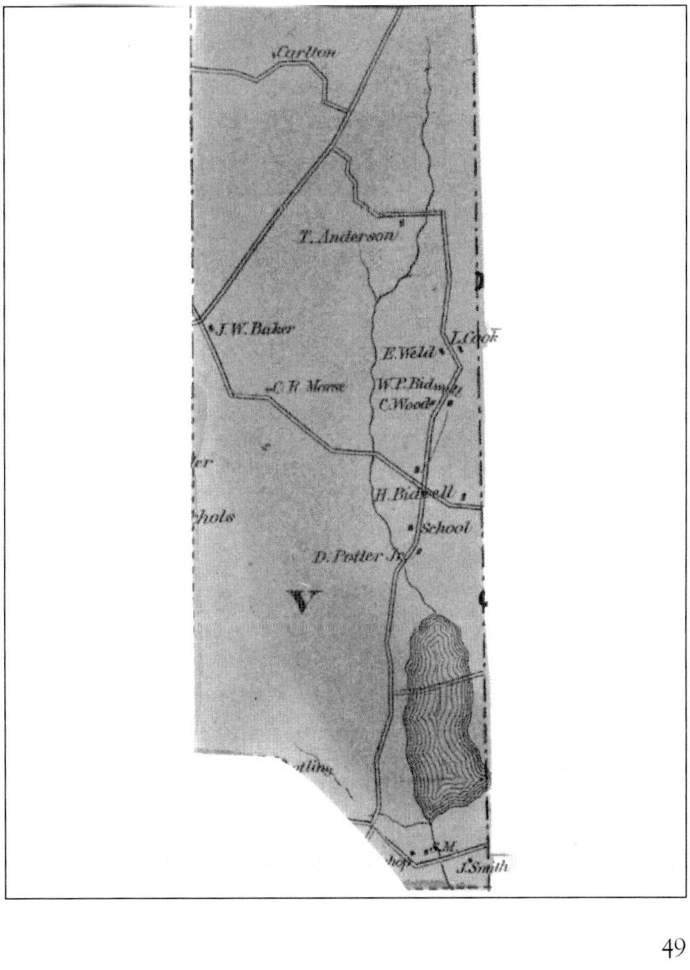

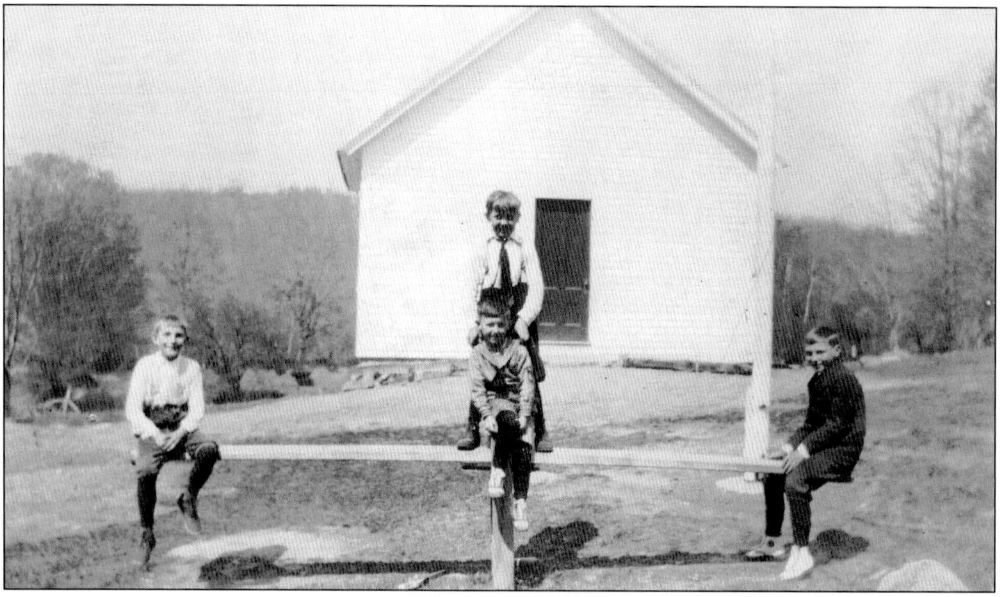

On July 3, 1914, the town voted to build a schoolhouse at a cost of not more than $1,000 in Willington's northernmost corner, bordered by Union to the north and Ashford to the east. The Potter School building committee consisted of W.C. Ruby, C.S. Amidon, and William Eldredge. The boys in this undated photograph are unidentified.

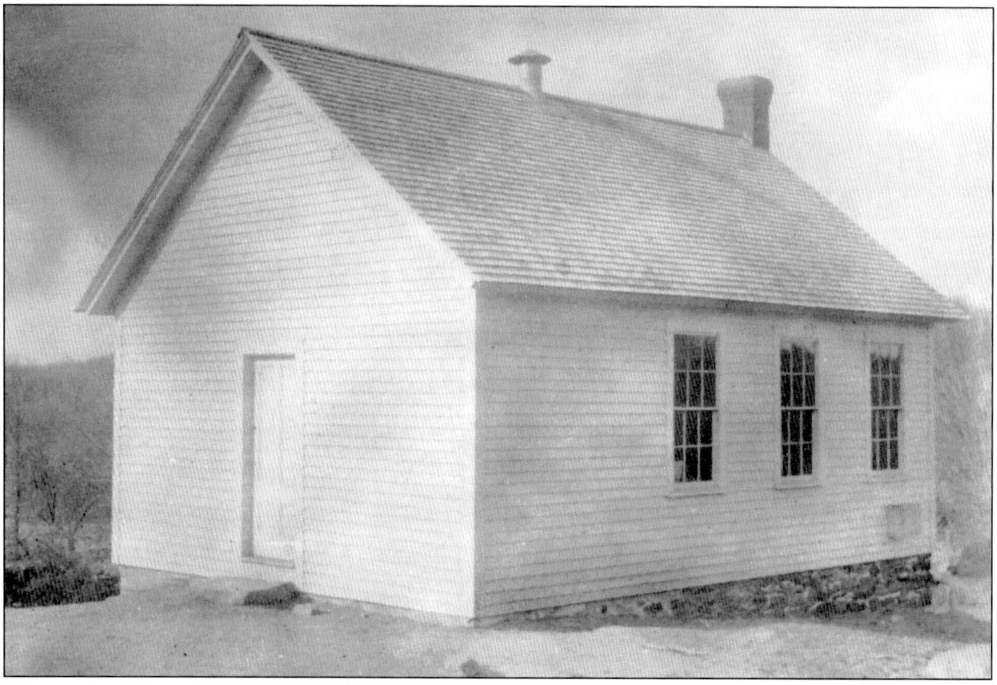

The original one-room Potter School, seen here in the early 1920s, is now a private home, and the owners through the years have added multiple sections. Among the earliest students were Helen, Kate, and Wilhelmina Balazs, who lived on the neighboring farm. Each of the girls earned certificates for perfect attendance at various points during their education. The current home is located on the corner of intersecting roads named after the Potter and Balazs families.

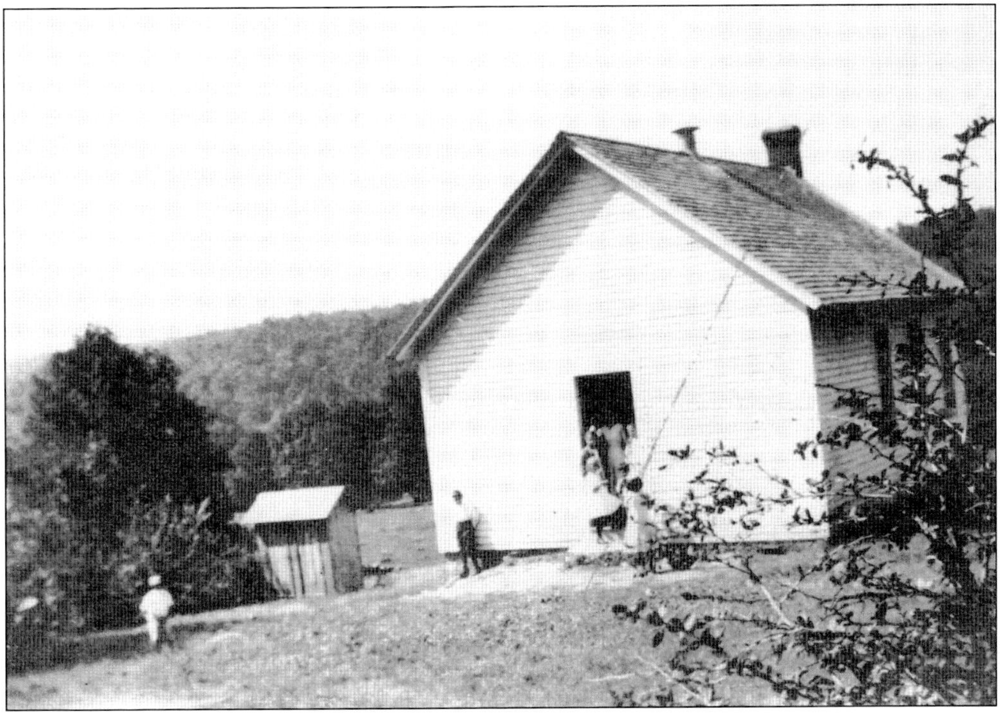

The unidentified students in this photograph, taken in 1917 or 1918, attended the newly built 24-foot-by-30-foot one-room schoolhouse. The school eventually became the home of Albert and Magda Balazs. As a child, Albert attended the Potter School, where he was known for starting the fire early each morning. He later served in World War II and as one of the town's selectmen from 1959 to 1965.

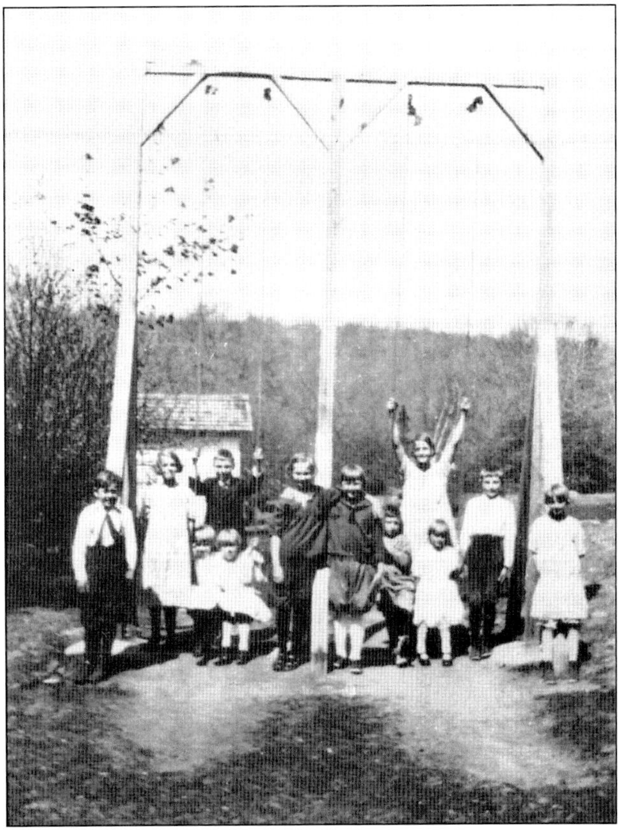

The Potter School District was a very rural area. The Fenton River begins there and flows into Bissonette Pond. This section of Willington retains its rural character today. It appears that the unidentified students in this early 1920s photograph are thankful that someone built a swing set at the school.

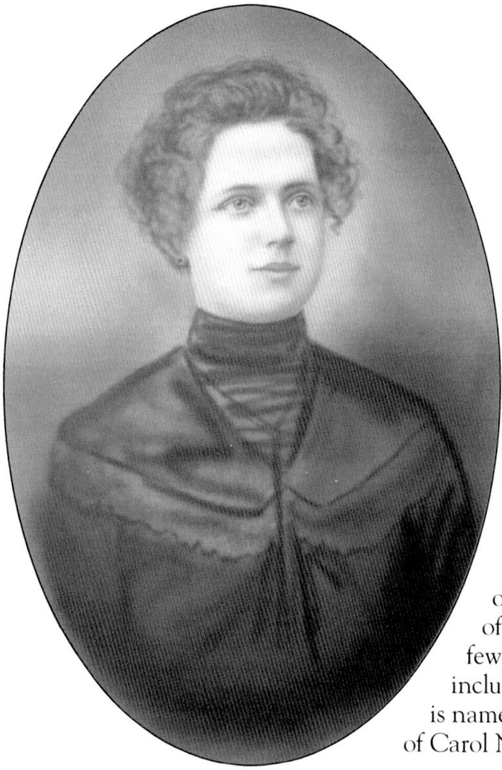

The descendants of Katherine and Andrew Balazs, seen here, cherish these portraits. Katherine was born Katalin Vidinszky in 1883 and came to the United States in 1905 from Hungary. Andrew was born in Hungary in 1883 and came to the United States in 1902. Their marriage produced seven daughters and one son. Katherine and Andrew had a large piece of property in the northeast section of Willington on which they operated a poultry farm. The area of their farm is now heavily wooded. In 1989, a few homes were built on the former Balazs farm, including one on the site of the former barn. The road is named in honor of the Balazs family. (Both courtesy of Carol N. Kelley.)

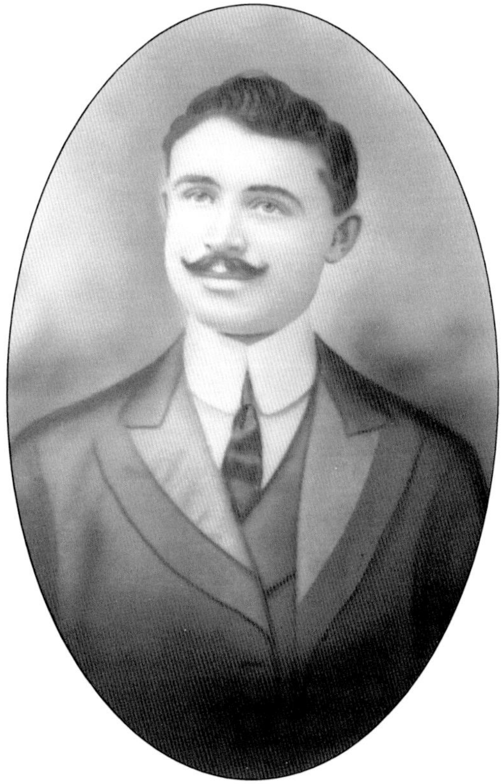

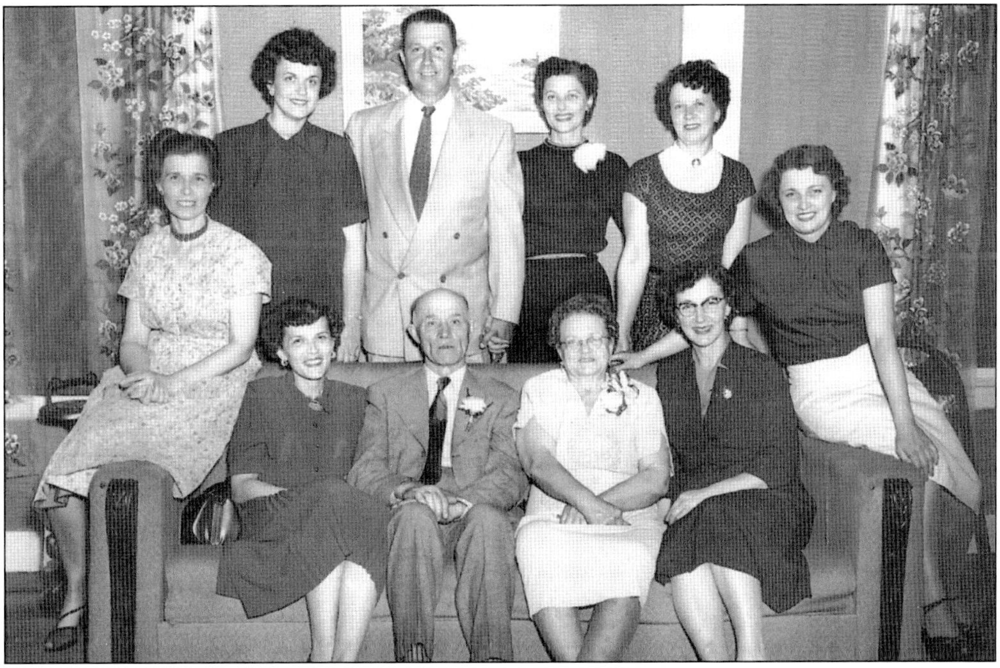

Andrew and Katherine Balazs celebrated their golden wedding anniversary at their Willington home in 1954 with their family. From left to right are (first row) Claire Balazs Coleman, Andrew Balazs, Katherine Balazs, and Katherine Balazs Guzzo; (second row) Ann Balazs McDermott, Wilhelmina Balazs Lee, Albert Balazs, Margaret Balazs Clear, Helen Balazs Levering, and Elsie Balazs Norval. The girls were dubbed the "Balazs beauties." (Courtesy of Carol N. Kelley and John Balazs.)

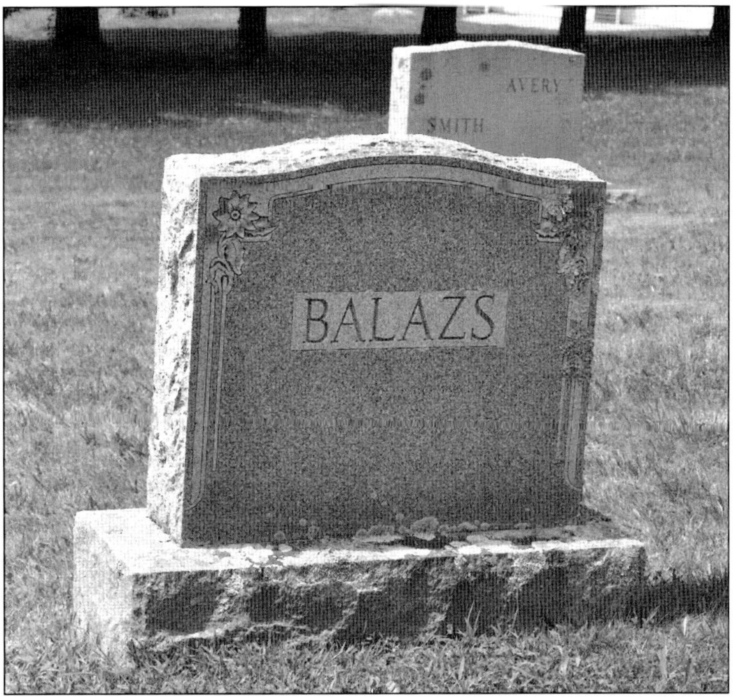

The Balazs family was prominent in the Potter School area. Andrew and Katherine Balazs purchased the former Potter School as a wedding gift for their son Albert. Andrew and Katherine's daughter Wilhelmina Balazs Lee lived on Balazs Road until her death in 2003. Their youngest child, Elsie Balazs Norval, lived in neighboring Stafford Springs until her death in April 2013 at the age of 92. (Courtesy of Marion Cullimore.)

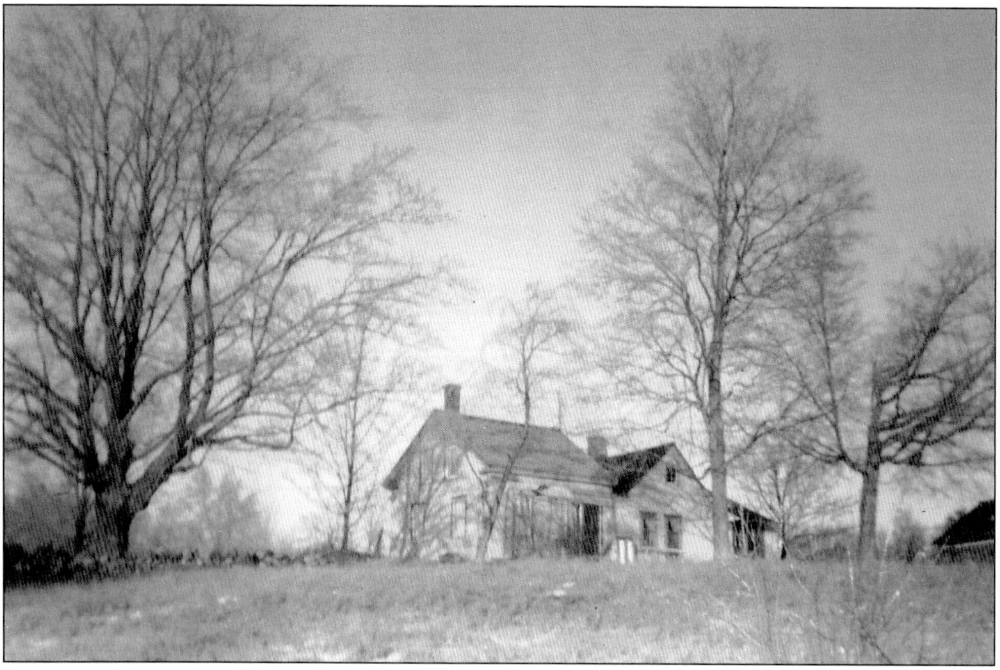

Born in 1871, Andrew Kubacka came to the United States from Czechoslovakia with his wife, Johanna. They raised their six children in this house on Balazs Road. Andrew was a farmer. The home, which was valued at $1,000 in 1940, was ultimately destroyed by fire. It dates to the 1760s and originally belonged to members of the Potter family. (Courtesy of Ann M. Kubacka.)

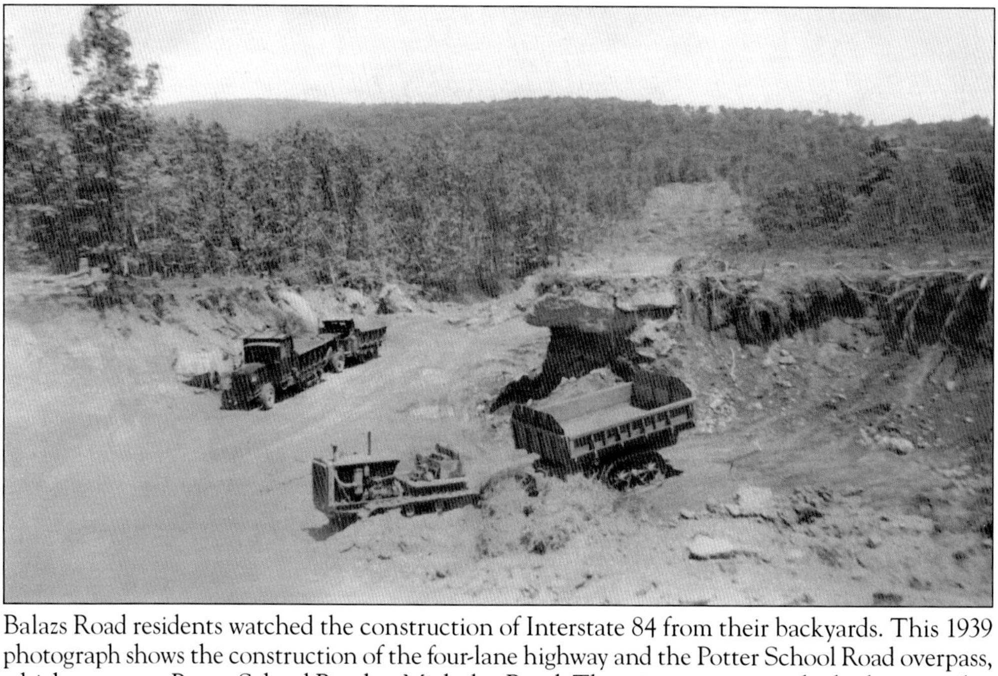

Balazs Road residents watched the construction of Interstate 84 from their backyards. This 1939 photograph shows the construction of the four-lane highway and the Potter School Road overpass, which connects Potter School Road to Michalec Road. There is no access to the highway in this area, and the landscape surrounding Interstate 84 today remains largely unchanged from this photograph. (Courtesy of Ann M. Kubacka.)

Six

Roaring Brook School District

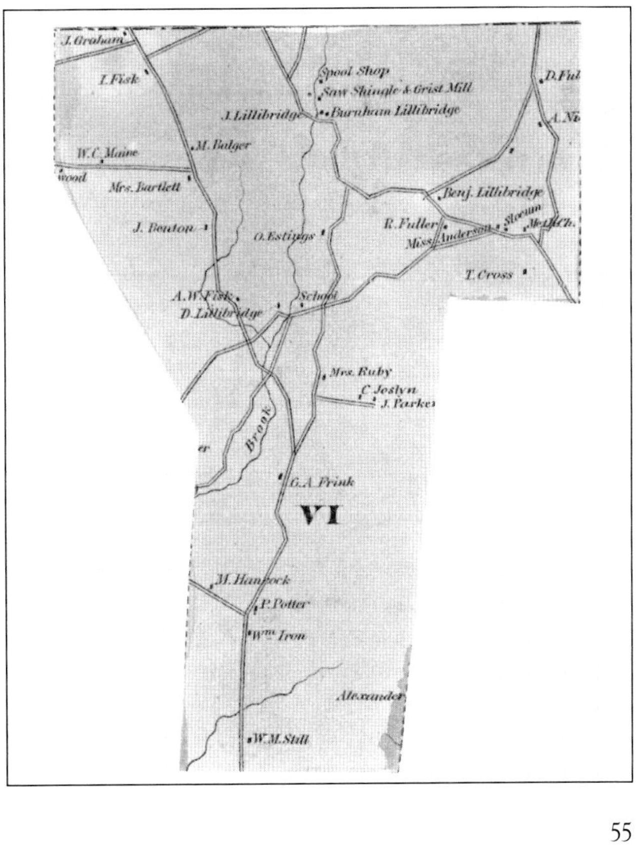

The young man who drowned his bride on June 2, 1859, in the brook for which this area is named was sent to the state prison for 52 years. It has since been a peaceful area and is now best known for the TA truck stop and FedEx ground shipping depot at exit 71 on Interstate 84.

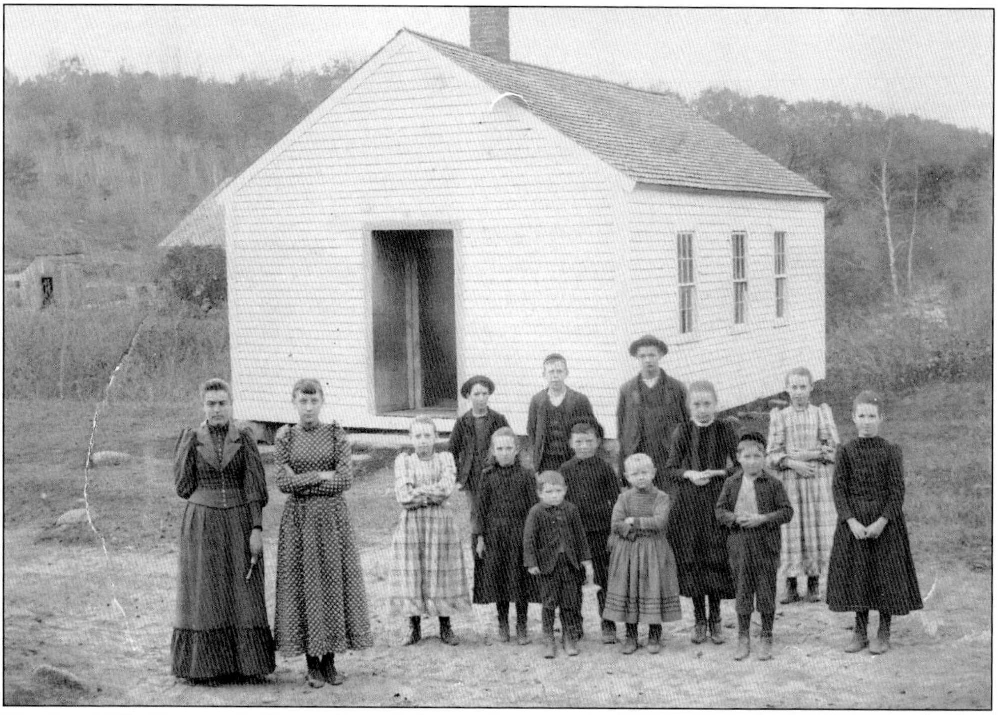

Teacher Lillia Fenton (left) stands with her students in this undated photograph of the original Roaring Brook School. A new school for the Roaring Brook School District was completed on December 4, 1920. The school district, sometimes known as District 6, was located in the north-central section of Willington and was bordered by the town of Stafford to the north.

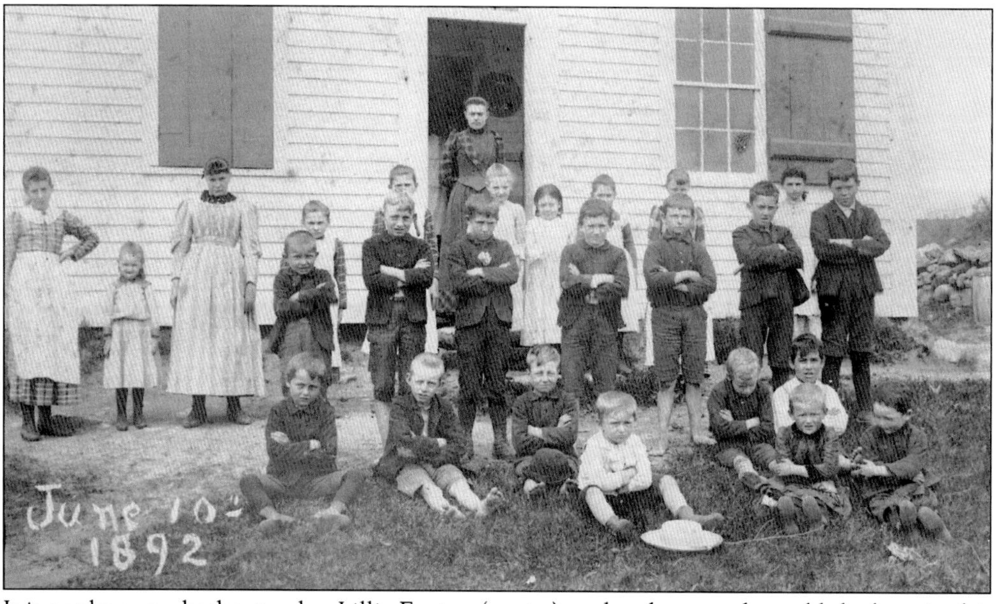

It is not known whether teacher Lillia Fenton (center) or the photographer told the boys in this class to cross their arms or if they decided to do so by agreement. Fenton taught at various one-room schools during her career. She boarded at the home of Edward and Emma Burdick, in the Moose Meadow section. After Emma's death, Lillia became Edward's housekeeper.

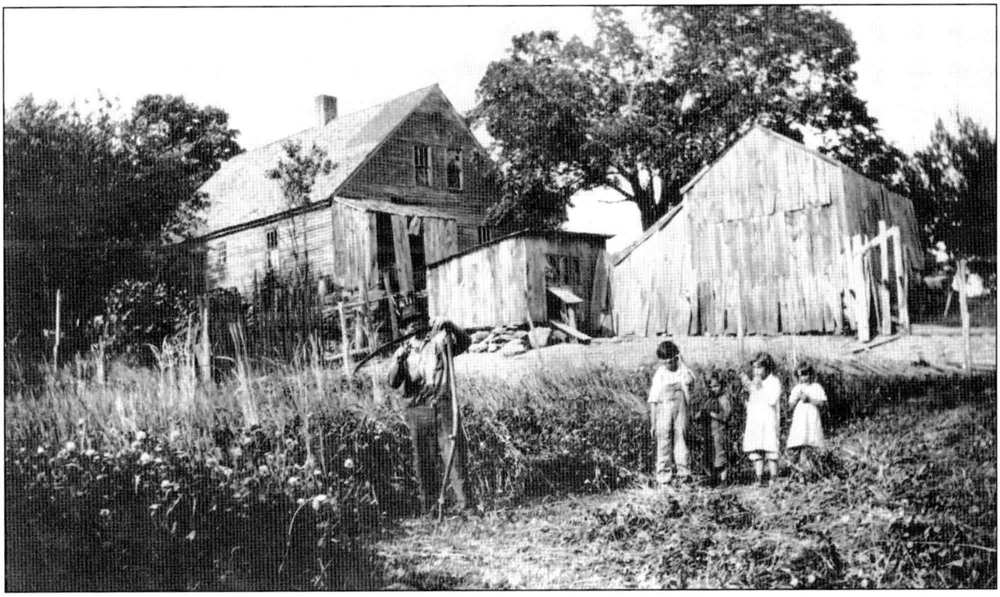

John Malack came from Austria in the late 1800s with his wife, Anna. They raised a family on the Polster Road farm seen here in 1929. This homestead was built in 1720 and razed in 1938. From left to right are John Sr., John Jr., Frank, Rose, and Ann Malack. (Courtesy of Ann M. Kubacka.)

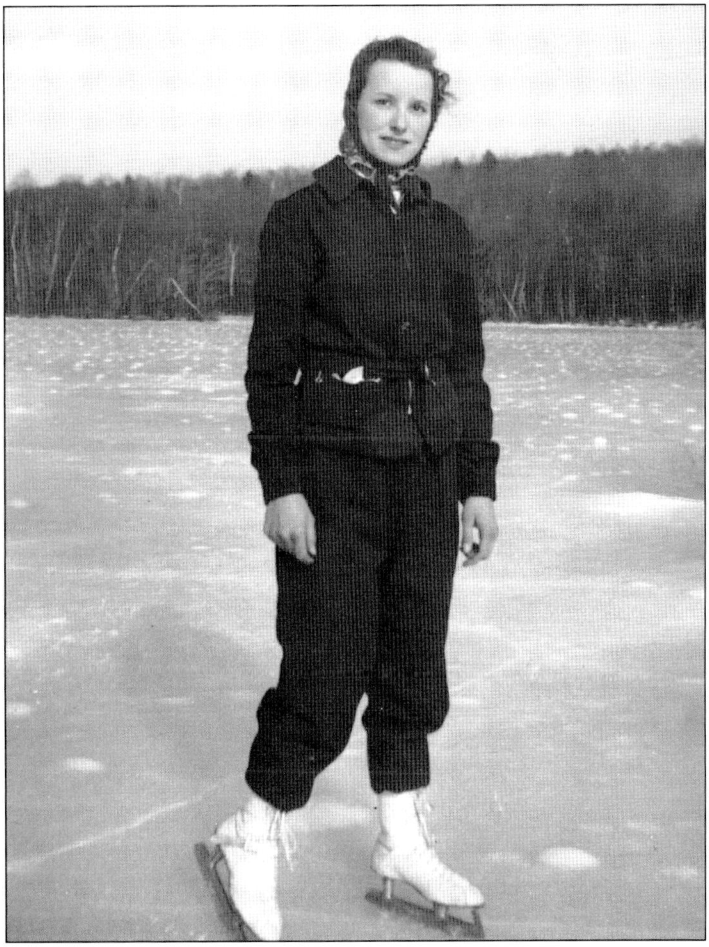

Ann Malack skated on Morey Pond when she was a young girl. The pond is located in nearby Union. Ann was raised in the Roaring Brook section of Willington. She is about 17 years old in this undated photograph. In October 1943, she married Edward Kubacka, a mechanic in the Air Force. (Courtesy of Ann M. Kubacka.)

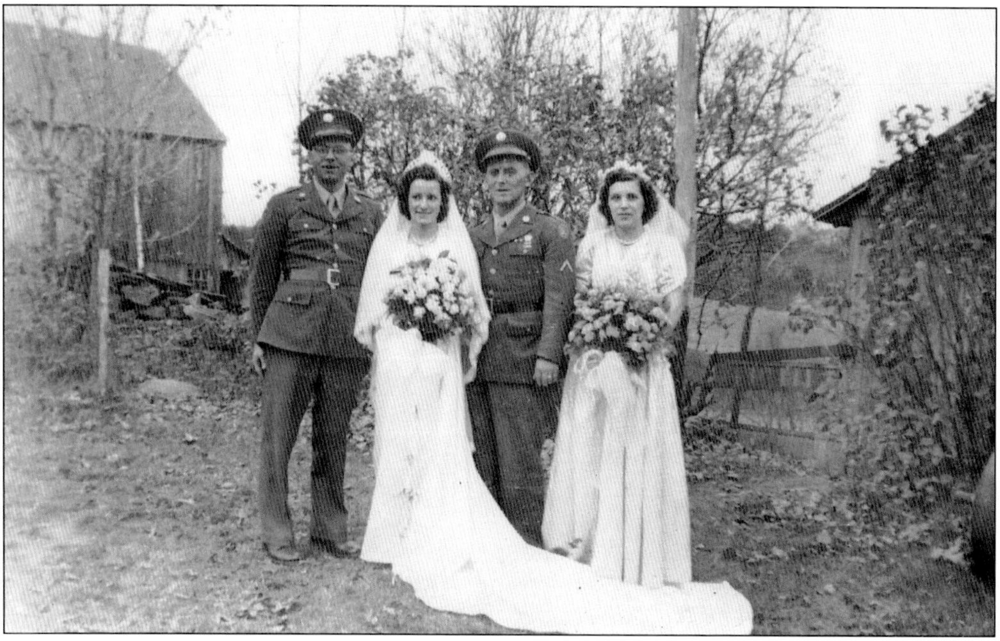

Seen here from left to right are best man Frank Kubacka, bride Ann Malack, groom Edward Kubacka, and maid of honor Rose Malack at the October 1943 wedding held on the Malack family property on Polster Road. The property is in the area that may soon be home to Willington's second truck stop. (Courtesy of Ann M. Kubacka.)

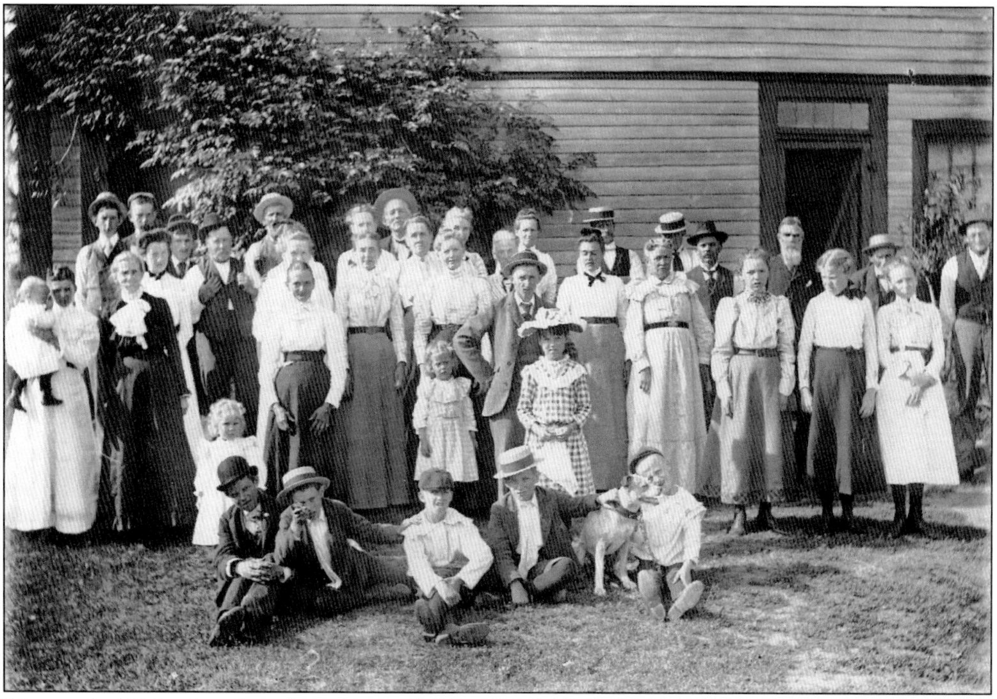

This early 1900s church gathering was held at the Ruby house in the Roaring Brook area. It is speculated that the majority of these people worshiped at the Methodist church that existed in Willington at one time. The house on Ruby Road was in the Ruby family for at least 150 years.

Seven

Village Hill School District

Northwest Willington's early industry was clustered together. The area's distance from the town common must have made it challenging for early residents to attend town events and meetings. Today, the Village Hill section is home to the Wilderness Lake Campground, a large equestrian center, and the town's recreation fields, all of which are easily accessible from Interstate 84.

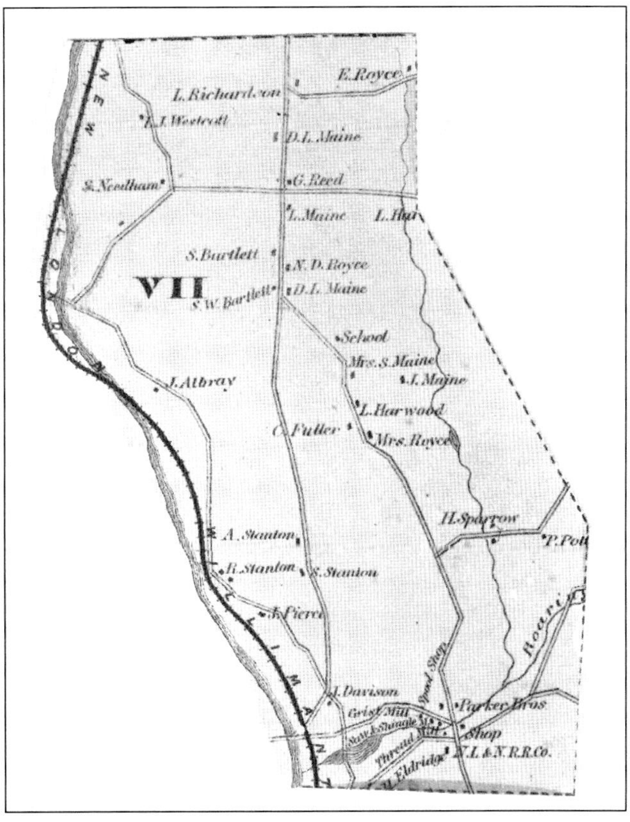

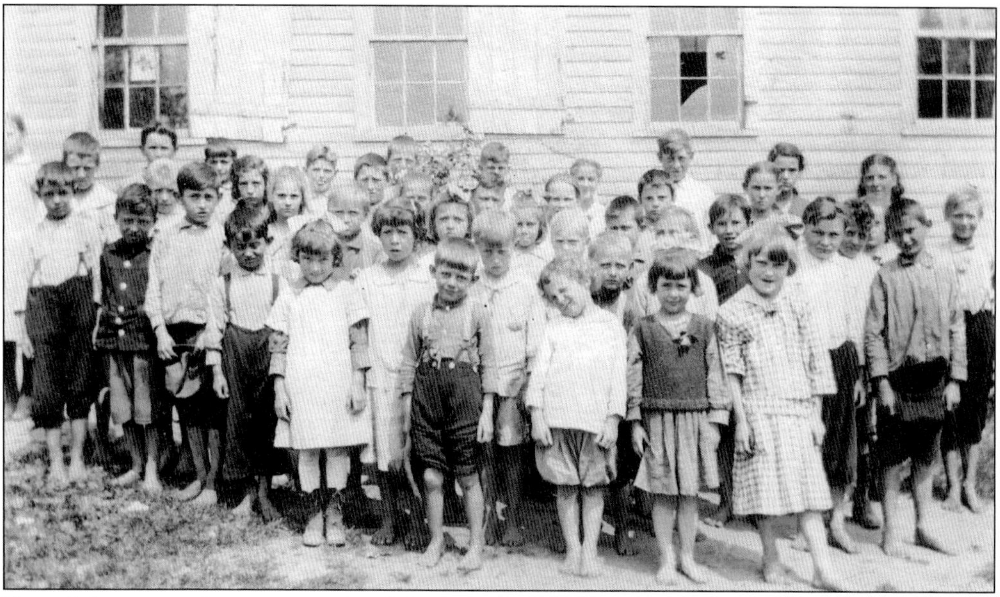

Two of the original one-room school districts, 7 and 11, were combined into the Village Hill School after a vote on December 30, 1784. During the winter, male teachers earned between $10 and $14 per month; in the summers, female teachers earned only $5 or $6 per month. This 1919 photograph of the Village Hill School and its barefoot students illustrates the rural nature of this district.

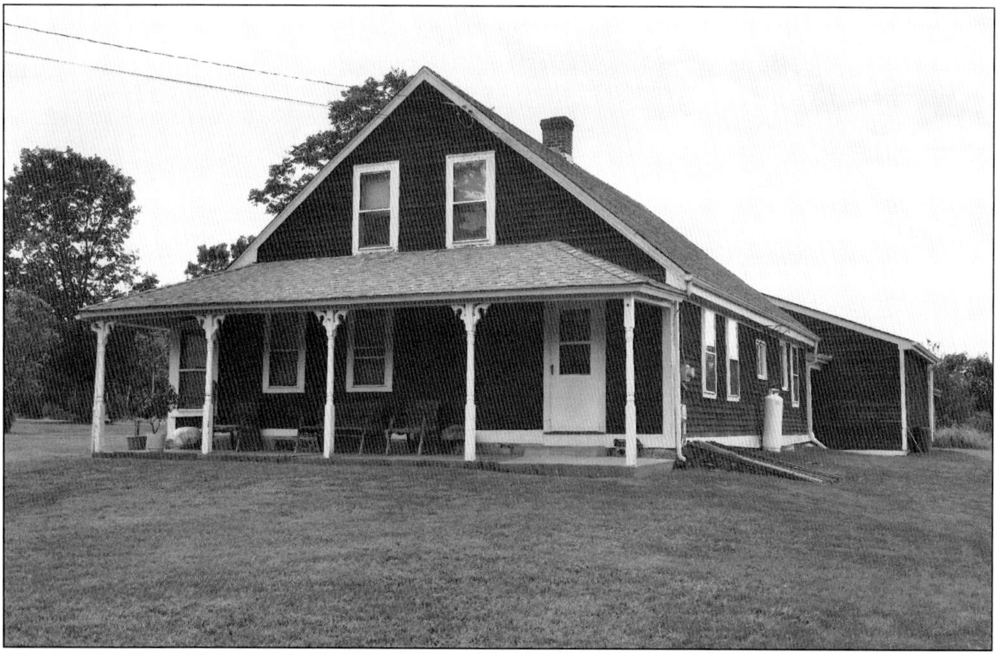

The house Samuel Johnson built between 1770 and 1810 on what is now Schofield Road remains today. Johnson was a soldier in the Revolutionary War, fighting first in Lexington and later in the Battle of Bunker Hill. Like other residents, Johnson marched from Willington to Massachusetts. The Schofield family purchased the home in 1876, and it is still owned by the family today. (Courtesy of Marion Cullimore.)

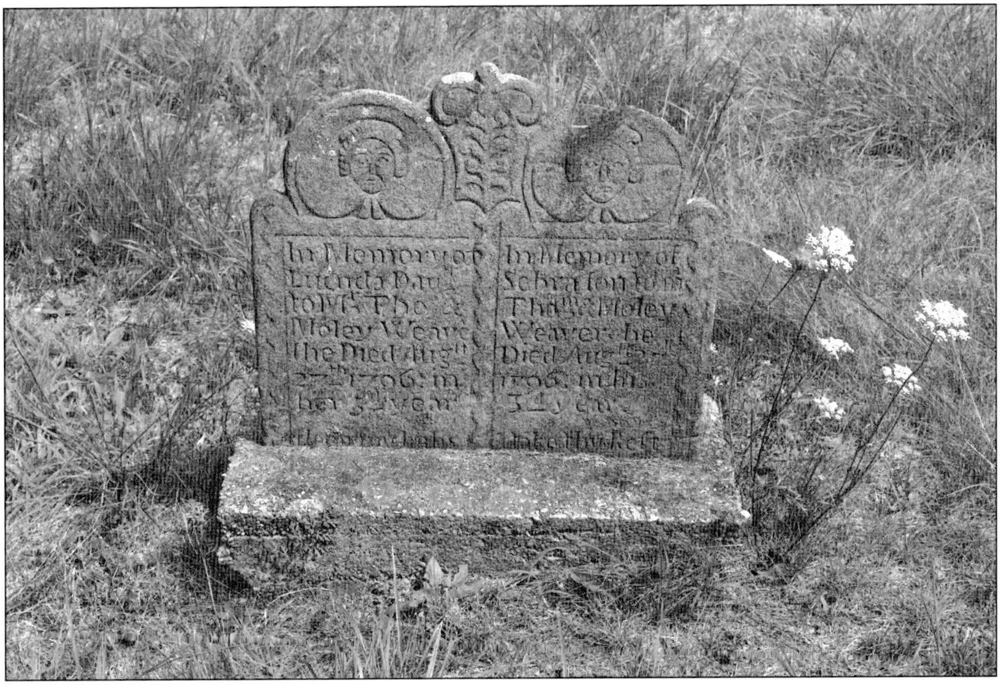

The oldest remaining tombstone in the Village Hill Cemetery commemorates the August 2, 1796, death of two young children from the same family who died on the same day. Their final resting place is on a steep hill in the cemetery, surrounded by a forest. (Courtesy of Marion Cullimore.)

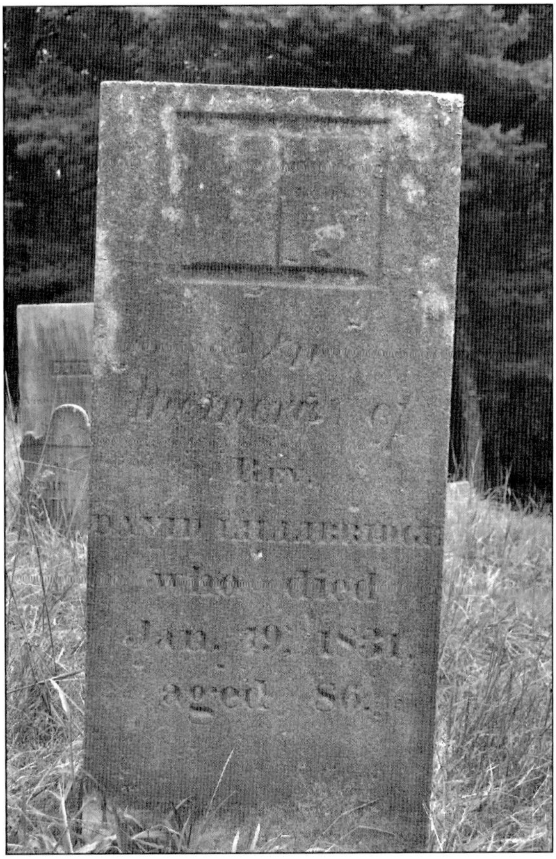

Rev. David Lillibridge was a Baptist minister who established a church in the Village Hill section in 1777. The church building itself was built in 1780. He remained pastor for over 50 years until his death in 1831. When he arrived in Willington from Rhode Island in 1777, he paid $4,000 for a farm and a house. He served in the French and Indian War. (Courtesy of Marion Cullimore.)

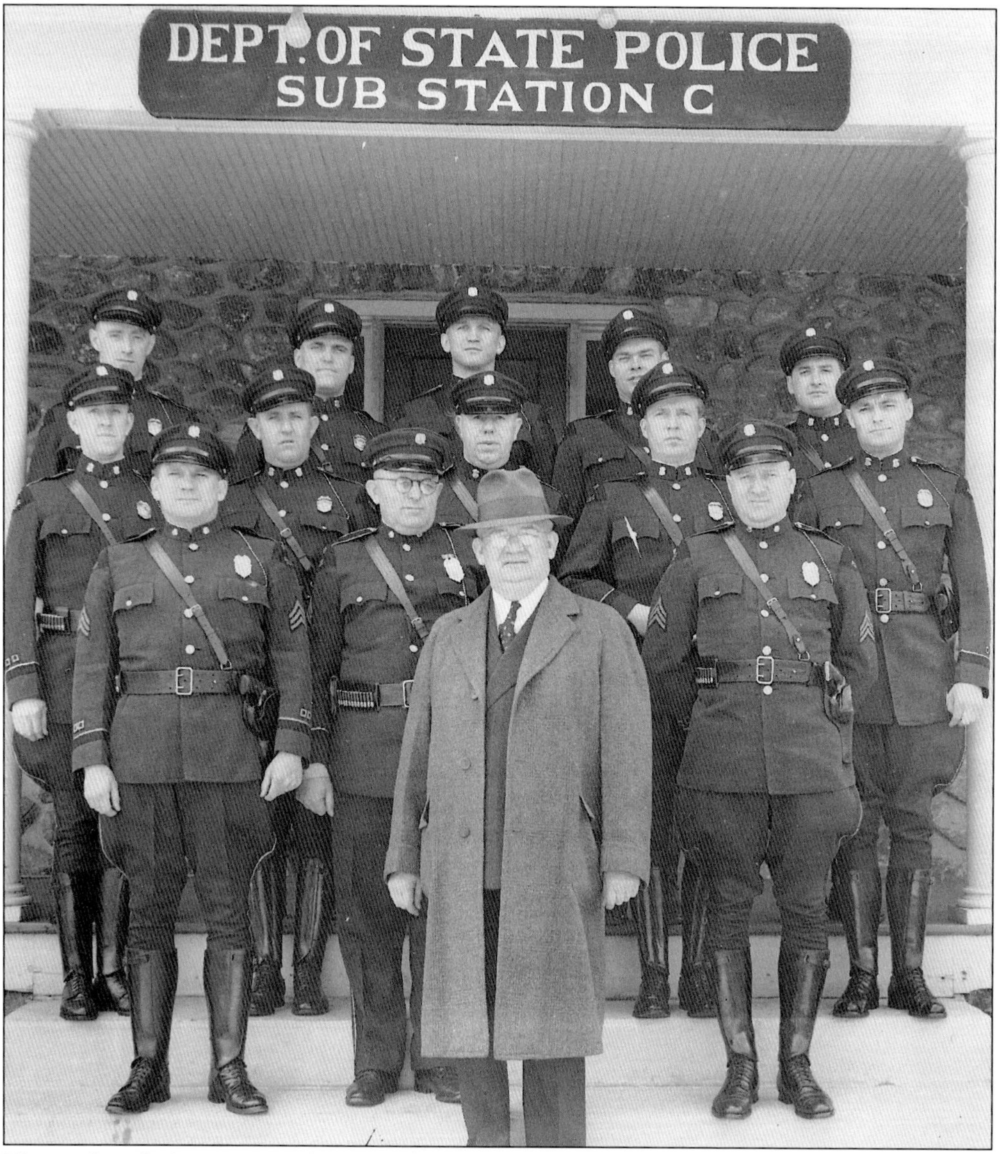

The unidentified troopers in this 1939 photograph, taken in front of the barracks in neighboring Stafford, were routinely dispatched to assist Willington residents and business owners, since Willington did not have its own police department. The organization now known as the Connecticut State Police, established in 1903, prides itself on being the first state police organization in the United States. What was once known as Sub Station C is now called Troop C. The names of the other substations in Connecticut have also been changed to "troop" and identified by a letter. Troop C is now located in Tolland. The uniforms have changed, the building in which Sub Station C was located is now the Stafford Senior Center, and the name of the department has changed, but troopers are still routinely dispatched to assist Willington residents and business owners. (Courtesy of the Connecticut State Police Alumni Association.)

Eight

Glass Factory School District

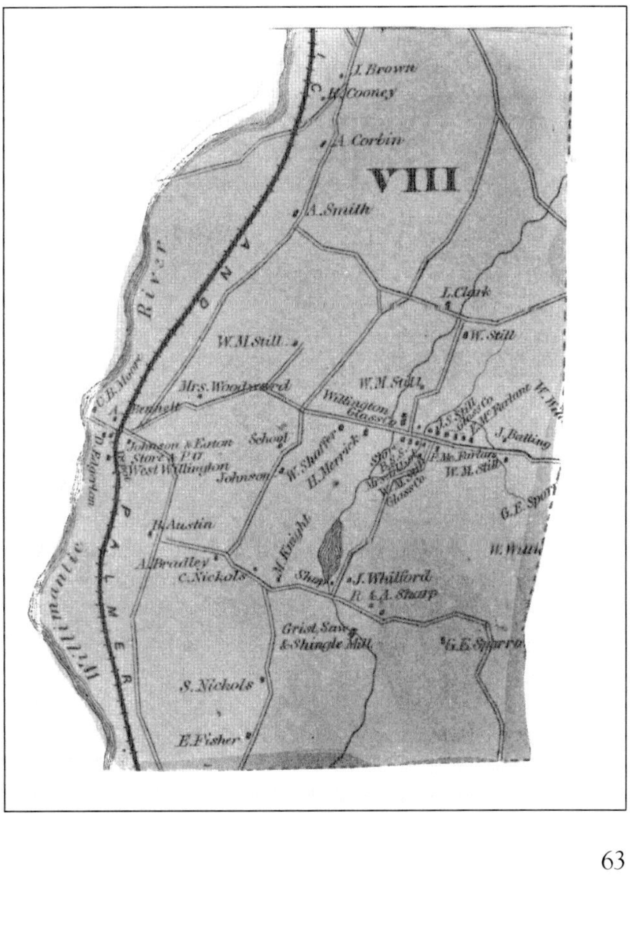

This western section of town is bordered by the Willimantic River. The factory that produced a variety of glassware in the 1800s was created by men who brought their trade from Eastern Europe. There was also a button factory on the adjacent property. Today, West Willington features small businesses, restaurants, a fitness center, and the post office.

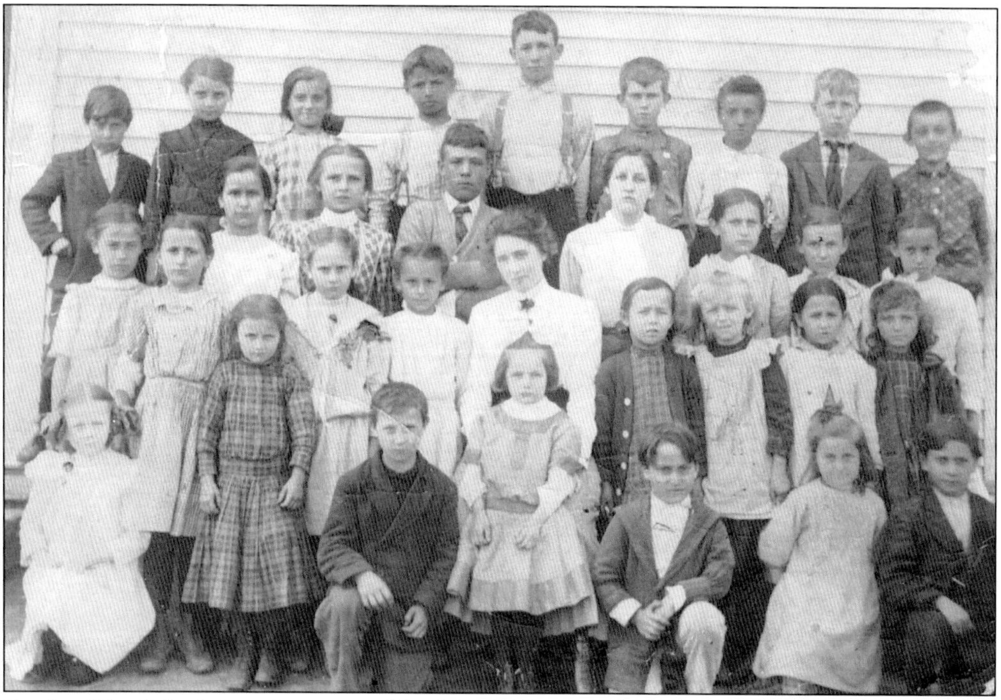

Teacher Olga Pobuda is in the center of this May 1912 postcard of a class of unidentified pupils at the Glass Factory School. Pobuda later noted on the back of the postcard, "This was taken a long time ago when Emily and Carrie went." The identity of the two girls to whom she refers is unknown.

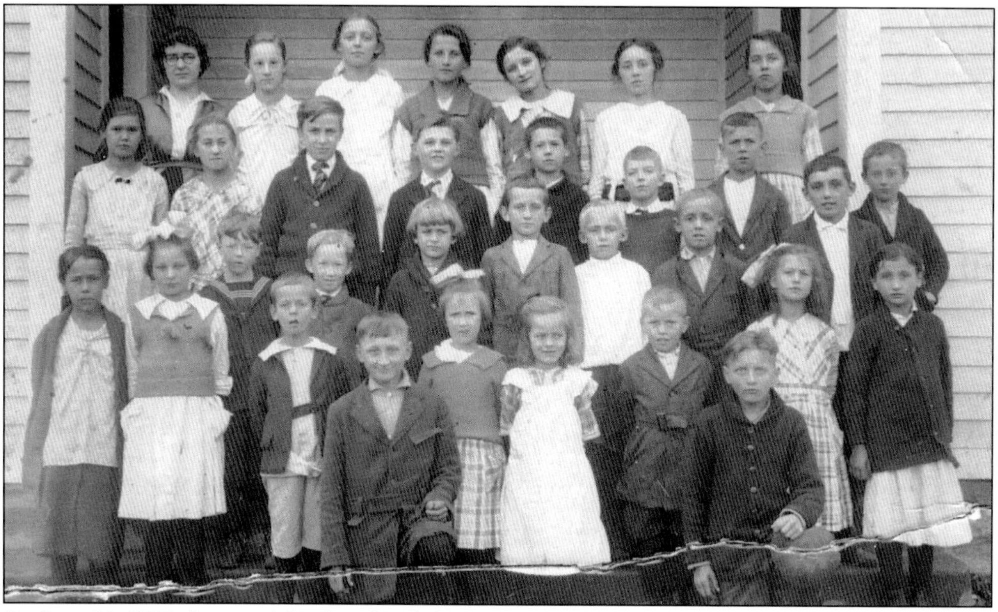

On June 21, 1727, the town's leaders decided to raise £20 to build a schoolhouse. The Glass Factory School is said to have been the first one built, although the original building was replaced by a new building in 1858. Esther Hanson Phelps, seen in the center of the first row with a bow in her hair, was seven years old when this photograph was taken in 1920. In 2013, she was the only surviving pupil.

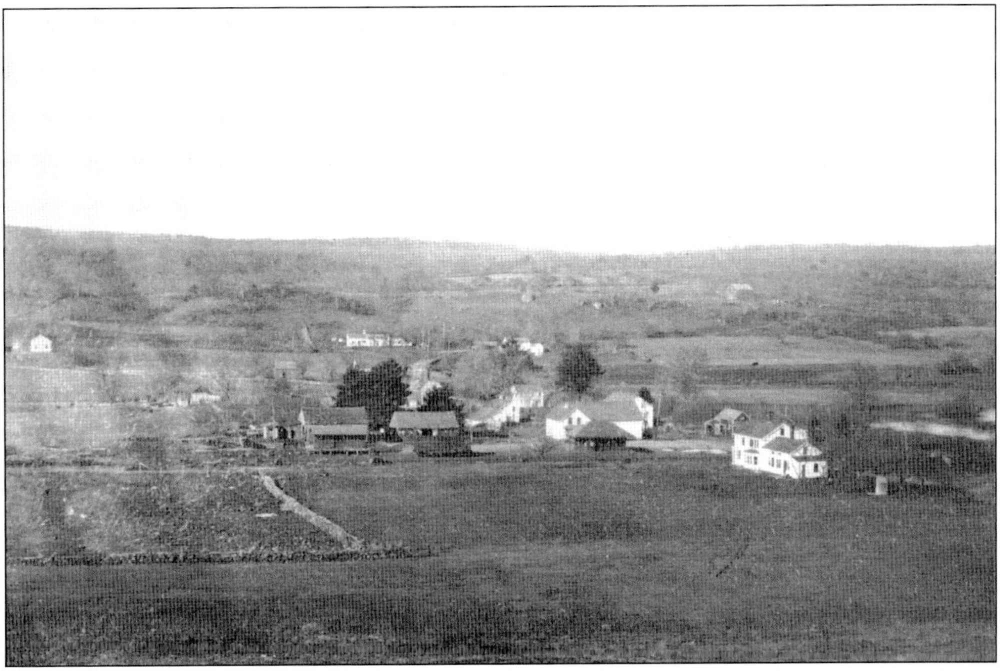

The relationship between sender Mrs. M. Jacobsen and the recipient of this postcard, Edith Robinson of Newburyport, Massachusetts, is unknown, but the September 1, 1906, postmark is from West Willington, where Willington's only post office is located today. The bird's-eye view appears to be of the area where Phelps Plaza is now located. (Courtesy of Stuart Cobb.)

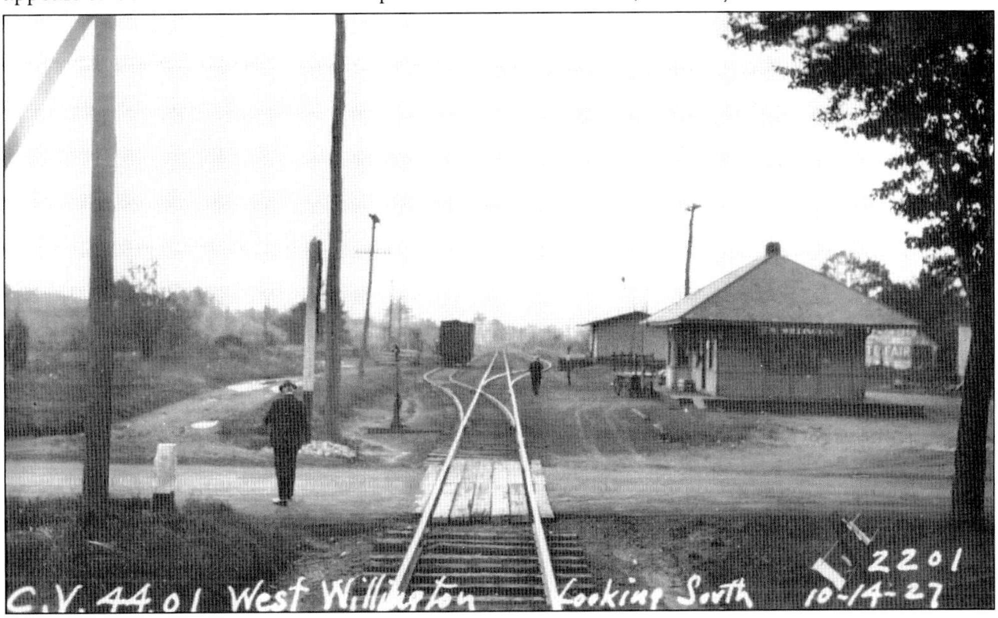

In 1850, the New London, Willimantic & Palmer Railroad was the first to travel through Willington. In addition to passenger rail service to and from the West Willington depot, there was a stagecoach that traveled daily from West Woodstock through Westford, Moose Meadow, East Willington, and Willington. By the time of this 1927 postcard, West Willington's depot was well established. (Courtesy of Richard N. Symonds Jr.)

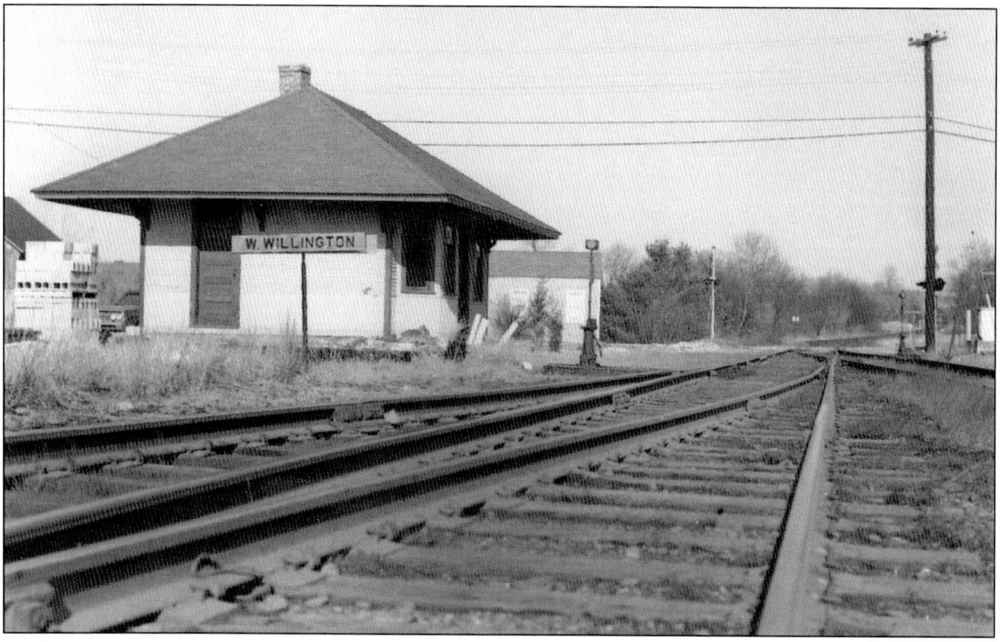

Rail service through Willington allowed residents to travel more easily and helped the local economy, as trains carried away lumber products for sale. Passengers were confused because the depot was originally known as Tolland, the county name. The original building burned in 1894. When the new one was built in 1895, it was renamed the West Willington depot, as seen on this undated photograph. (Courtesy of Richard N. Symonds Jr.)

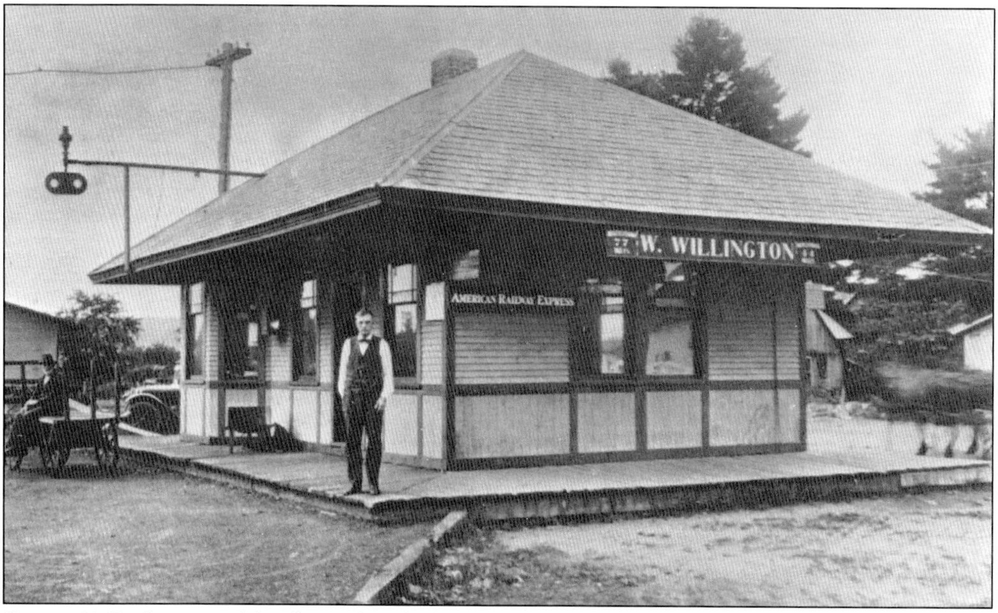

George P. Bugbee posed for the undated photograph that became this postcard. He served as the stationmaster in Willington from 1900 to 1937. The depot closed two years later, and passenger service to and from Willington ended in 1947, in part due to the prevalence of automobiles in the area. Since then, the building has housed the Savings Bank of Tolland and David Wright Jewelers. (Courtesy of Richard N. Symonds Jr.)

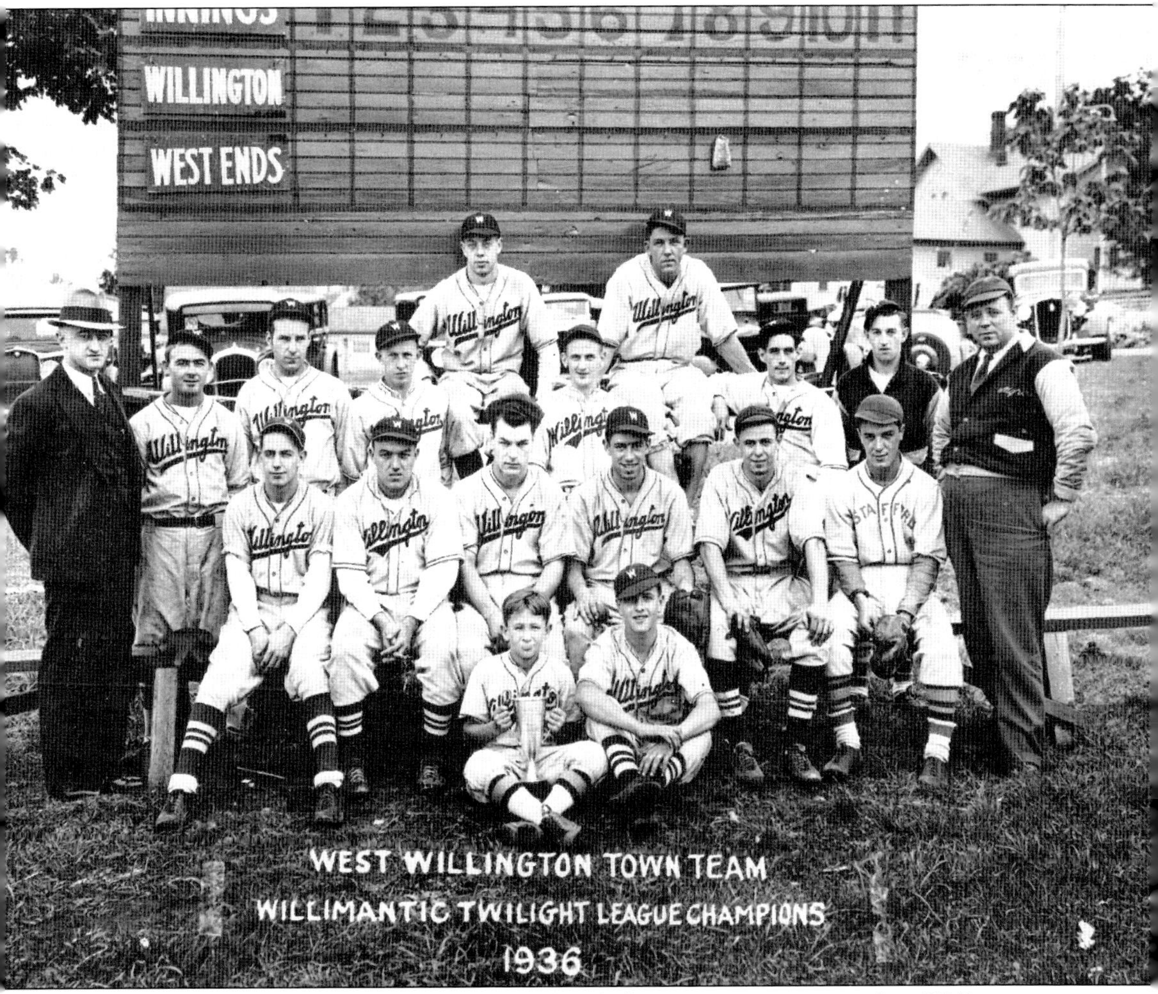

This 1936 photograph of the West Willington baseball team commemorates their Willimantic Twilight League Championship. Willimantic is approximately 15 miles from Willington. This photograph was taken at the conclusion of the trophy-winning game. Identified mostly by their last names, the team included, from left to right, (first row) team mascots Meyers and Hockla; (second row) Squires, Connors, Marko, F. Prochaska, Dempsey, and Julian; (third row) team sponsor Frank Parizek, Miske, Fligel, Potter, Herman Usher, Defosse, Woodworth, Ashley, Dadolt, and manager Tony Prochaska. Dr. Frank Converse assisted the team throughout the season. In addition, a Mr. Ruby and a Mr. Wochumurka assisted the team's members. Herman Usher was known to friends and family as Hi. On September 8, 2001, he and his wife, Marjorie, donated his West Willington baseball team uniform to the Willington Historical Society.

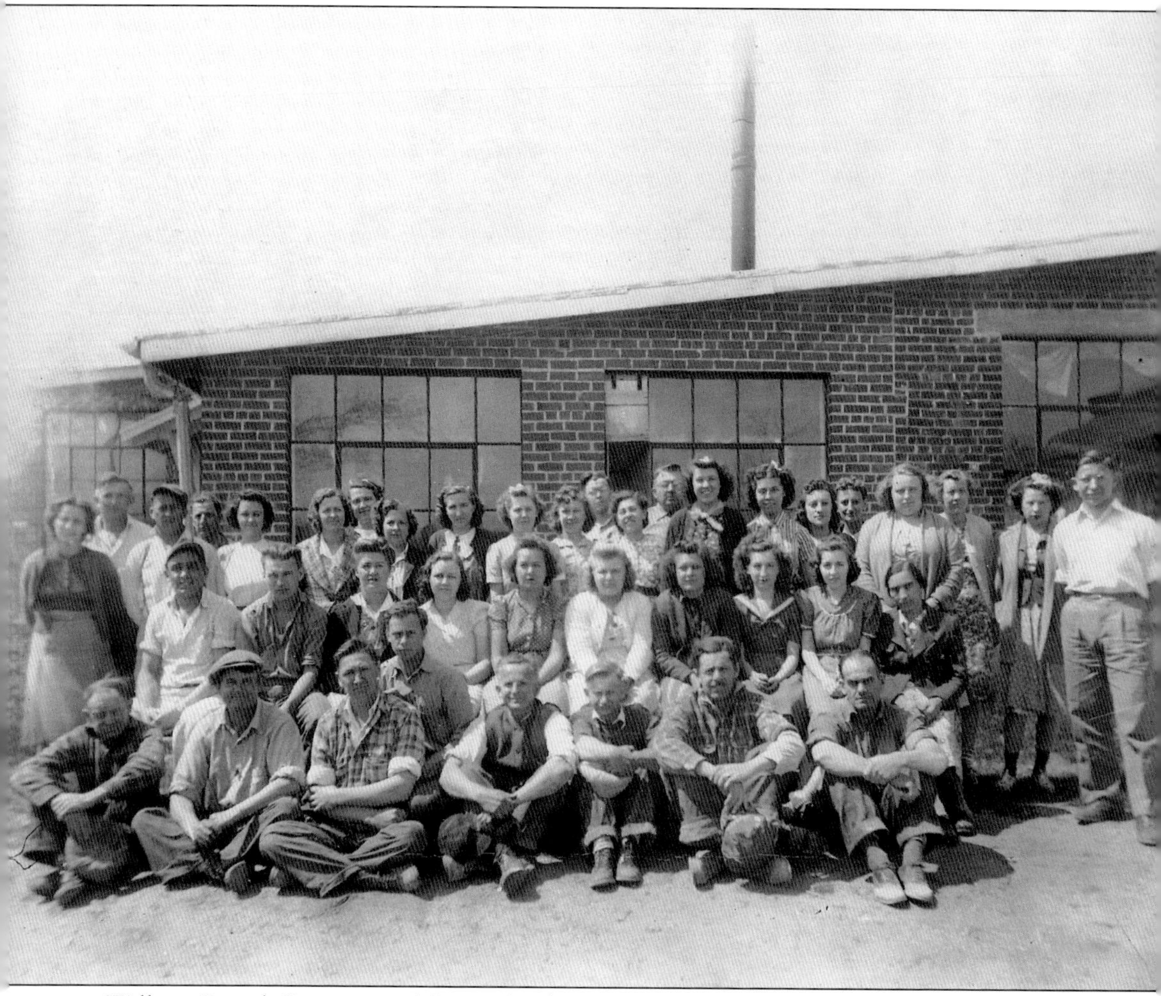

William Parizek Sr. emigrated from what became Czechoslovakia in 1907 and later opened a button shop in Willington. He built this large brick factory adjacent to the old glassworks and produced ocean pearl buttons using seashells imported from Australia. One can only imagine the time it must have taken in the days before high speed transportation to get those shells from Australia to Willington. The employees who posed for this 1930s photograph are, from left to right, (first row) Arthur Merrifield, Michael Sapoznik, Andrew Palocko, unidentified, Charles Parizek, John Marowsky, Armide DaRos, and unidentified; (second row) Emil Adamec, Jerry Sykora, Wilhemina DaRos, Ruth Krivanec, unidentified, Tessie Marowsky, Mary Chilkowitch, and unidentified; (third row) Amelia Hipsky, Ralph Parizek, Frank Triska, George Cheman, Anna Triska, Susie Halchek, Emily Rudnasky, unidentified, Margaret Dunay, Shirley Hansen, Fedora Spak, Charles Tranka, Mary Simon, William Parizek, Ella Mottarelli, unidentified, Margaret Dunay, unidentified, Helen Kania, unidentified, Bertha Tranka, and Peter Majnich. (Courtesy of Brenda LaFemina-Weber.)

Employees at Parizek's Button Shop on Trask Road were assigned to operate various portions of the complicated manufacturing equipment used to produce the buttons. Assignments included button cutter, splitter, sorter, slicer, driller, facer, and backer. In the early 1940s, employees worked 50 hours in a five-day week. The equipment in this undated photograph remained intact long after the factory closed. (Courtesy of Katarin A. Parizek.)

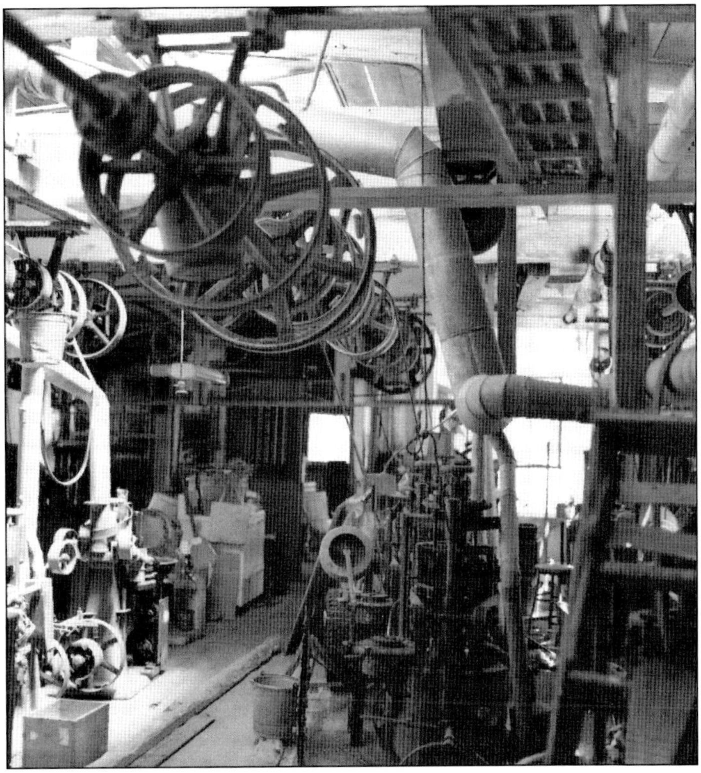

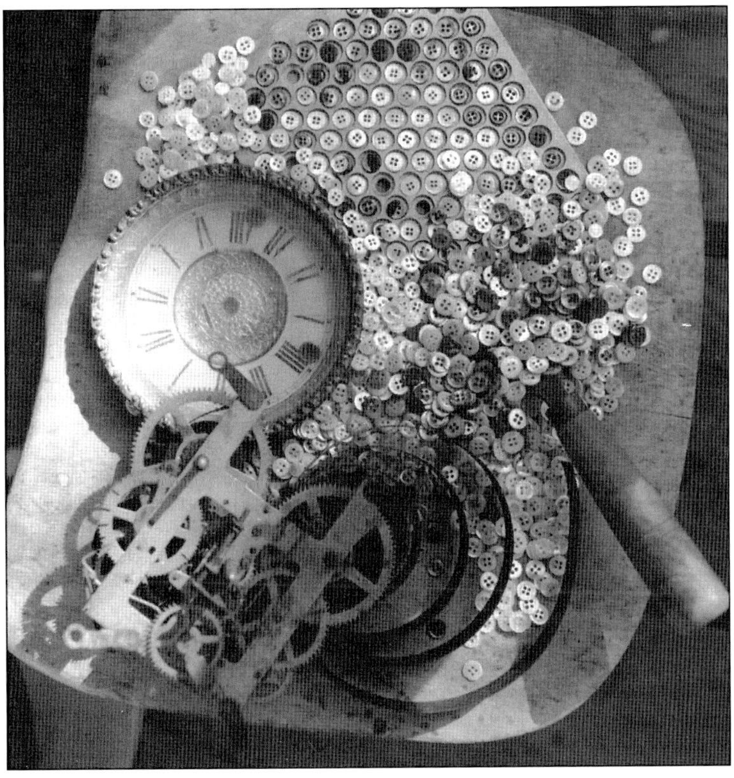

The assortment of buttons in this undated photograph from the Parizek Button Shop on Trask Road are the result of an 11-step process that started with cutting a core based on the size of the button needed. The process also included slicing, sizing, sorting, and drilling holes before the buttons were washed, rinsed, and polished. Many buttons were manufactured for men's shirts. (Courtesy of Katarin A. Parizek.)

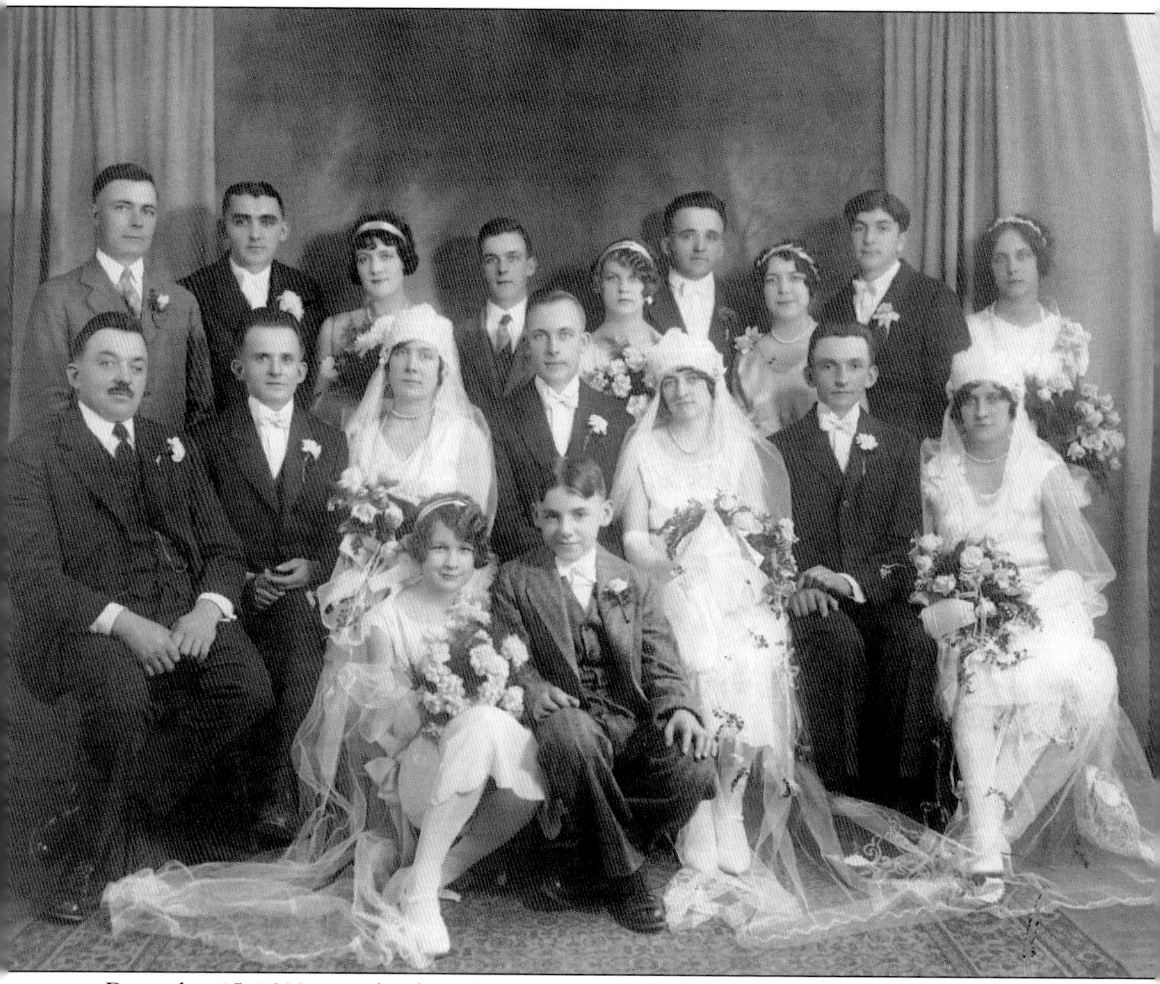

December 15, 1928, was the day of a gala event in Willington, a triple wedding at which the Rev. Edwin Sundt of the Federated Church performed the ceremony for members of the Hipsky and Parizek families. The large wedding party shown in this photograph is, from left to right, (first row) Bertha Novotny and William J. Parizek; (second row) William Parizek, groom Charles Parizek, bride Arlene Hipsky Parizek, groom Paul Hipsky, bride Barbara Parizek Hipsky, groom Ralph Parizek, and bride Amelia Hipsky Parizek; (third row) John Hipsky, Emil Adamec, Emily Dittrich, Joseph Hipsky, unidentified, Jerry Parizek, two unidentified, and Vilma Duhansky. The ceremony took place at the Federated Church on the town green, also known as the Hill Church. The couples extended more than 250 invitations to the reception, which was held at the bungalow, also known as the Czechoslovak Society of America Lodge. (Courtesy of Evelyne A. Parizek.)

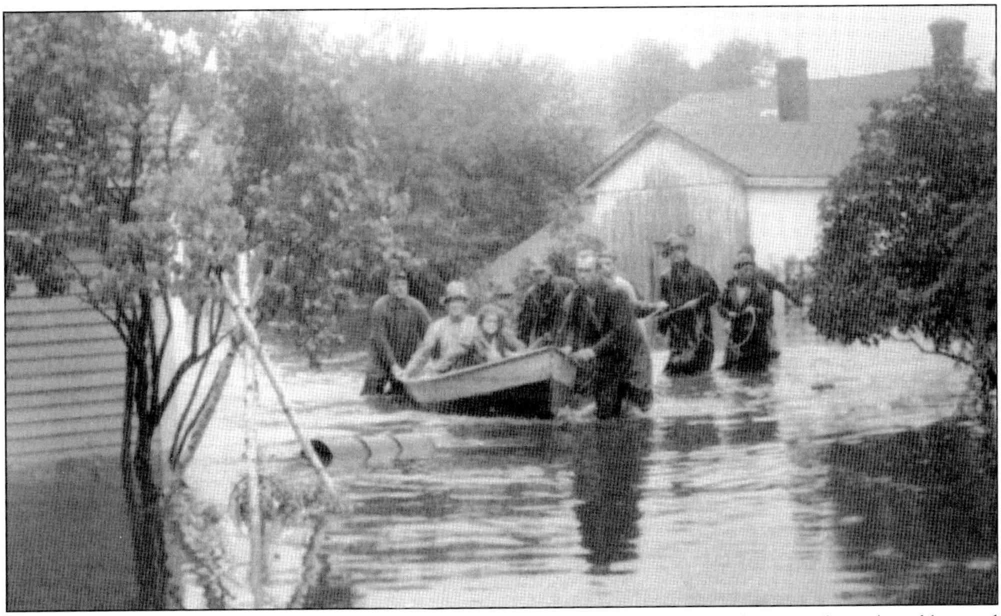

In an effort to assist those who were most affected by the 1938 flood, residents gathered and braved the rising waters after the hurricane that caused the Willimantic River to overflow its banks. Here, unidentified rescuers help Allen and Jessie Bennett escape their flooded home.

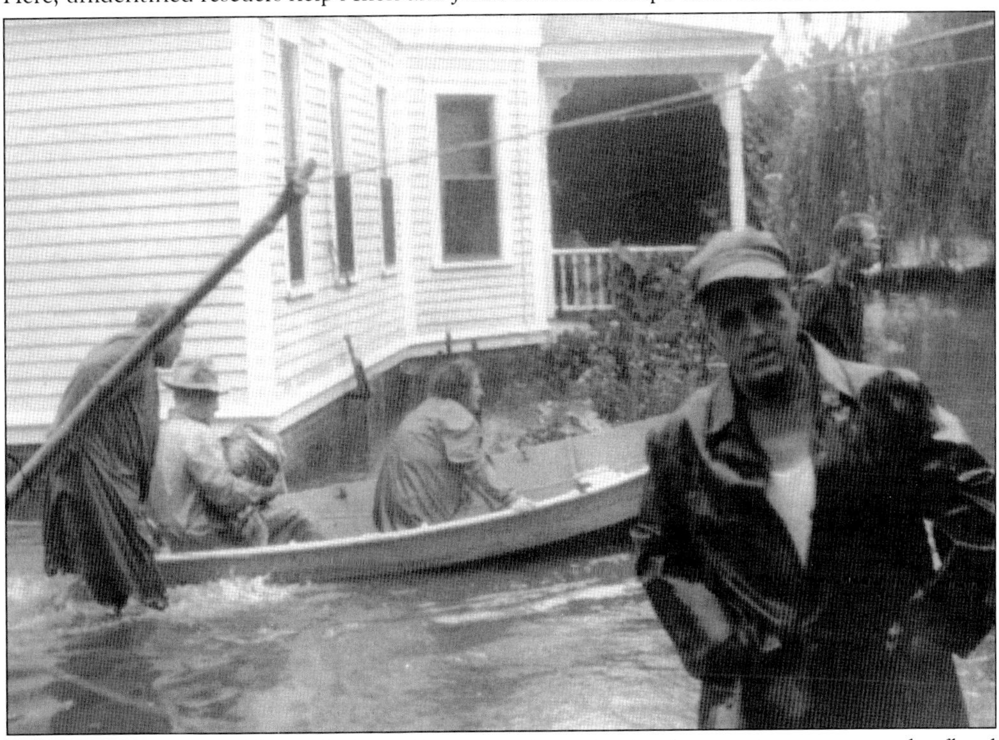

Allen Bennett, 47, and his wife, Jessie Bennett, 40, are in this boat trying to escape the flood that resulted from the 1938 hurricane. Allen worked as a chauffeur for Jessie's father, Willington doctor Frank Converse, with whom the couple lived. In the right foreground is Bill Bowler, a 39-year-old auto mechanic. The other two men are unidentified.

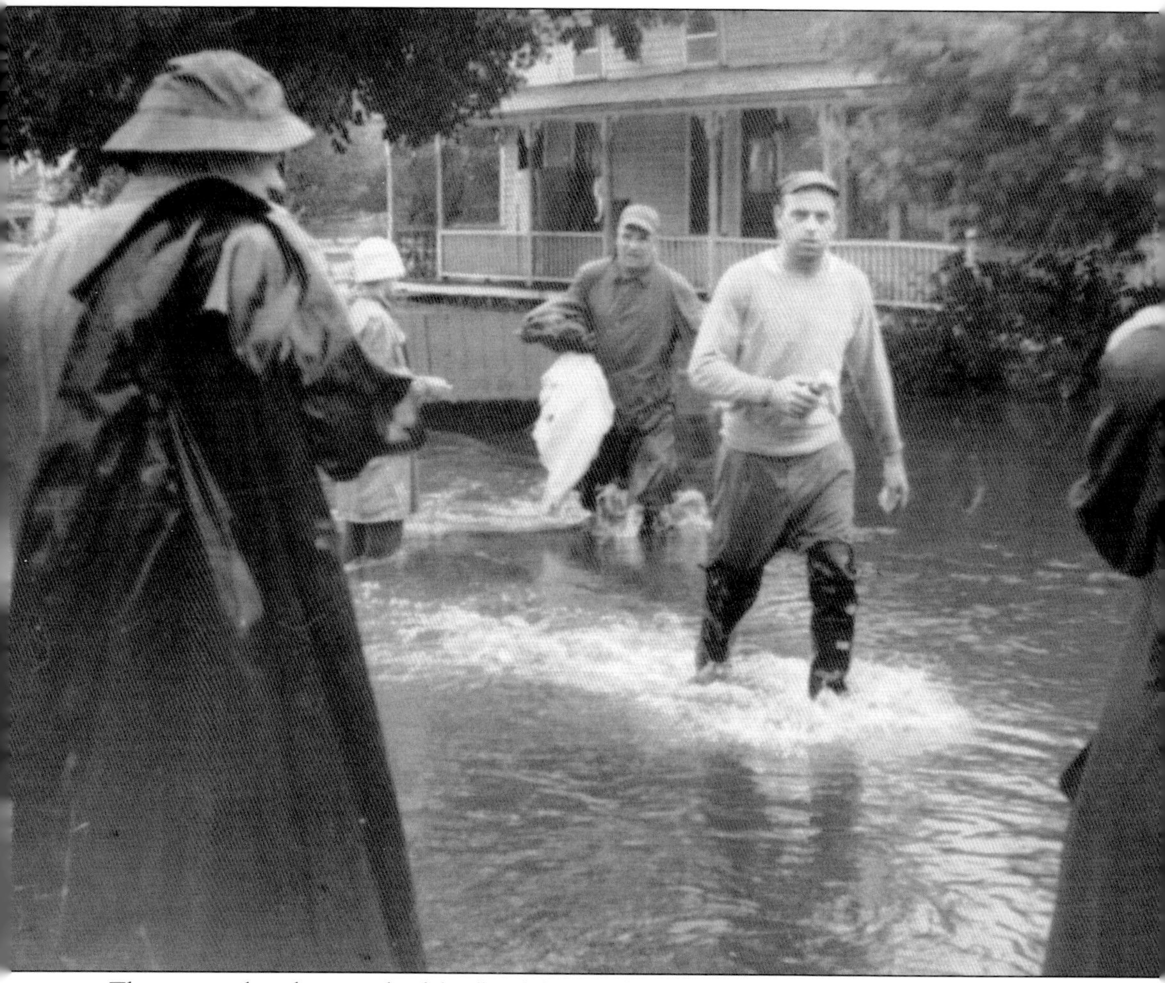

The men in this photograph of the flood that resulted from the 1938 hurricane are mobilizing in order to provide assistance as quickly as possible. The fact that one man has not even finished donning his rain gear demonstrates the urgency with which people reacted to the natural disaster. West Willington was severely affected because of its location adjacent to the Willimantic River. It is unknown how the residents were able to get to higher ground when they were evacuated.

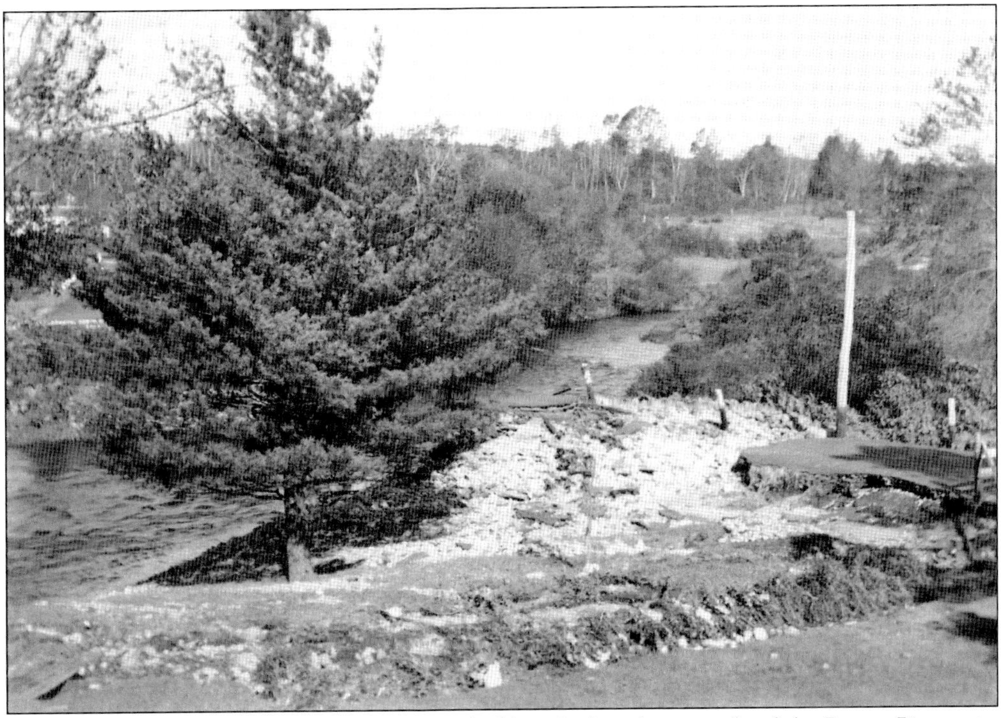

A member of the Dr. Frank Converse household took this photograph of the Route 74 area in West Willington after the flood of 1938. The photograph was taken from a bedroom window in the Converse house, which had been flooded after the hurricane because of its proximity to the Willimantic River.

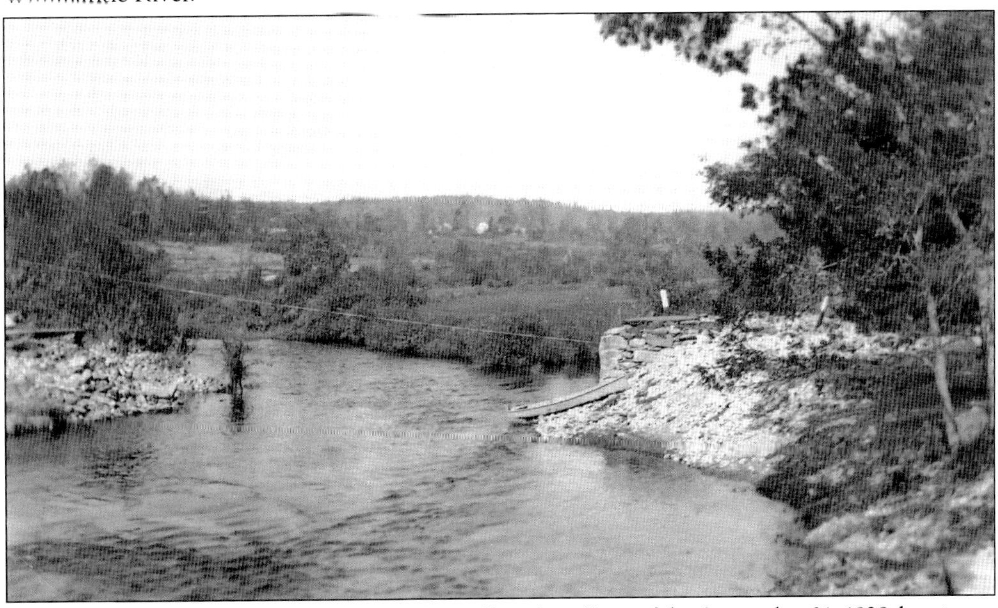

Resilient, creative Willington residents did not allow the effects of the September 21, 1938, hurricane to defeat them. After the Willimantic River overflowed its banks and destroyed the steel bridge, the residents used a rope to carry mail and groceries across the river. The canoe was used for residents and construction engineers who needed to travel between Willington and Tolland.

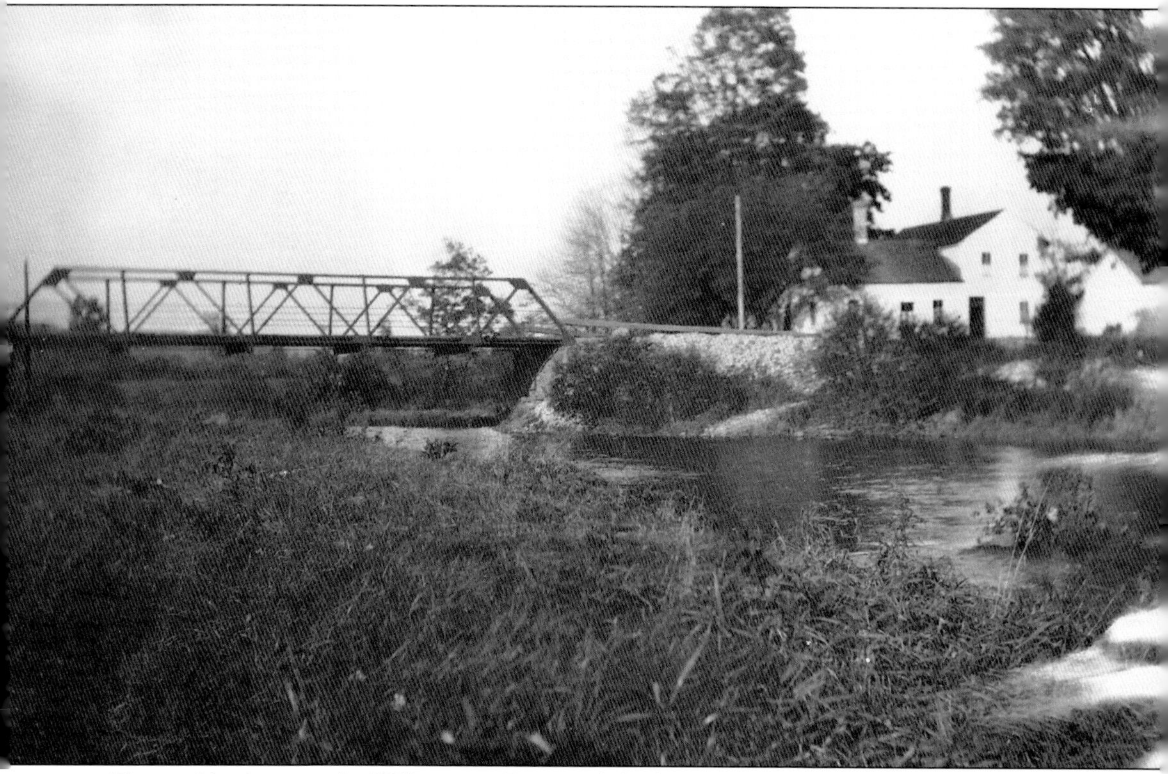

The steel bridge over the Willimantic River and the home of Alfred and Amorette DeWolfe are seen here in 1919, years before they were subjected to the fierce winds and rising waters of the 1938 hurricane, which destroyed the bridge. The DeWolfe house is on the Willington side of the river. The home where they raised their three children, Edwin, Esther May, and Eleanor, was also where those who crossed the bridge paid their toll. It is unknown who actually collected the toll and during what hours. There are no longer tolls on Connecticut roads. Eleanor DeWolfe became a teacher in the Willington schools and married Hans Hanson Jr. Their daughter Esther Hanson Phelps followed in her mother's footsteps and also became a teacher in the Willington schools.

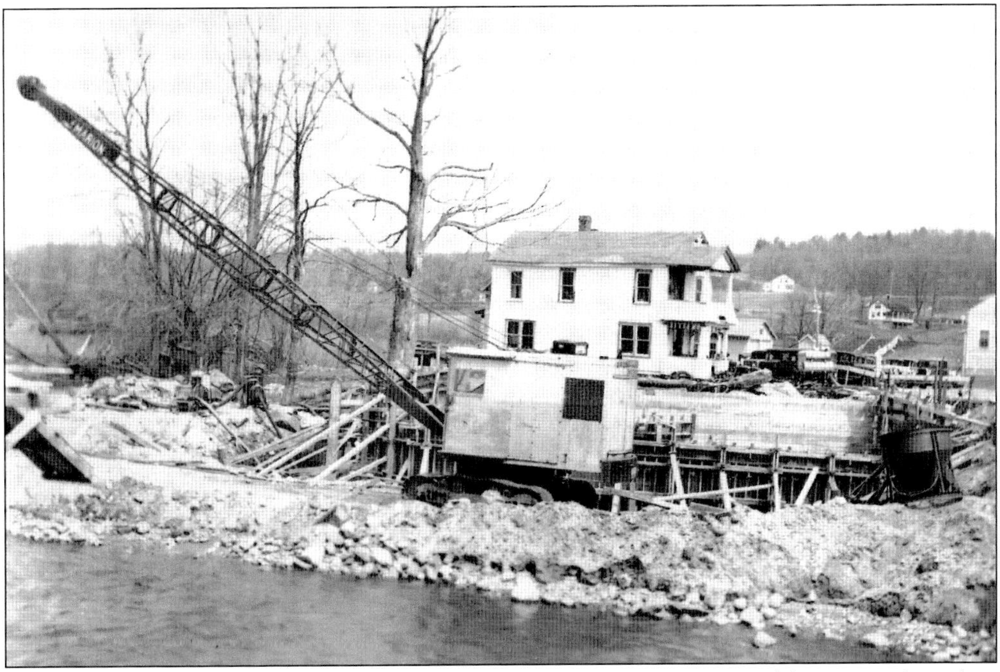

The devastation, cleanup, and renovation of a bridge collapse is unimaginable even in these days of technological equipment. It is incomprehensible and inspiring that the citizens rallied together to ensure that their community was safe and that their roads were passable less than one year after the hurricane of 1938 destroyed the bridge over the Willimantic River in West Willington.

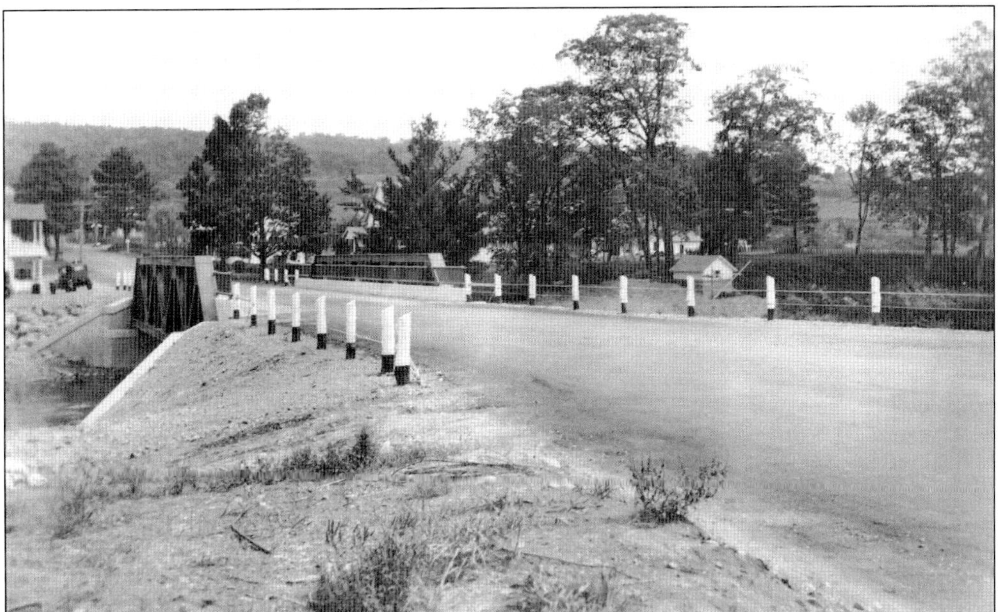

After the damage from the flood, and after a great deal of effort on the part of local and state officials and employees, the new bridge over the Willimantic River in West Willington welcomed locals and visiting travelers alike. By the summer of 1939, the new bridge was completed and accessible to all.

W. C. RUBY & SON

Lumber and Building Materials
FUEL

•

Breeder of Hereford Cattle
Registered Stock

Dependable Courteous Service

WEST WILLINGTON CONNECTICUT

Telephone Office: Will. 9916. Residence: Will. 9445

In the early 1900s, Wilbert C. Ruby operated a sawmill. By the time of this 1941 advertisement, he had opened a lumber company with business and home telephone numbers made available to all who perused the brochure. Wilbert's business interests also included agriculture, although it is unknown what fuel he sold. The business was located next to what is now the Track Nine Diner.

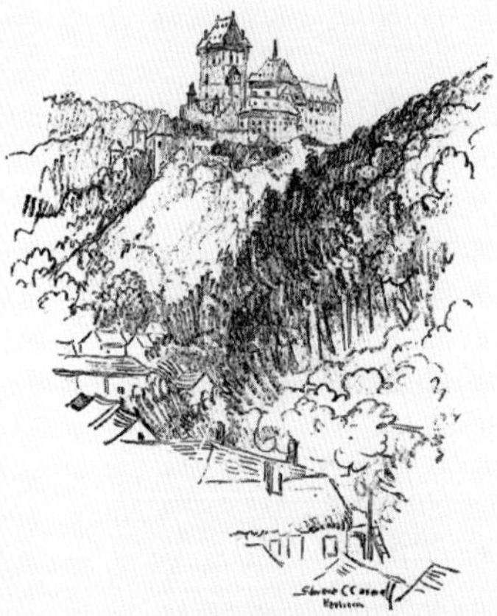

KARLŮV TÝN

THE FRANK PARIZEK

MANUFACTURING COMPANY
Manufacturers of
OCEAN PEARL BUTTONS

•

WEST WILLINGTON CONNECTICUT

Frank Parizek's advertisement in the program for the 1941 Czechoslovak Day, held in nearby Stafford Springs, announced not only his pearl button manufacturing business in West Willington but also his heritage. The sketch is a depiction of Karluv Tyn castle in Czechoslovakia.

Like many Willington residents, William F. Masinda was of Czechoslovakian descent. In this undated photograph, he is approximately 25 years old. His father, William T. Masinda, founded one of Willington's button factories in the early 1900s. The button business was not an enduring one, however, and the younger William did not follow in his father's footsteps. (Courtesy of Maureen Gantick.)

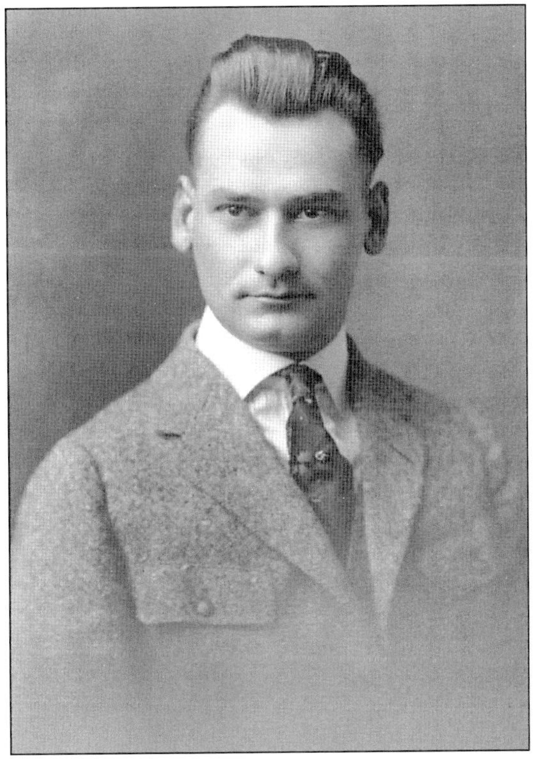

The two-story building in the center of this 1979 photograph of the Masinda property may have been built in the late 1790s by Abel Johnson. Robert Sharp bought the property in 1815. Besides operating a gristmill, he was also an undertaker who made coffins, sliding them from the upstairs door. In the late 1800s, the building in the left background was the dance hall for Bohemian immigrants. (Courtesy of Maureen Gantick.)

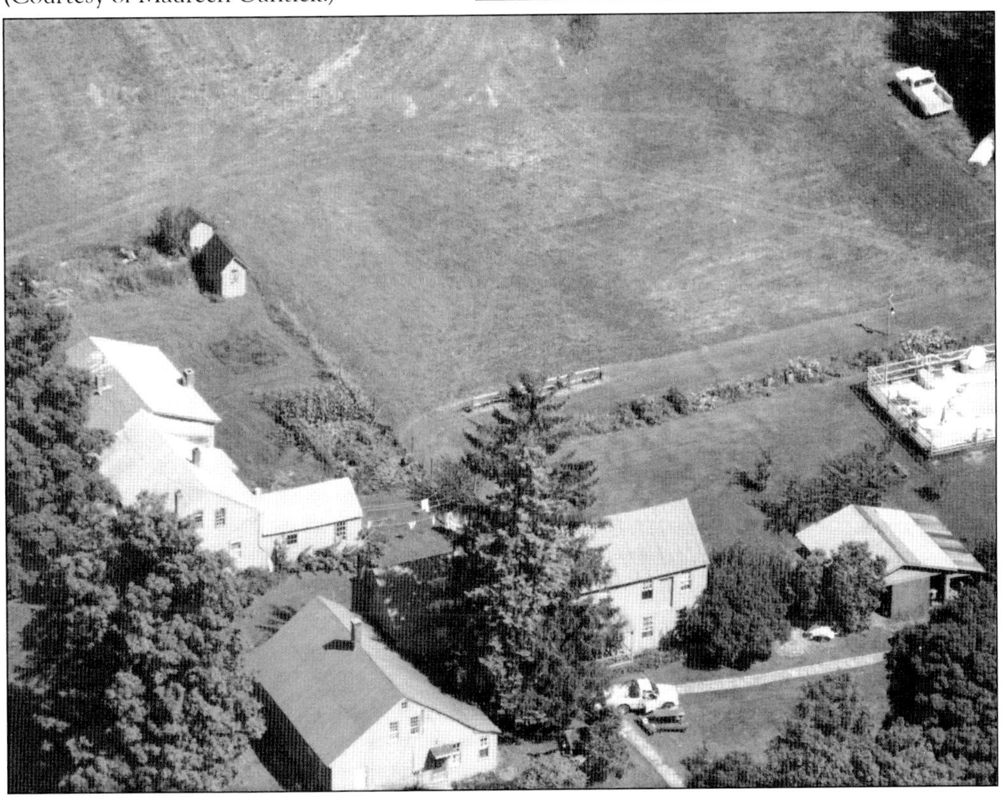

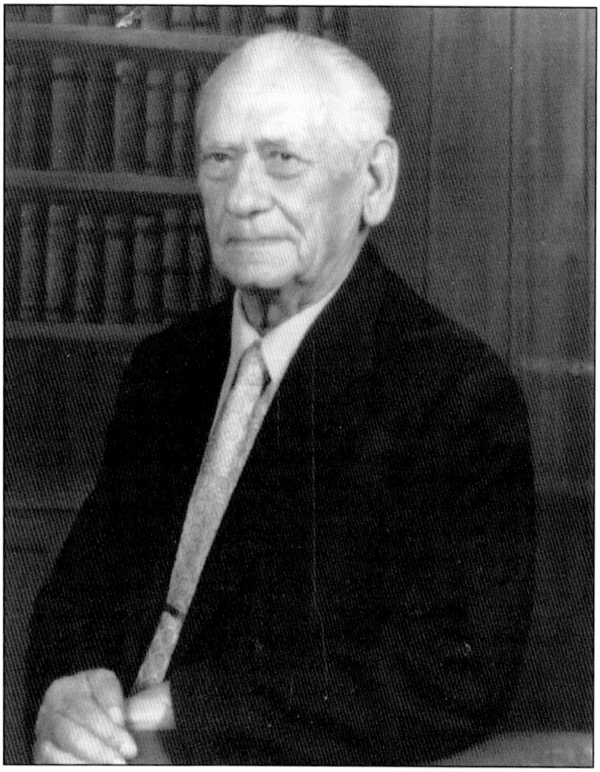

These undated photographs show William F. Masinda much later in his life, as well as his wife, Johanna. Instead of pursuing his father's button business or another manufacturing enterprise, he became active in local politics, serving from 1961 to 1965 as one of Willington's assessors. He also served for many years as the sealer of weights and measures, and represented Tolland County at the 38th National Conference on Weights and Measures in Washington, DC, in 1953. He also served as the Tolland County sheriff. He married the former Johanna Hauschild, who was born in 1894. She was a woman of faith, good humor, and talent who enjoyed writing poetry. She died in 1990, shortly after William's death at the age of 90. (Both courtesy of Maureen Gantick.)

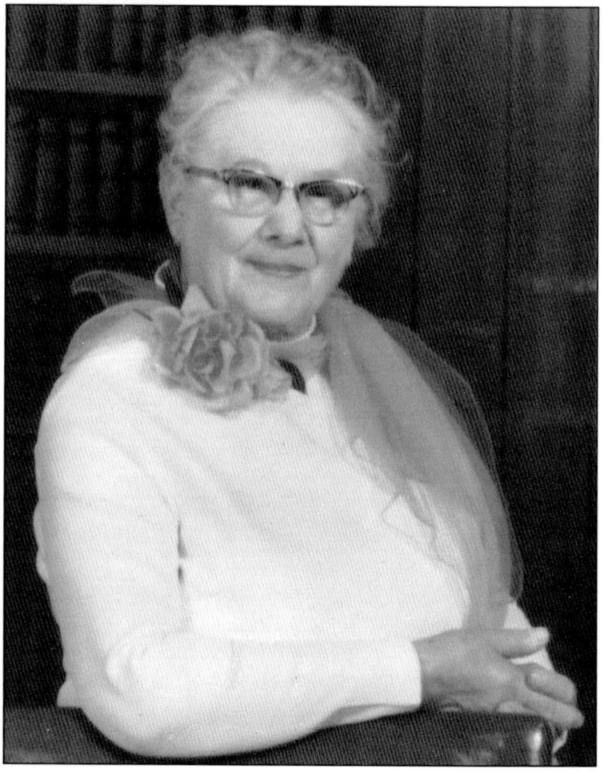

Emil Masinda was the youngest of William T. and Rose Masinda's four children. He was 29 years old when he enlisted in the Army on February 28, 1941. After serving his country during World War II, he returned to his family's home in Willington, where he is seen in this 1950 photograph with his girlfriend Rita Caisse, whom he married a year later. (Courtesy of Maureen Gantick.)

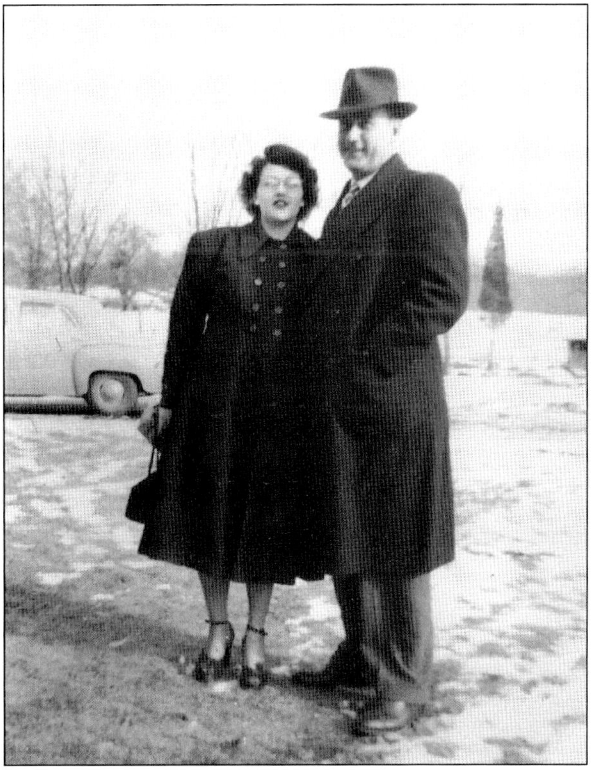

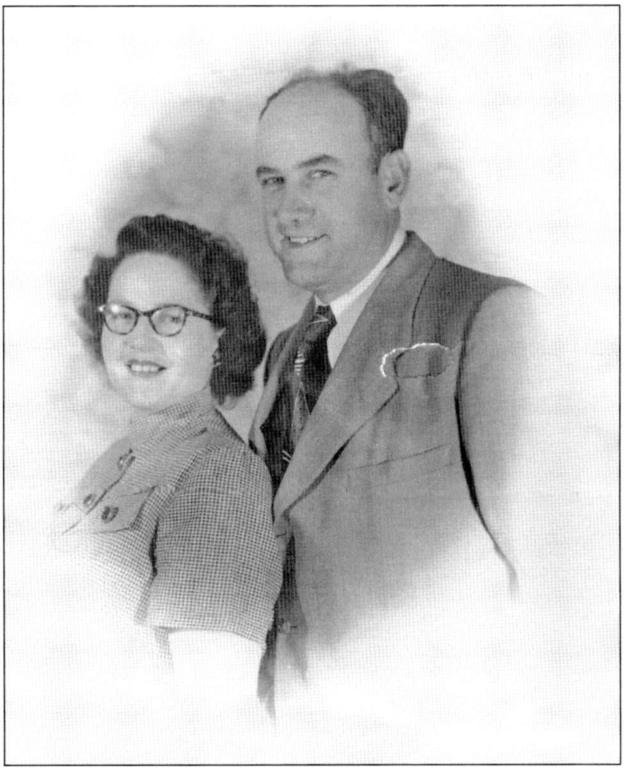

Rita Caisse married Emil Masinda in 1951. She worked as a secretary at the nearby University of Connecticut, and Emil worked for the Connecticut Department of Transportation. Emil spent almost his entire life living on the family property in Willington. They had three children, Maureen, Doreen, and Mark, two of whom still live in buildings on the family property. (Courtesy of Maureen Gantick.)

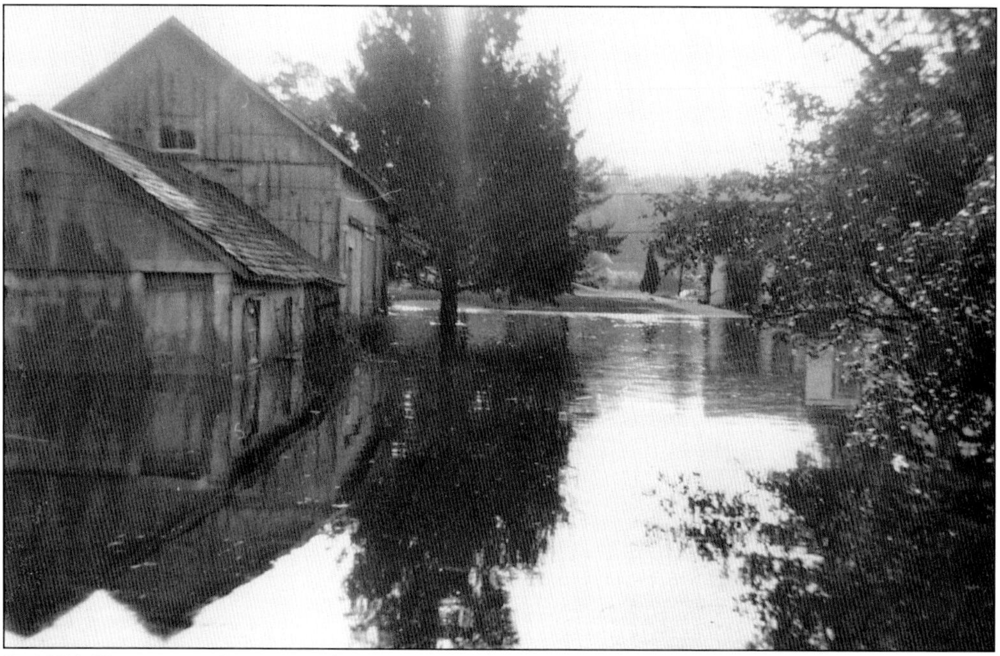

In 1955, Hurricanes Connie and Diane swept through Connecticut, dumping between 4 and 24 inches of rain in just a few days. The barn in this photograph still stands on Tolland Turnpike (Route 74). It was once owned by Arthur Devereaux, the first Willington school bus driver.

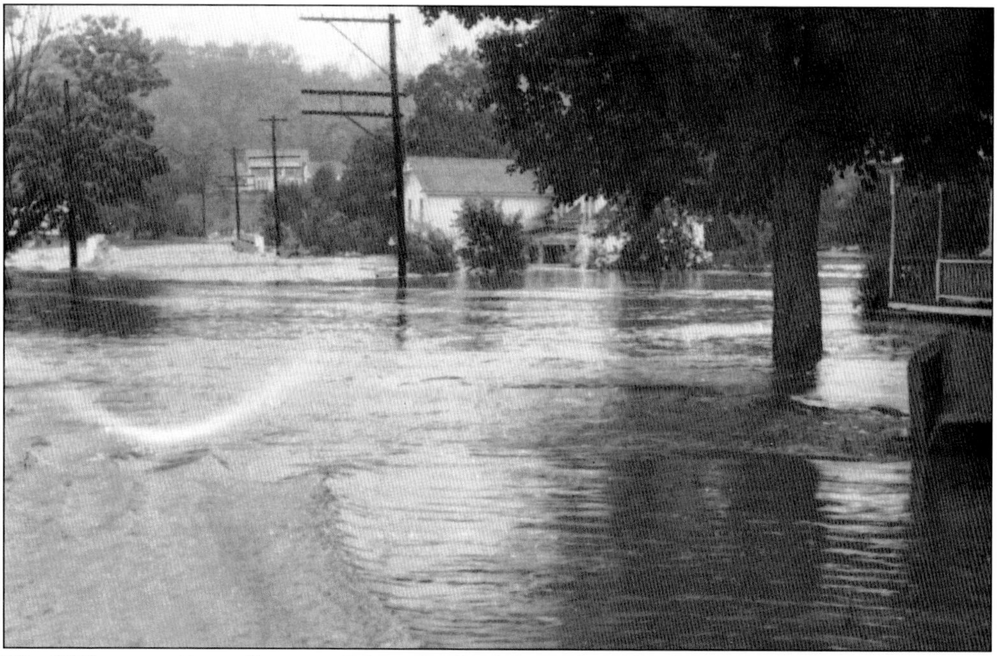

The Willimantic River flows south from Stafford through Tolland and forms the border between Tolland and Willington. Route 74 crosses over the river, connecting the two towns. The Willimantic River overflowed its banks in August 1955 as a result of Hurricanes Connie and Diane. This photograph of Route 74, looking west toward the Nye-Holman house, shows some of the damage.

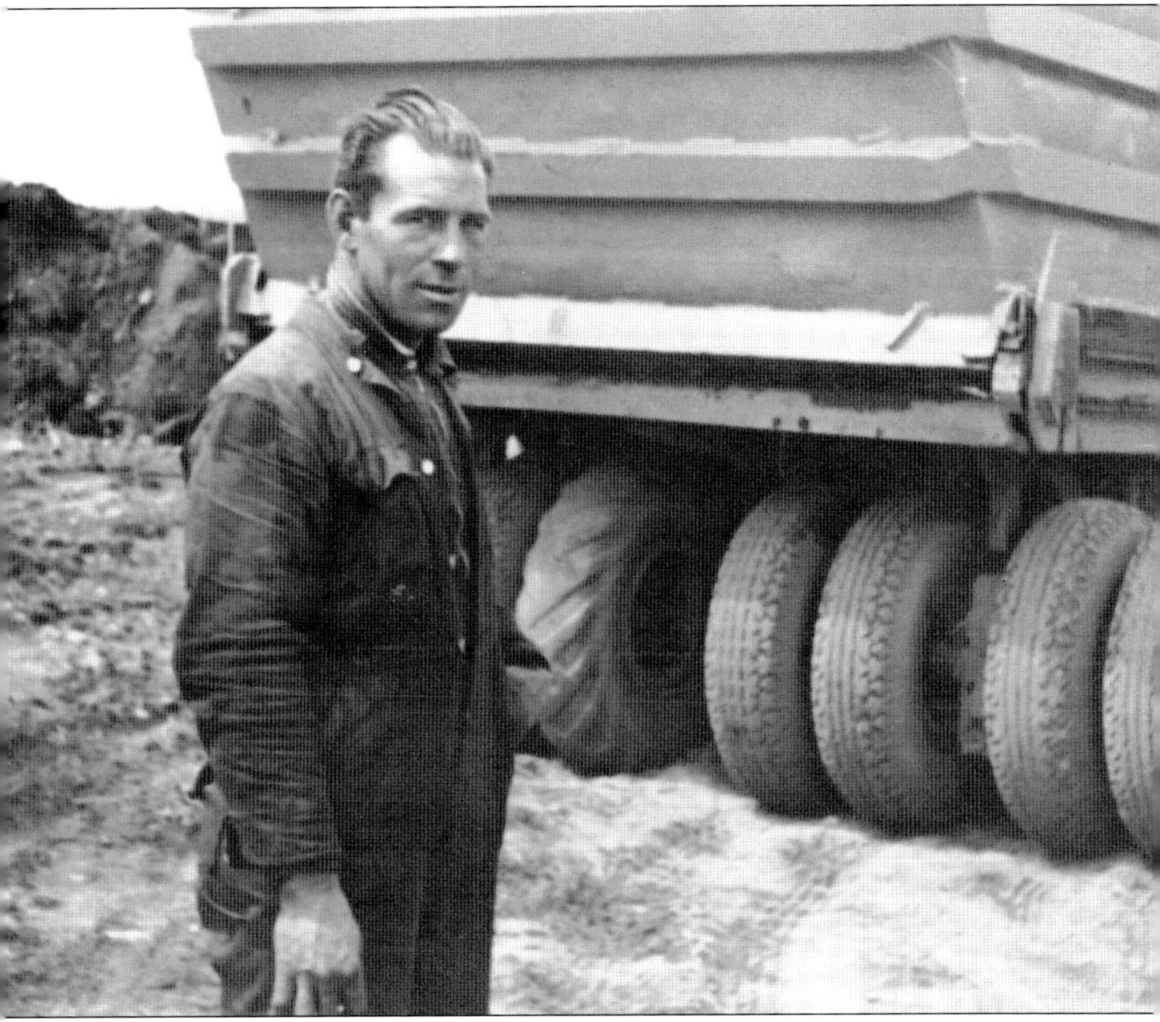

Here, on April 25, 1940, an unidentified construction worker pauses while working on the section of the Wilbur Cross Parkway that travels through West Willington. Extensive blasting was required for the construction of the four-lane divided highway. In 1970, the road was known as Interstate 86. This section of what is now Interstate 84 features eastbound and westbound rest areas. There are two entrances and exits to the interstate in West Willington. Exit 69 provides direct access to the existing post office, shops, and restaurants in Willington, as well as access to the Connecticut State Police troop in Tolland via Route 74. Exit 70 provides access to Willington, Mansfield, Willimantic, and Stafford via Route 32. New England winters mean that today's travelers still often face traffic challenges on this heavily traveled route along the New York-to-Boston corridor.

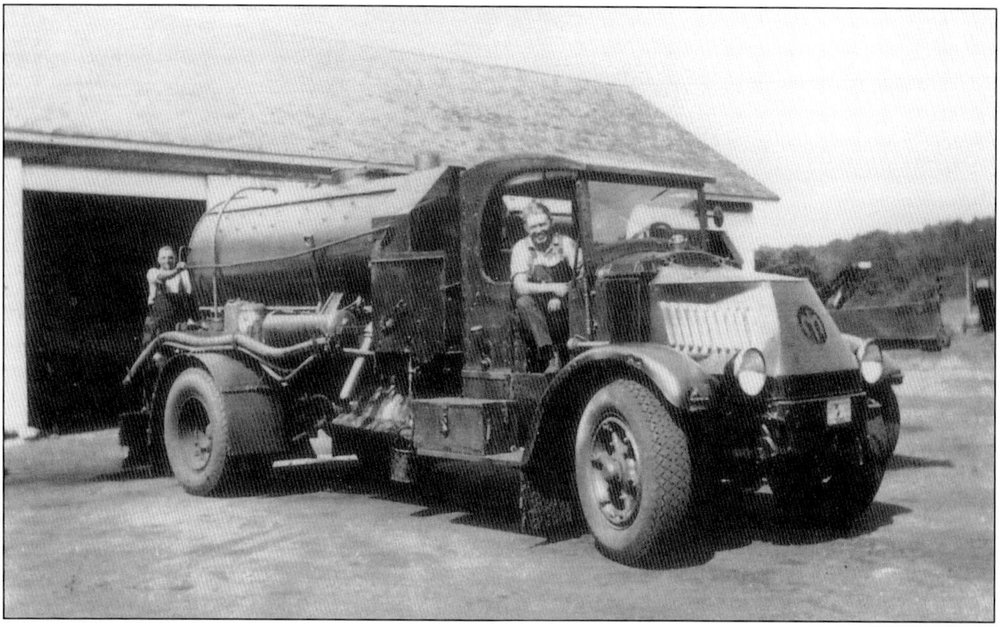

In 1910, the state highway department, now known as the Connecticut Department of Transportation, established district headquarters on what is now Route 74 in Willington. This occurred just five years after the town first received state aid for road construction, and it increased the number of state highway workers in Willington. Edward Ehret stands on the back of the tanker in this undated photograph; the man in the cab is unidentified.

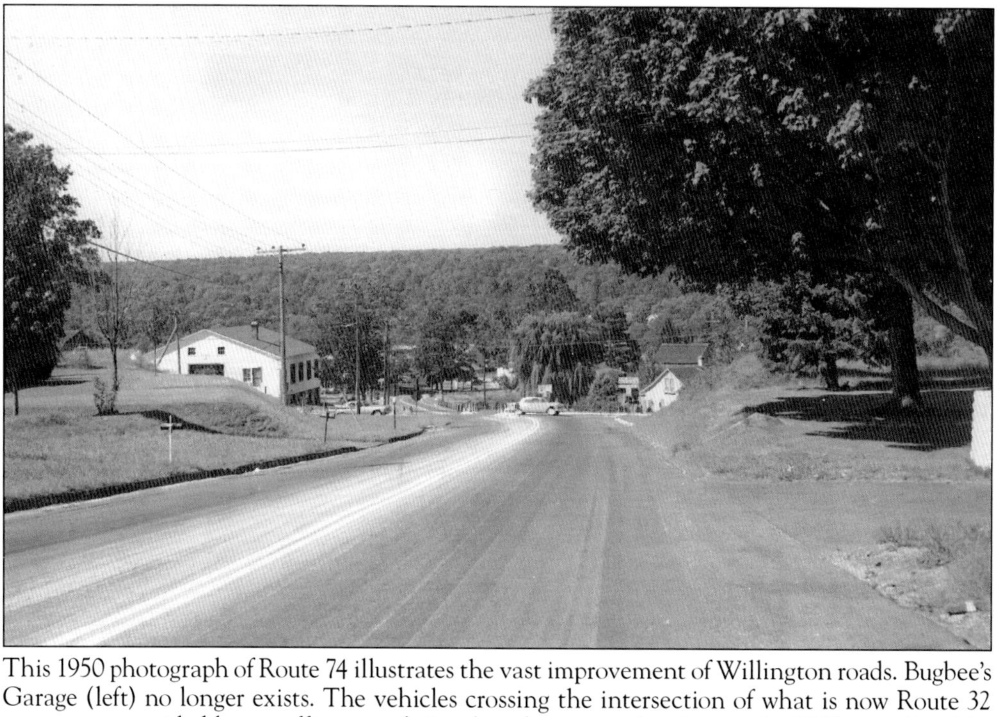

This 1950 photograph of Route 74 illustrates the vast improvement of Willington roads. Bugbee's Garage (left) no longer exists. The vehicles crossing the intersection of what is now Route 32 were not yet guided by a traffic control signal as they are today. Currently, Willington's public works department maintains more than 70 miles of roadway.

Nine

South Willington School District

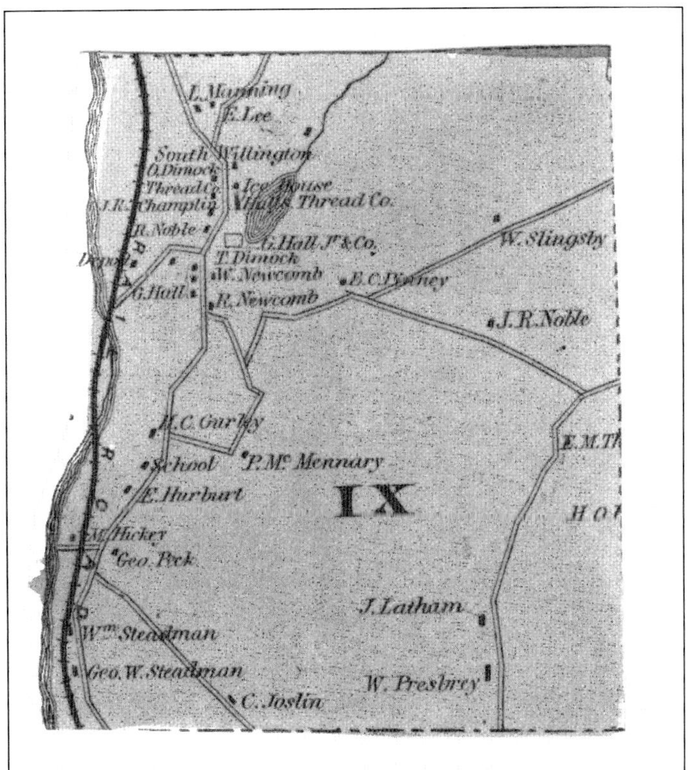

South Willington was the manufacturing hub of town from the mid-1800s through the mid-1900s; thus, there are more photographs of this area than others. There are varying schools of thought regarding company housing and company stores during the Industrial Revolution, but it cannot be disputed that the Hall family's businesses benefited Willington's residents. The existing Hall Church and Hall Memorial School are examples of this generosity.

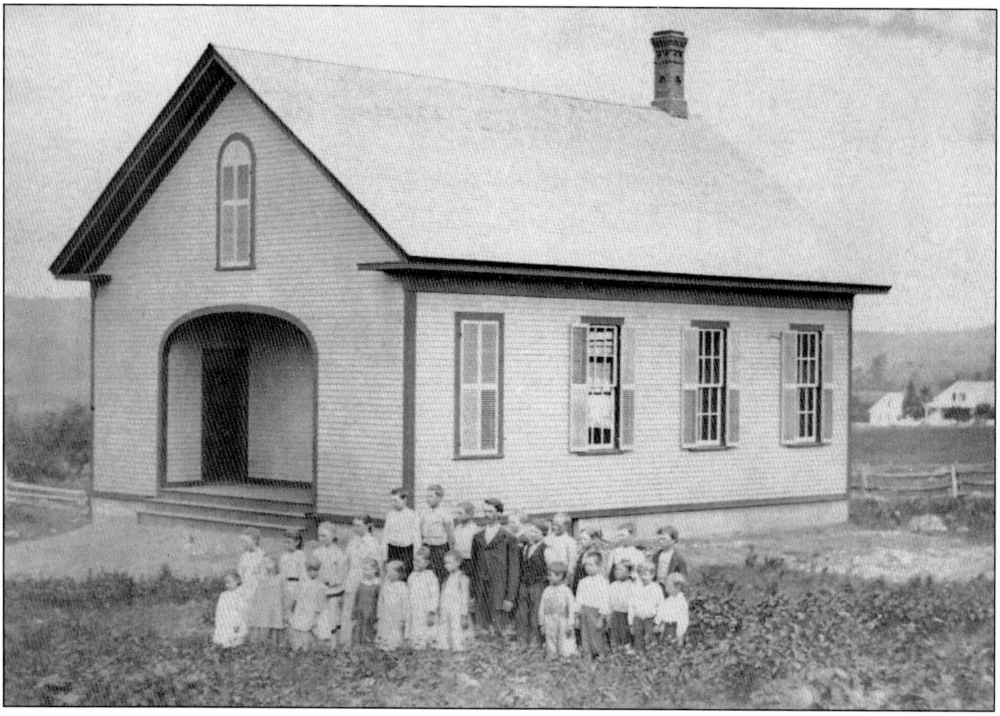

The Pinney Hill School was built in 1877. The male teacher and his students standing outside the one-room schoolhouse are unidentified. The photograph was taken before 1900, when renovations were made, including equipping the schoolhouse with a hot-air furnace, painting the interior, and raising the roof.

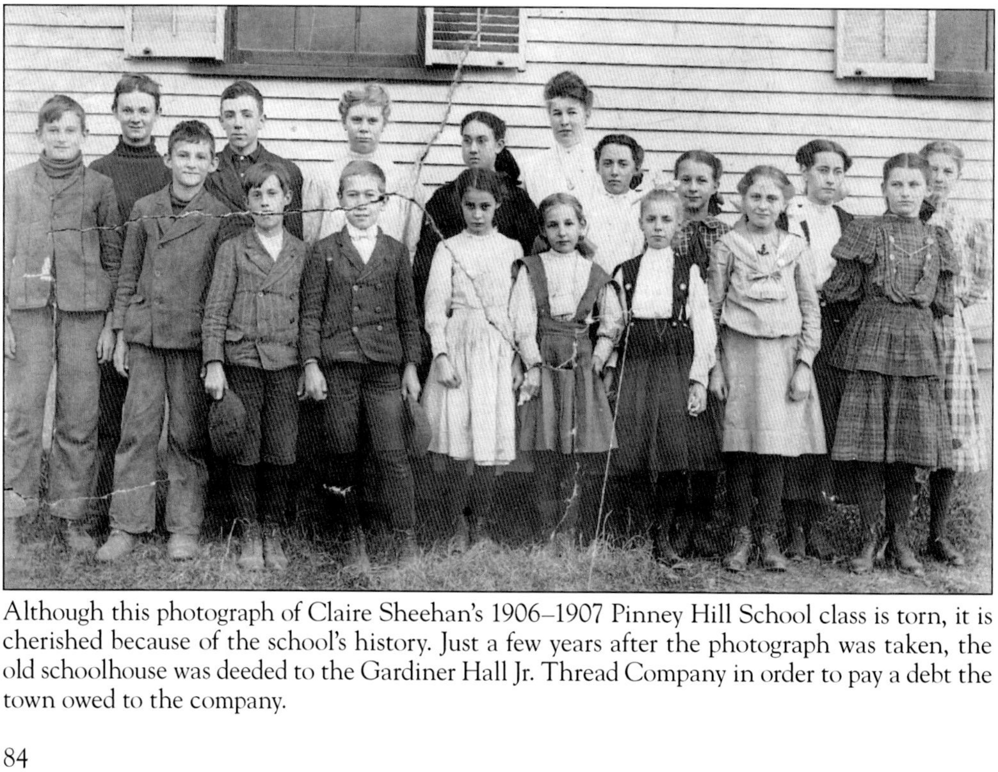

Although this photograph of Claire Sheehan's 1906–1907 Pinney Hill School class is torn, it is cherished because of the school's history. Just a few years after the photograph was taken, the old schoolhouse was deeded to the Gardiner Hall Jr. Thread Company in order to pay a debt the town owed to the company.

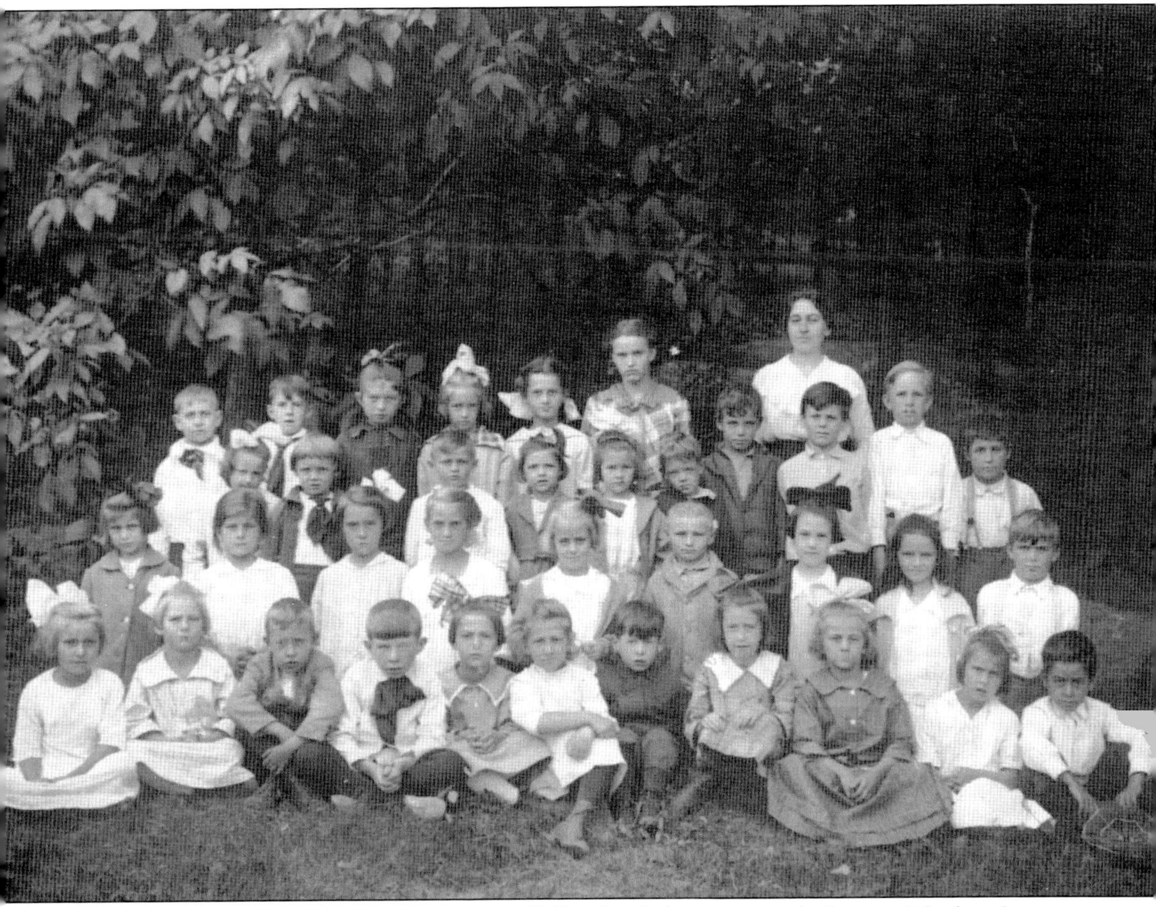

Teacher Elizabeth Green's 1917–1918 Pinney Hill School class consisted of more girls than boys. This may be because some boys were required to work in family businesses. From left to right are (first row) Frances Bartek, Rose Novak, William Potter, William Ceaser, Mary Nedwied, Mildred Hatak, Edward Ladr, Helen Potter, Clara Toberman, Lena Cahoon, and Alphonse DeCicco; (second row) Elsi Pardus, Mary Hatak, Grace Service, Annie Novak, Carolyn Warden, Frank Zemec, Beatrice Malo, Jeanette Nichols, and Ralph Cahoon; (third row) unidentified, James Wolsterholm, Romaine Toberman, Frieda Woodworth, Edith Nichols, Herman Usher, Nelson Usher, Peter LaRoss, Arthur Benson, and ? Maturo; (fourth row) Frank Pardus, John McLean, Mary Ceasar, May Cahoon, Helen ?, Ina Snow, and Elizabeth Green. The large number of pupils is evidence of the greater population in South Willington than in the more rural, remote school districts. The pupils of varying ages who attended this one-room schoolhouse soon become aware, whether directly or indirectly, of the effect of World War I upon their lives.

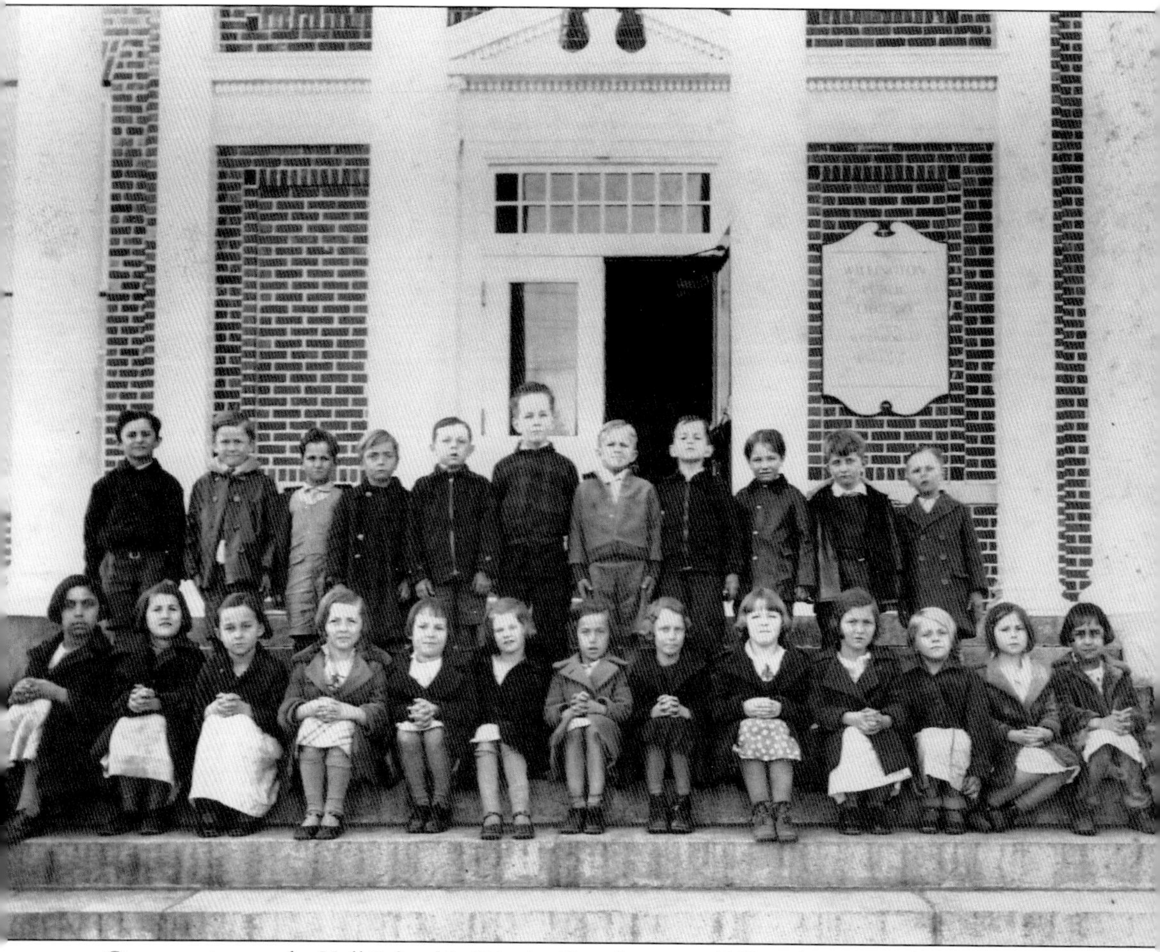

Construction on the Hall School in District Nine began in 1922 and was completed in 1923. The students in this 1924 class were among the first to attend the Hall School, which was the first Willington school to have more than one classroom and to officially separate students by grades, unlike the one-room schoolhouses in the other districts. The members of this class, along with their families, would grow up to face the realities of the Great Depression in the 1930s. Many Willington residents remained employed during the Depression, in large part because of the success of the Gardiner Hall Jr. Thread Company. The sign on the wall on the right announced that the school also housed the Willington Public Library. It was not until 2006 that the library moved into a large, modern building at the corner of Ruby Road and Route 74. Its resources rival those of libraries in more urban areas, but because of its courteous employees, it retains the feel of a small-town library.

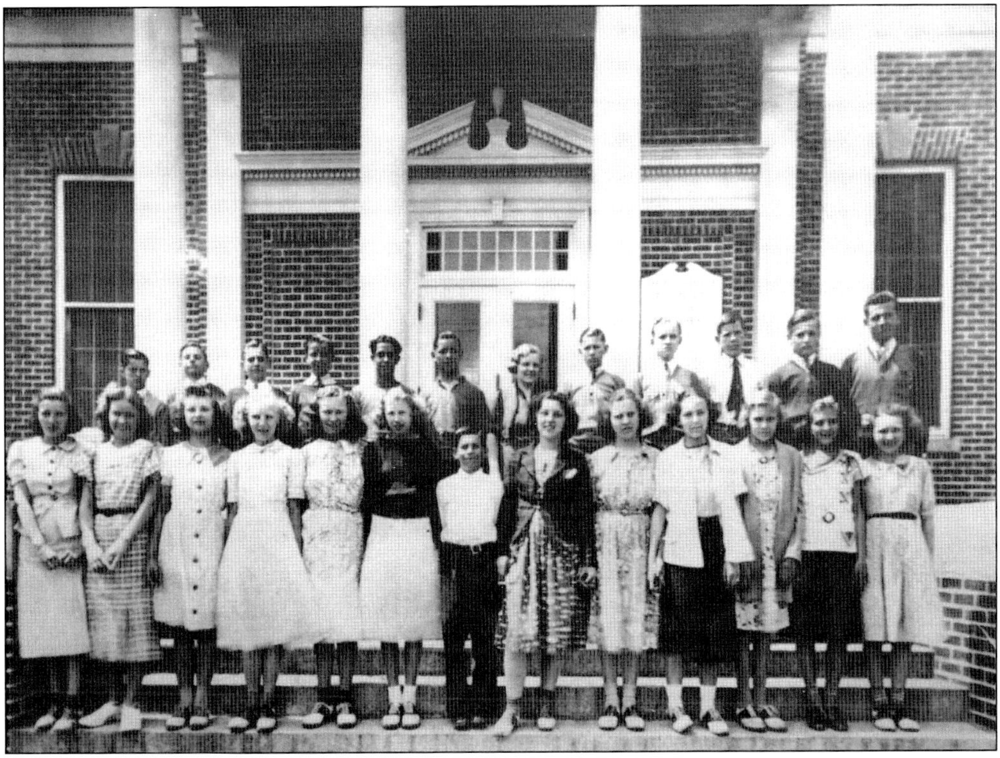

The Hall School class of 1939 included, from left to right, (first row) Ruth Krivanec, Evelyn Dailey, Stella Petrovic, Anna Kowalyshyn, Esther Brndiar, Mary Safranek, Raymond LaBonte, Stella Kulakowski, Margaret Hockla, Hazel Fisher, June Amidon, Laura Safranek, and Sophia Mroczkowski; (second row) Arthur Davis, George Bazala, Franklin Navratil, Leonard Todd, William Downes, Francis Malack, teacher Caroline Mirtl, Edward Ehret, Russell Vonasek, William McBee, Charles Wochomurka, and Charles Kresnowski.

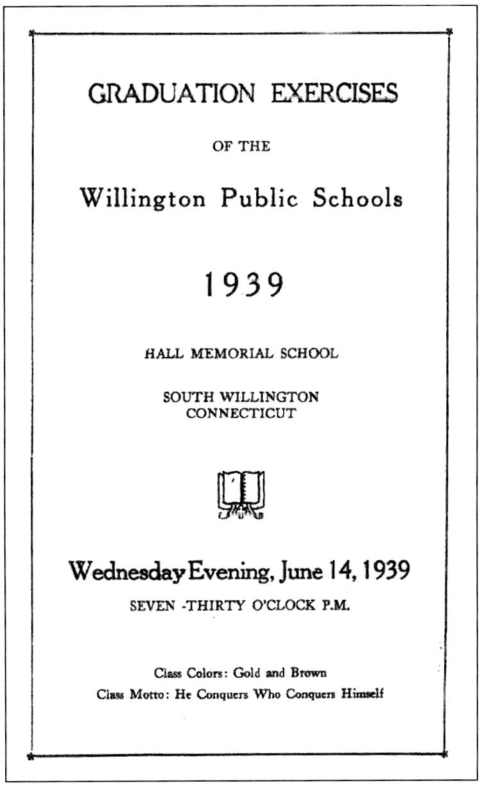

GRADUATION EXERCISES

OF THE

Willington Public Schools

1939

HALL MEMORIAL SCHOOL

SOUTH WILLINGTON
CONNECTICUT

Wednesday Evening, June 14, 1939

SEVEN -THIRTY O'CLOCK P.M.

Class Colors: Gold and Brown

Class Motto: He Conquers Who Conquers Himself

The 1939 graduation program from Hall Memorial School reveals that there were nine teachers, including Esther Phelps, who was herself a product of the Willington school system, having attended the Glass Factory School as a child. The graduating students performed *William Tell*, a three-act musical. Class members William McBee, Charles Kresnowski, and Laura Safranek wrote the words to the class song.

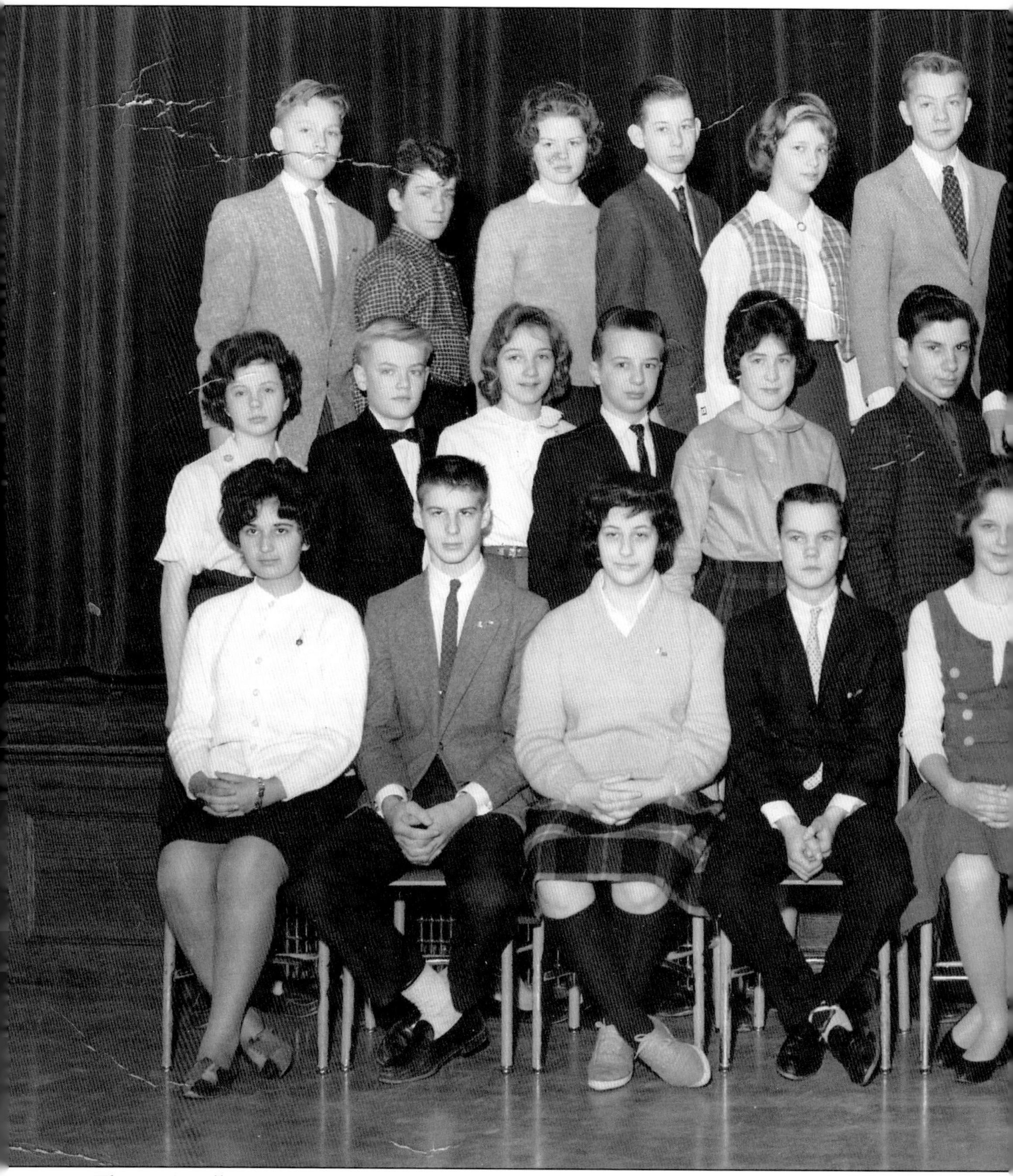

The 1963 Hall Memorial School graduating class included, from left to right, (first row) Regina Rovozza, Nicholas Marco, Lynn Mackovick, Michael Borovicka, Nancy Kristoff, John DuPilka, Linda Allard, James Hunyardi, Judith Vonasek, and Allen DaRos; (second row) Kathleen Olson, L. Thompson Wallis, Nancy Potz, John Howlett, Ellen DuPilka, Robert Mihaliak, Fred McIntosh, Pamela Standish, Bill Navratil, two unidentified, and Dale Dyer; (third row) unidentified, Thomas Farmer, Shirley Keenan, Charles Voboril, Cheryl Phelon, two unidentified, Ina Skinner, unidentified, Bridget Burke, Glenn Martin, and Dennis Hockla. While the faces differ each year,

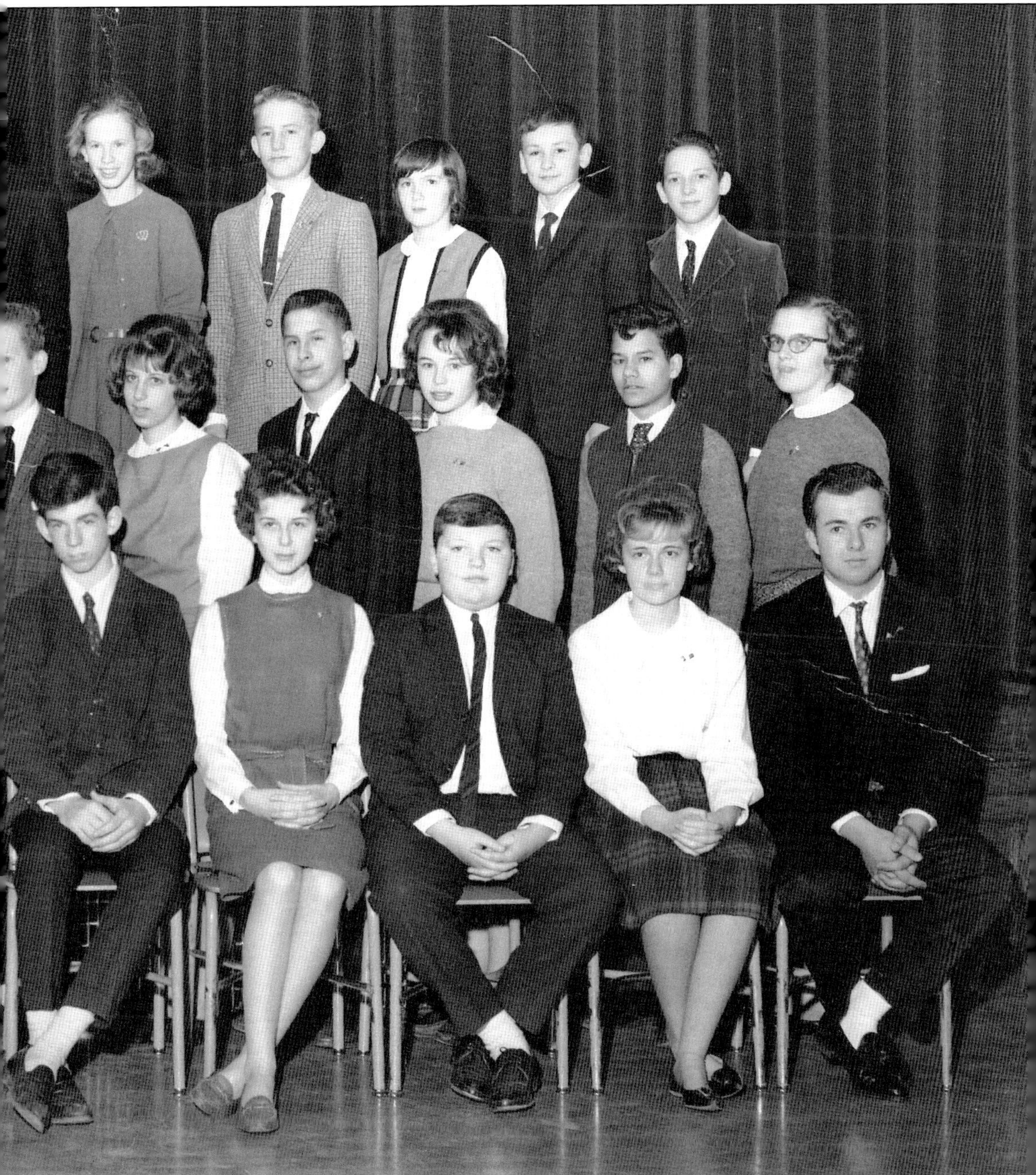

the eighth-grade graduation ceremony traditionally includes speeches from students who talk about their hopes and dreams for the future. The future for the class of 1963 included, among other dramatic and life-changing events, the Vietnam War, the musical revolution, the feminist revolution, protests, marches, assassinations, and the Civil Rights movement, the far-reaching effects of all of which forever changed a nation, a state, and even a small town in northeastern Connecticut. (Courtesy of Shirley Beyor.)

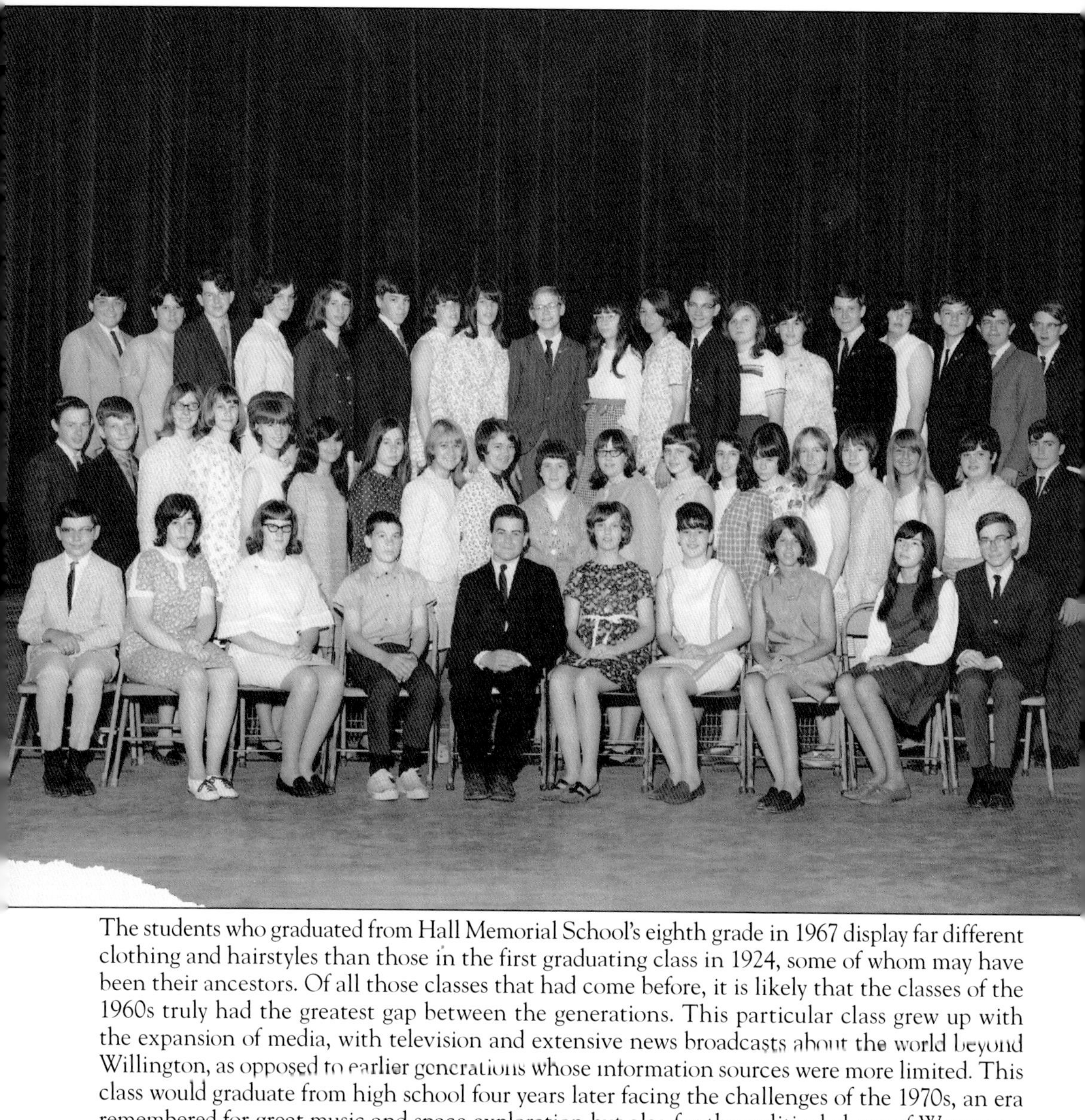

The students who graduated from Hall Memorial School's eighth grade in 1967 display far different clothing and hairstyles than those in the first graduating class in 1924, some of whom may have been their ancestors. Of all those classes that had come before, it is likely that the classes of the 1960s truly had the greatest gap between the generations. This particular class grew up with the expansion of media, with television and extensive news broadcasts about the world beyond Willington, as opposed to earlier generations whose information sources were more limited. This class would graduate from high school four years later facing the challenges of the 1970s, an era remembered for great music and space exploration but also for the political chaos of Watergate. More than clothing and hairstyles would change for these students; the world their ancestors knew was changing rapidly in ways that would affect Willington.

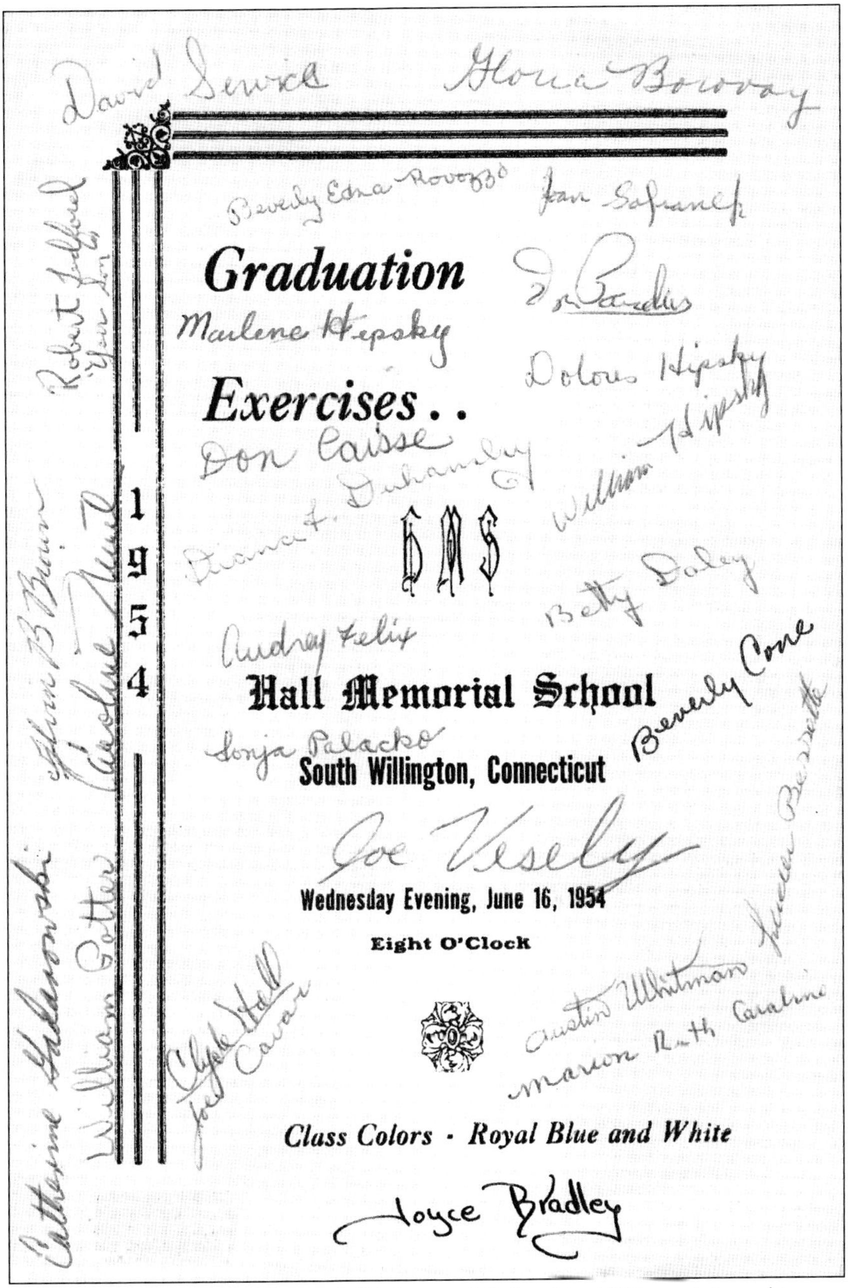

Graduation Exercises..

1954

HMS

Hall Memorial School

South Willington, Connecticut

Wednesday Evening, June 16, 1954

Eight O'Clock

Class Colors · Royal Blue and White

The 22 students who graduated from Hall Memorial School in 1954 participated in an original play, chose their class colors, and sang a song they composed. Tradition lives on today at this small school, where each class creates its own banner. Every year, members of previous graduating classes fill the auditorium and stand beneath their class banner, with even-numbered years hanging on one side of the room and odd-numbered years on the other. As one might expect, there are far fewer graduates standing under the banners of the graduating classes of the early and mid-20th century than from the later part of the century. Elsie Vesely LaBonte, however, stood proudly in June 2013 under the banner her eighth-grade graduating class created in 1933. Likewise, Elsie's niece Elizabeth Robertson smiled as she stood under the banner her class created in 1949.

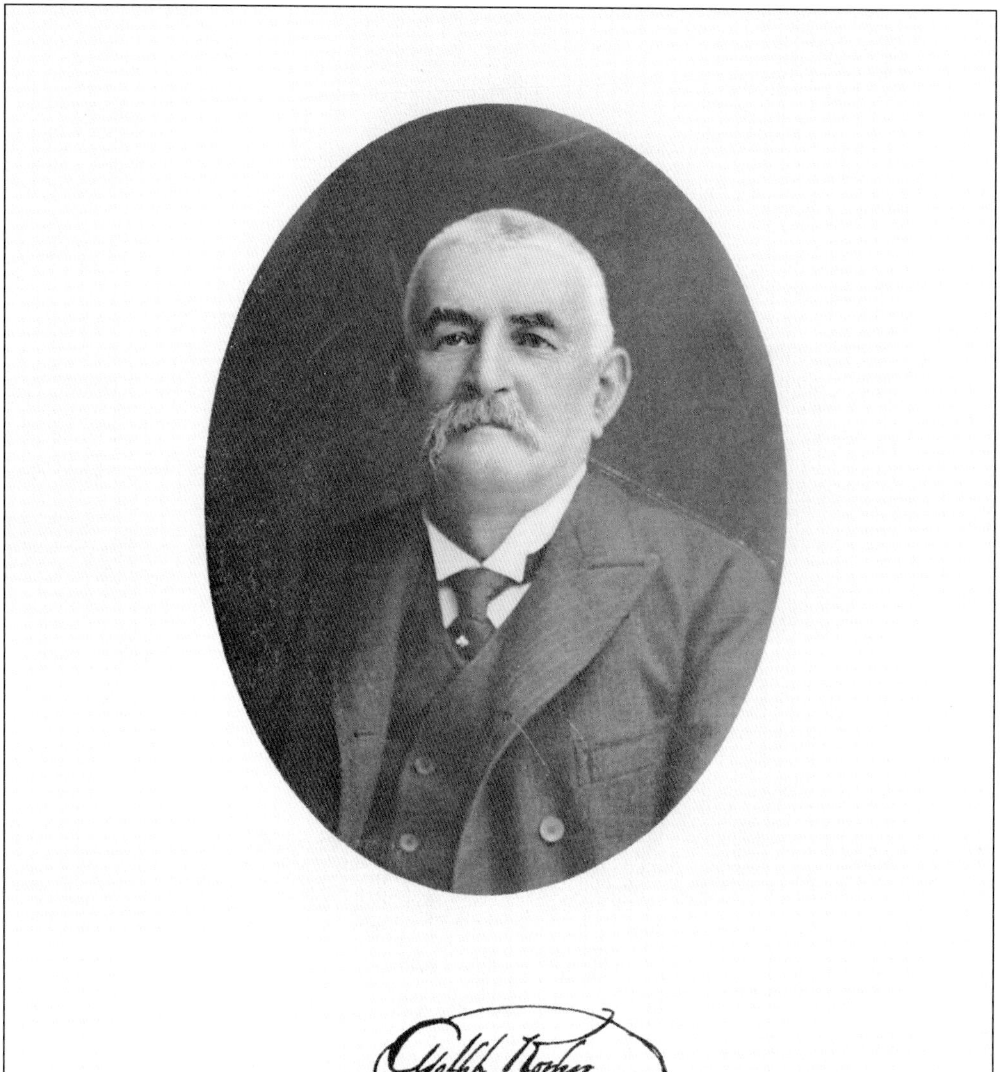

Adolph Korper, born on February 27, 1846, in Bohemia, is an example of the American dream. He came to Willington via Hamburg, Germany, in 1867 at age 21. He was a hardworking and progressive man who installed a windmill and a gasoline engine at his South Willington home. He worked as a shopkeeper at the Willington Glass Works and as a bookkeeper and paymaster at the Gardiner Hall Jr. Thread Company mill. His determination and dedication made him a role model for others, especially those born in foreign countries. When the South Willington post office opened in 1889, Korper was appointed postmaster, a position his wife assumed when his other duties prohibited him from giving the task his full attention. Korper was the first foreign-born resident to serve as a Willington official. He was elected as the town's first selectman in 1886 and was reelected 10 times, serving through 1911. He died on May 7, 1912, and is buried in Willington.

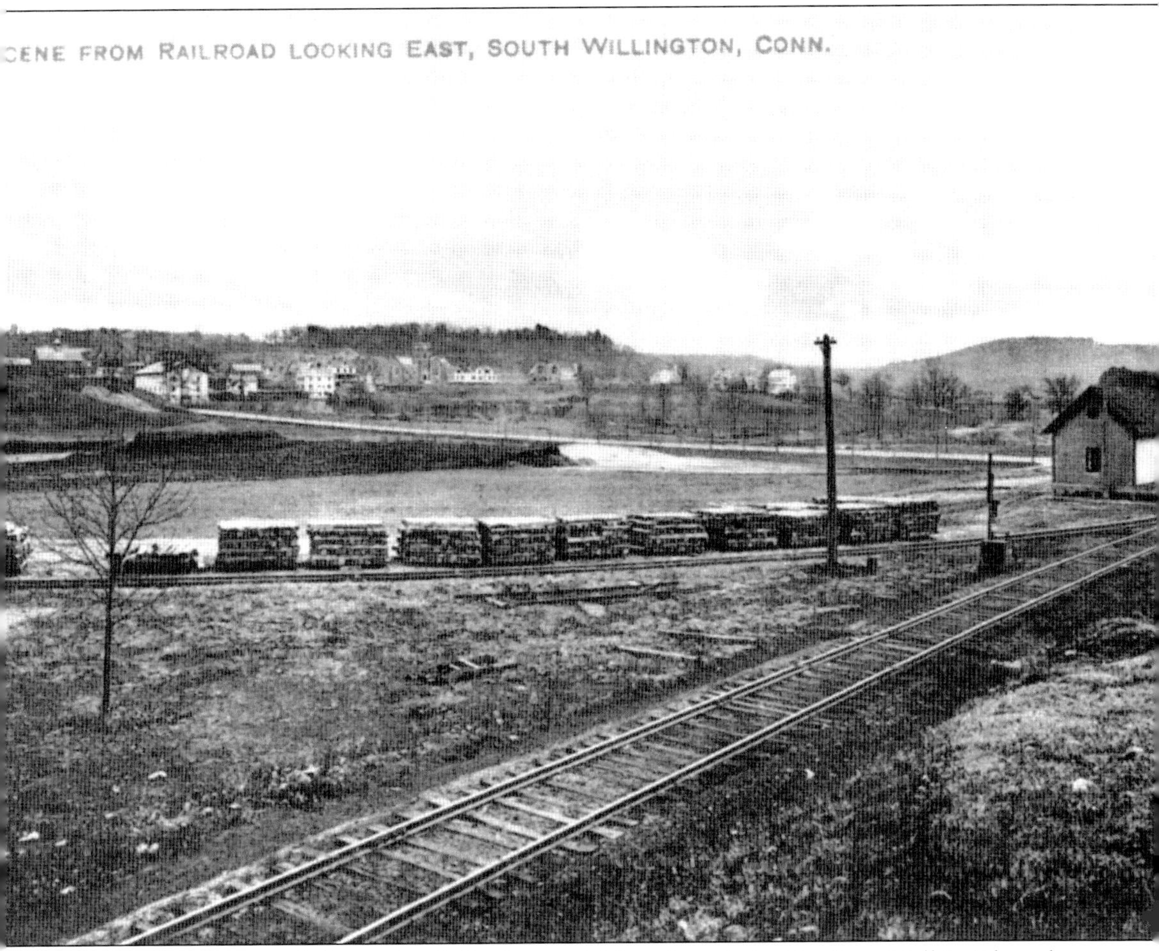

This undated postcard shows the Hall Memorial Church and the Gardiner Hall Jr. Thread Company in the background. The South Willington railroad station (right) was essential to the thread company because it provided transportation for the goods that were made at the company. There is currently no passenger or freight rail service that stops in Willington.

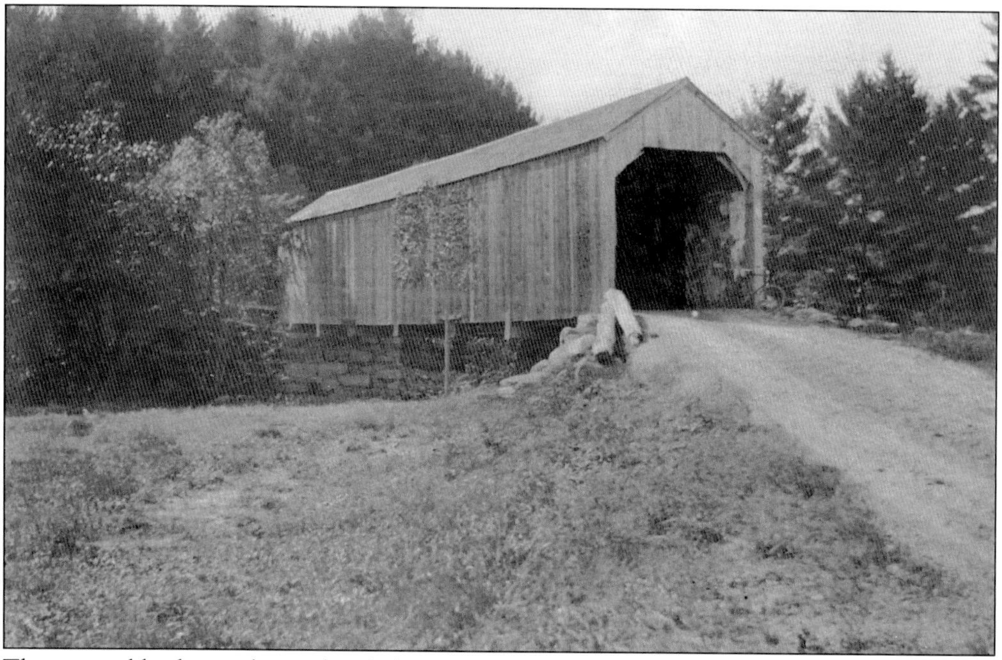

The covered bridge in this undated photograph crosses the Willimantic River, which serves as the border between South Willington and Tolland. The river parallels what is now River Road (Route 32). Although the bridge no longer exists, a person standing on Depot Road just off of River Road can easily see its stone foundation.

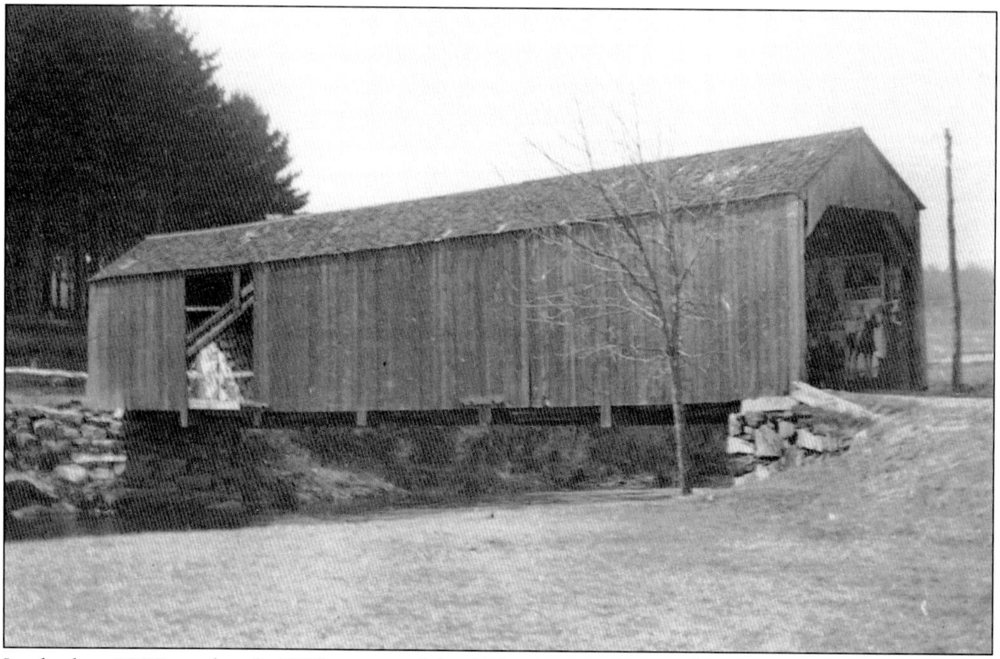

In the late 1800s and early 1900s, most of the 18 bridges in the small Willington community had been built between 1850 and 1913 and were covered. The bridges spanned the Fenton River, the Willimantic River, and Roaring Brook. Looking closely at the entry of the bridge in this undated photograph, one can see posters on the inside walls, precursors to today's highway billboards.

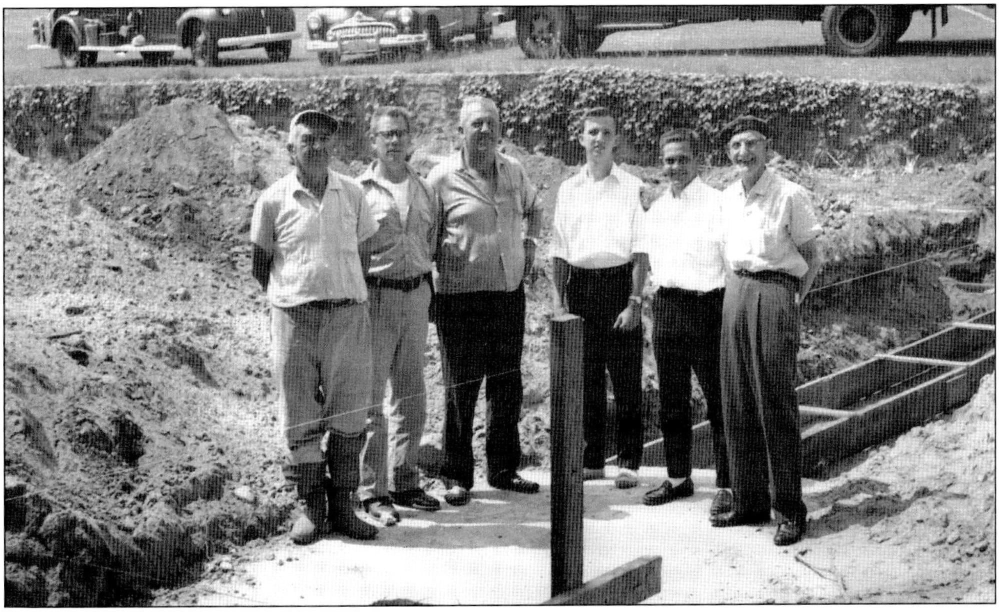

The Hall family donated land on Route 32 so the Willington Fire Department, incorporated in 1945, could build a new firehouse. From left to right in this June 16, 1962, photograph are deputy chief Frank Ladr, fire chief John Service, first assistant chief Earl Woodworth, fireman Gerry Hall, secretary Dave Service, and Gardiner Hall. Today's fire department consists of paid and volunteer firefighters and emergency medical personnel. (Courtesy of Tyler Millix.)

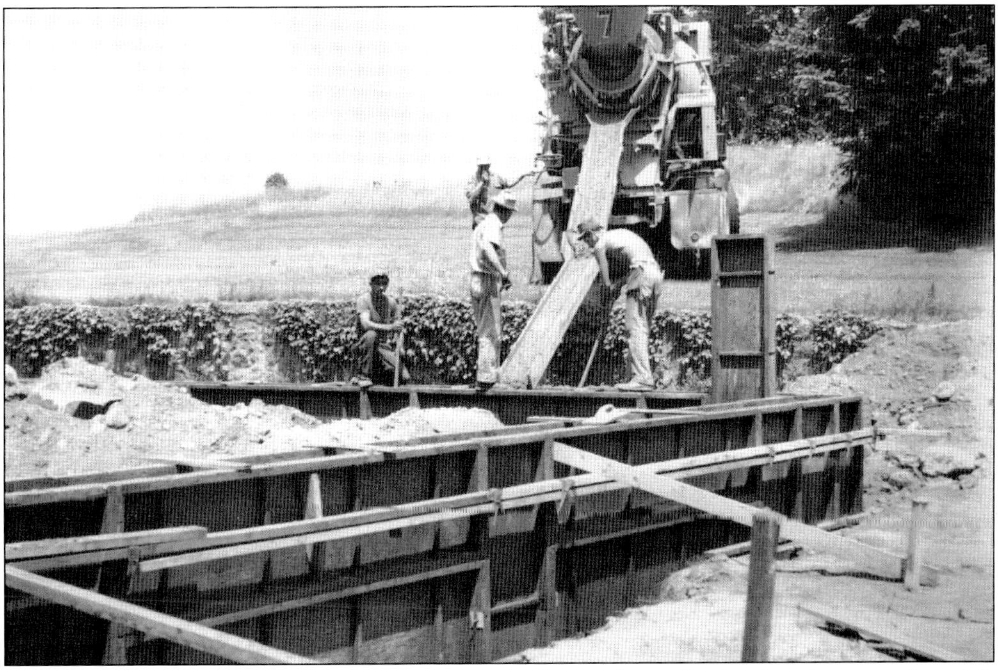

The fire department building process began with placing forms for the foundation on June 28, 1962, and continued with these unidentified workers pouring the foundation on the north side of the building two days later. This is one of two buildings this fire department uses today, both of which are on Route 32. (Courtesy of Tyler Millix.)

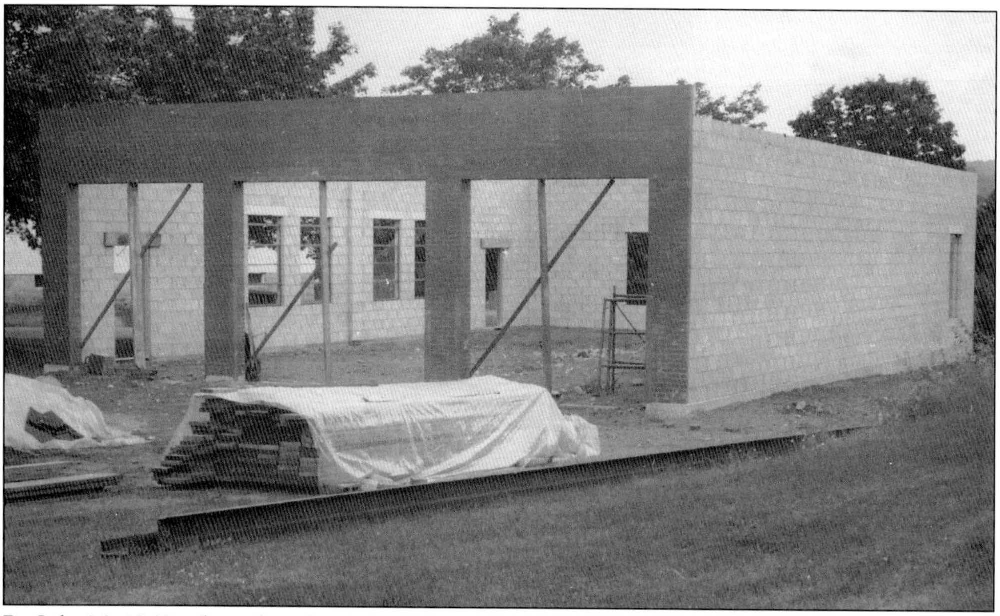

By July 26, 1962, when this photograph was taken, passing motorists could easily visualize the new firehouse. The fire department originally serviced only the nearby Gardiner Hall Jr. Thread Company. Its services were later expanded to the entire community. Today's residents benefit from modern ambulances and the dedication of those who respond to medical and fire emergencies. (Courtesy of Tyler Millix.)

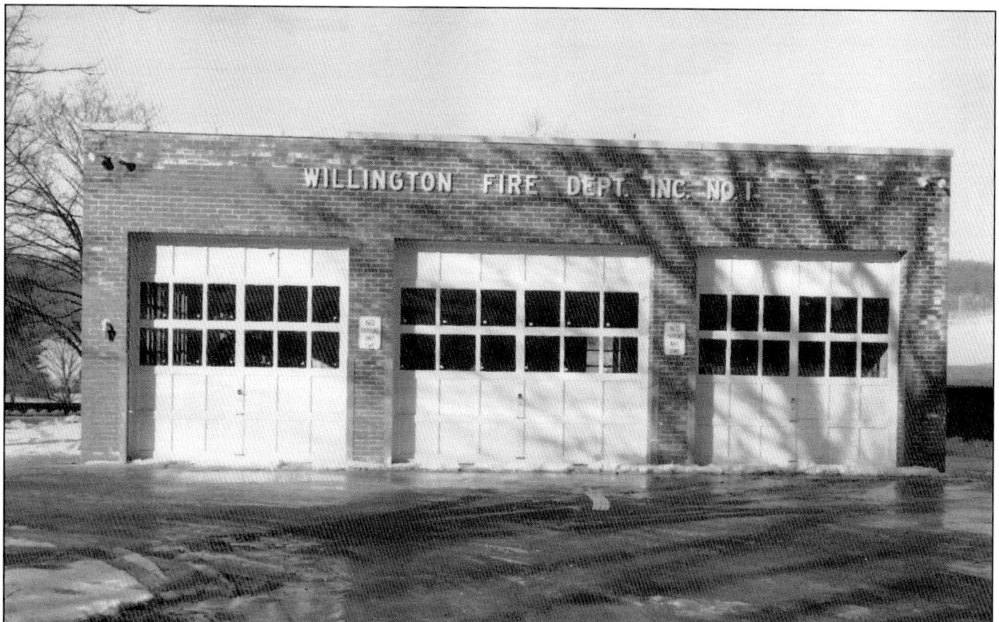

The firehouse, on Route 32 near Depot Road, was completed on December 21, 1962, just six months after the groundbreaking. Along with the Willington Hill Fire Department, dedicated public servants and volunteers respond to emergencies in town and on nearby Interstate 84. (Courtesy of Tyler Millix.)

Service of Worship

Praise and Thanksgiving

In observance of
The End of World War II

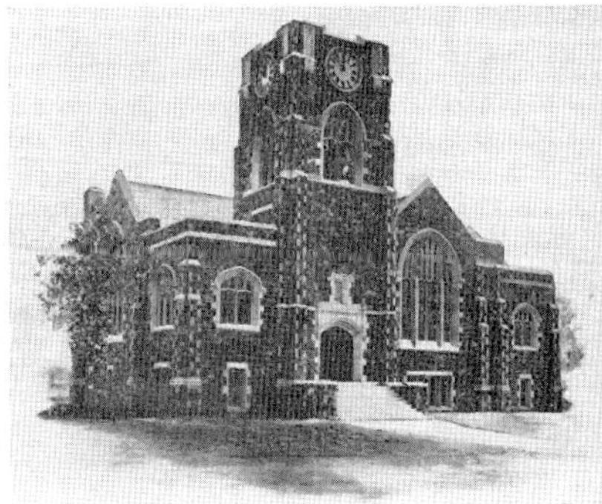

The Clara Hall Elliott Memorial Church
South Willington

Lord's Day, August 26, 1945, 10:30 a. m.

Auspices of
The Federated Churches of Willington
Rev. Alan T. Jones, Pastor

The Federated Church of Willington hosted a service in honor of the end of World War II and in memory of those local residents who lost their lives during the war. It was held just days after the victory over Japan. Though the town was jubilant that the war had ended, the joy was marred by the deaths of 11 men from Willington over the course of the war. The town's prewar population was just over 1,200, and many people knew each other. The program advised attendees that the congregation would donate all money collected during the traditional offering to the American Red Cross.

In Memoriam

MEMBERS OF THE ARMED SERVICE
OF THE UNITED STATES
FROM THE TOWN OF WILLINGTON
WHO GAVE THEIR LIVES IN WORLD WAR II

★ ★ ★

FRANK BECKER
JOHN BRNDIAR
STEPHEN BRNDIAR
FRANKLIN CONVERSE
JOHN HALCHEK
DANIEL LICHANEK
JOHN MACKOVICH
ARNOLD SAFRANEK
JOSEPH SOUKUP
ARTHUR SQUIRE
ADOLPH WOCHOMURKA

★ ★ ★

For the sacred and tender ties which bind us to the unseen world; and for the faith which frees us from our fears and fills us with the light of our immortal hope, thanks be to Thee, O God.

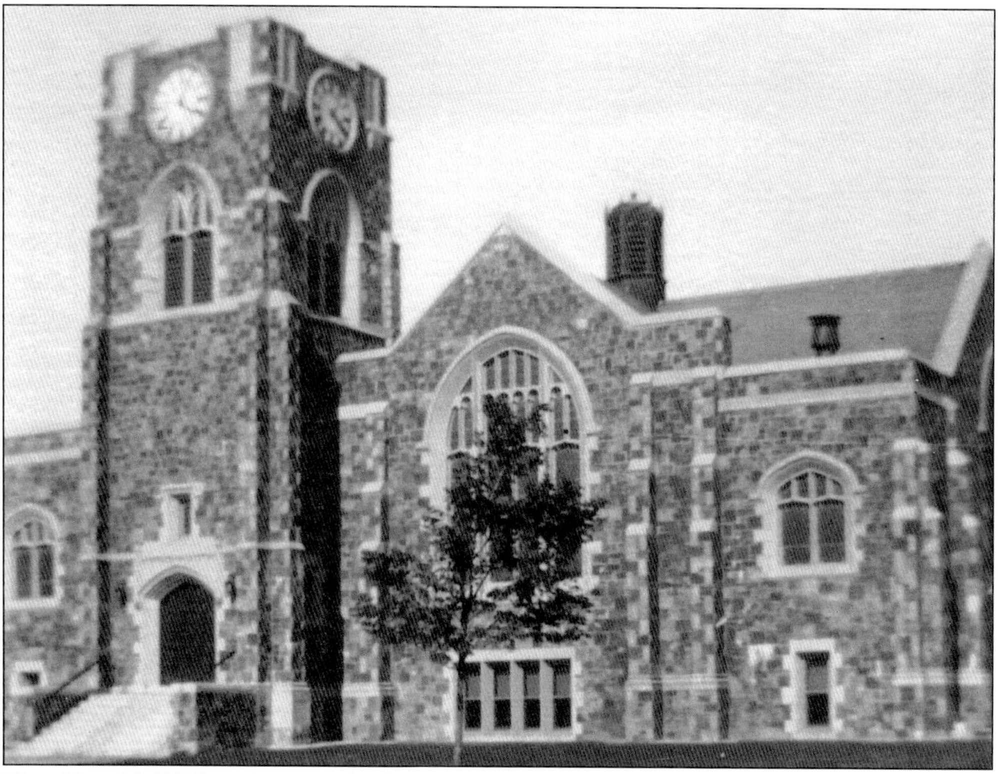

The Clara Hall Elliott Memorial Church was dedicated on October 22, 1911. It stands as a memorial to the daughter of Gardiner Hall Jr. and Fannie Parker Hall. The tree in this June 1924 photograph, like others on the property, is symbolic of the roots and the endurance of the members whose 1911 agreement to join a Baptist and a Congregational church together into one has survived to the present.

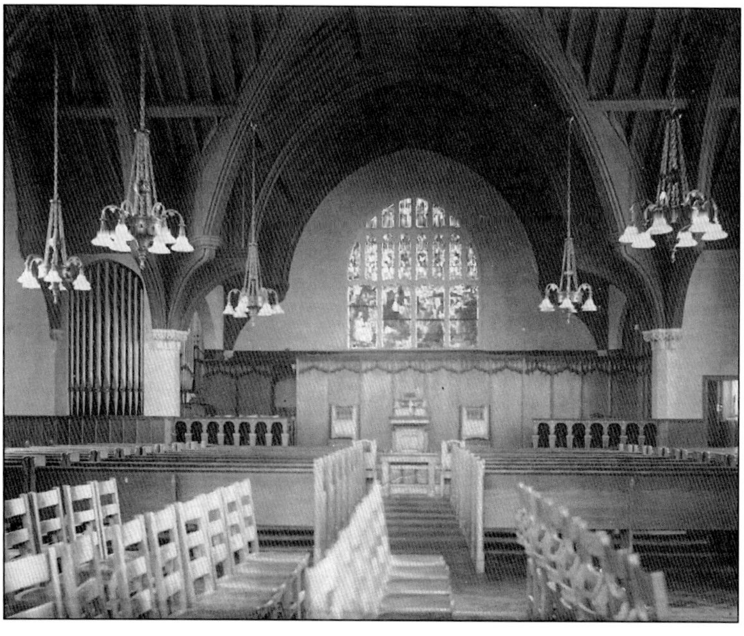

The sanctuary of the Clara Hall Elliott Memorial Church, seen in this undated postcard, provides an elegant and welcoming location for members and guests to worship. The 1911 dedication consisted of an early afternoon organ recital, a late afternoon service of dedication, and an evening service, each of which consisted of a variety of music and prayers.

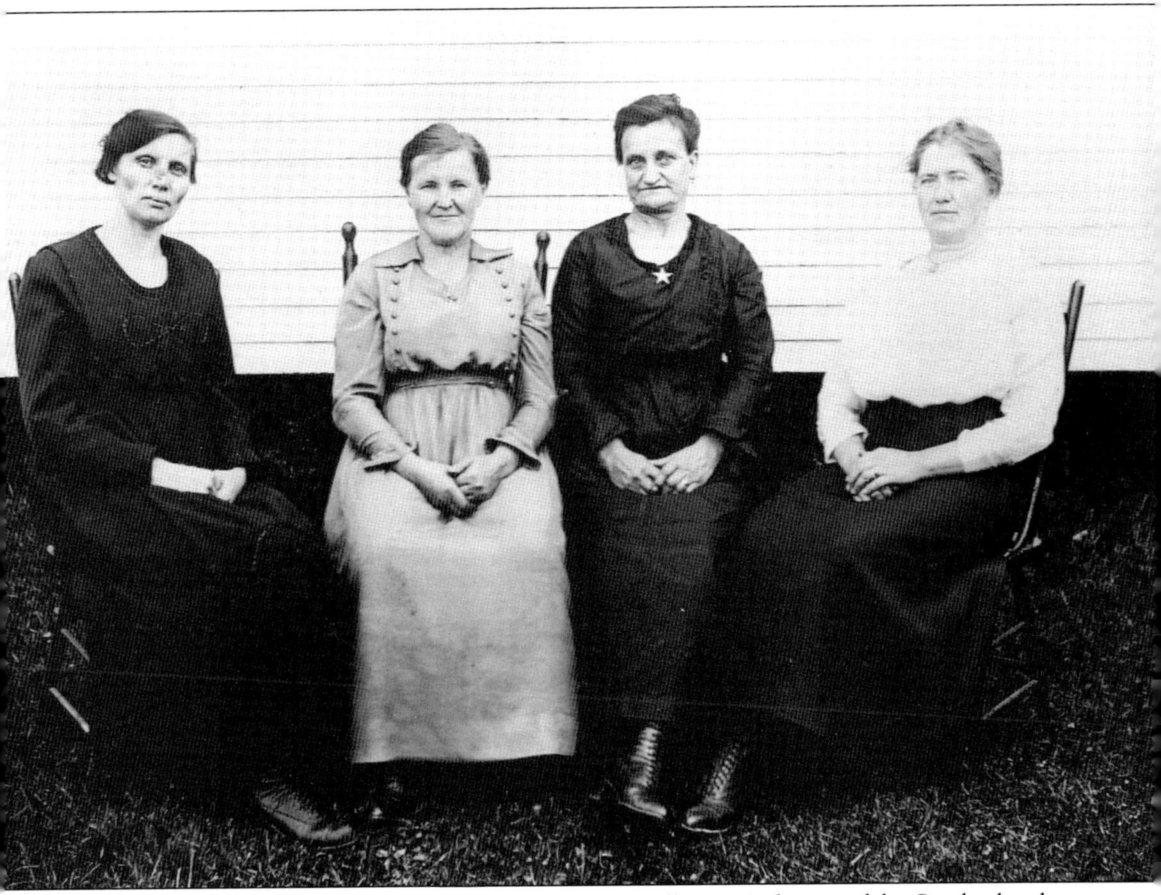

The Czech-Slovak Protective Society was a precursor to Willington's chapter of the Czechoslovak Society of America. The women in this 1919 photograph are, from left to right, unidentified, Rose Pobuda, Anna Parizek, and Bertha Wondrasek. They met regularly with other club members in an effort to ensure that Czech and Slovak traditions and customs continued to exist in their new homeland.

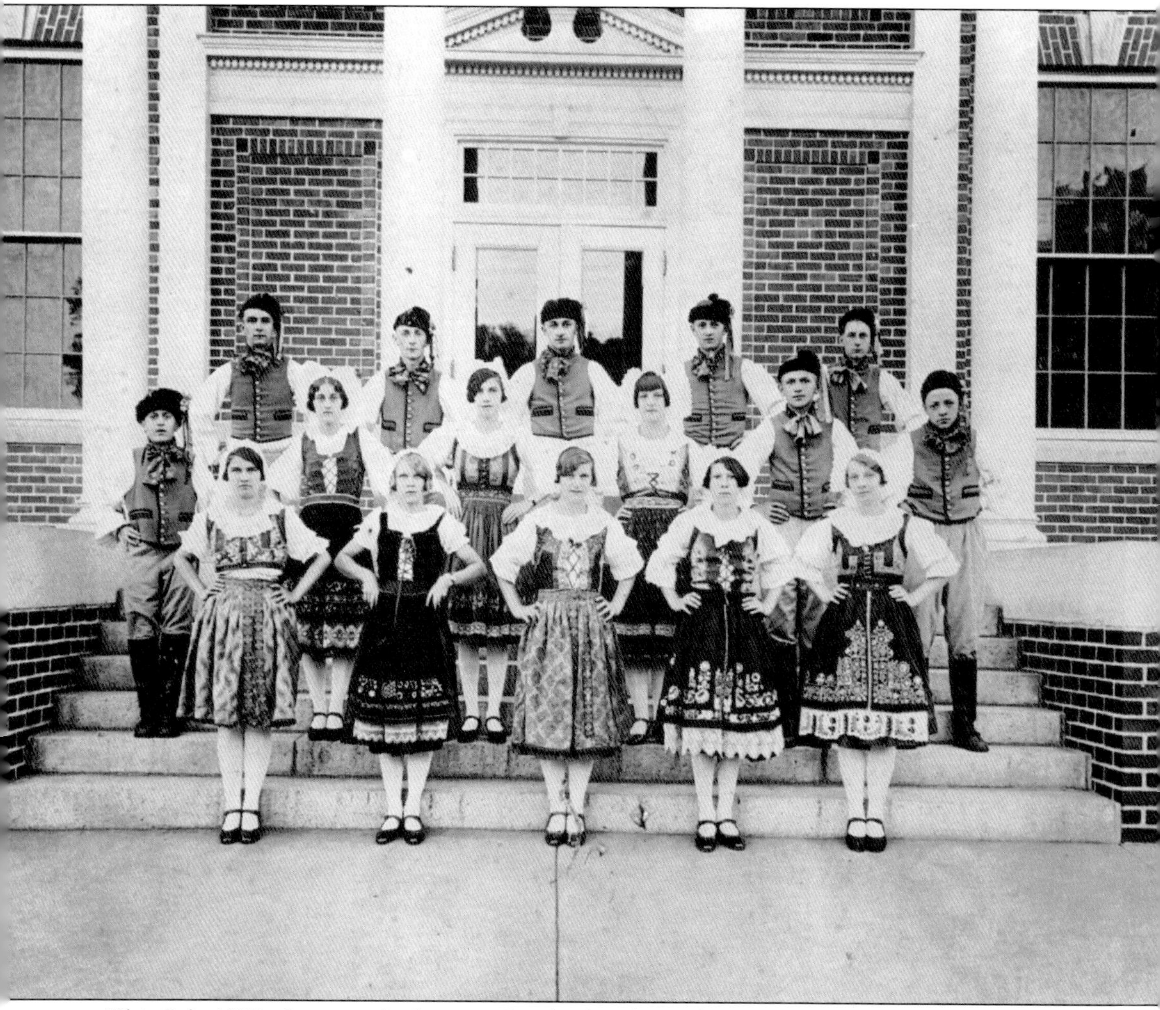

This July 1927 photograph shows a Czechoslovakian dance group celebrating Willington's bicentennial in front of Hall Memorial School. The dancers are, from left to right, (first row) Helen Safranek, Gerry Novotny, Frances Stross, Sophie Holub, and Alice Luchart; (second row) Charles Rada, Clara Toberman Beenk, Elizabeth Hrouda, Mary Nedwied, Daniel Lichanec, and Joe Cavar; (third row) Joseph Voboril, John Zemek, Frank Parizek, Otto Vonasek, and Charles Voboril.

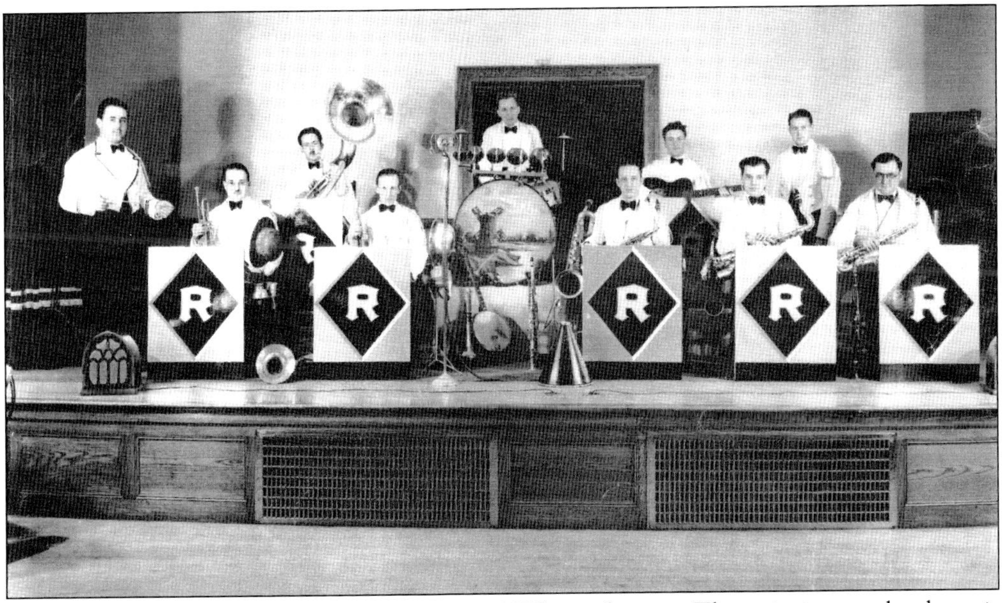

The purpose of this Reveliers performance in 1935 is unknown. The painting on the drum is possibly a tribute to the band's homeland. The Czechoslovak Society of America not only hosted meetings and fundraising events, it also rented out the Laurel Lodge for weddings and private parties. (Courtesy of Dawn Yedziniak.)

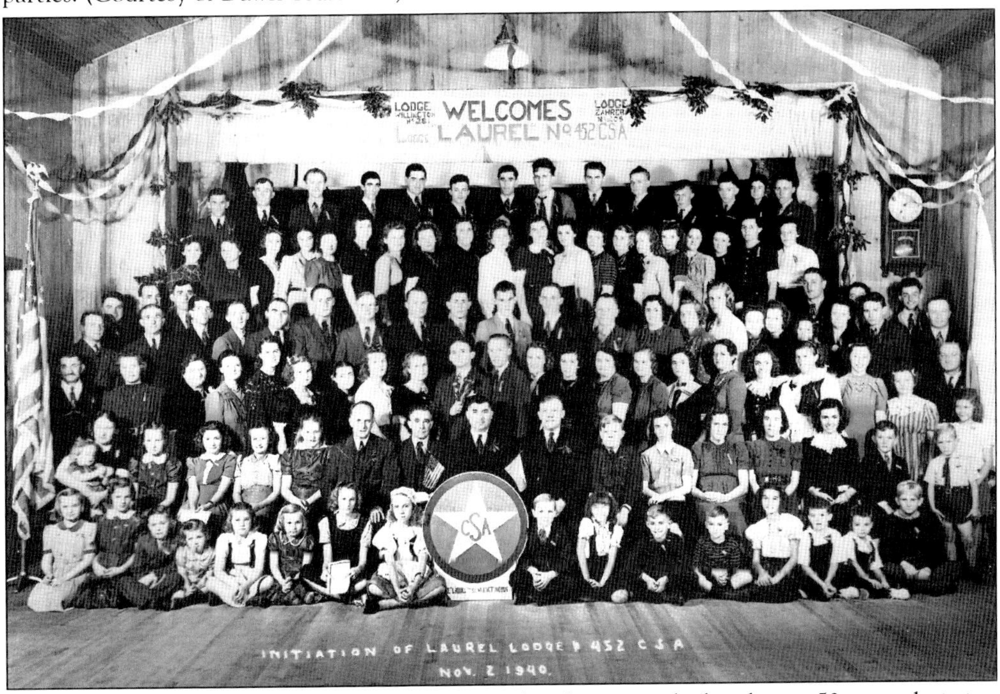

Those attending the Day of Initiation at the Laurel Lodge were asked to donate 50¢ per admission ticket. The more than 126 charter members of the Czechoslovak Society of America were treated to music by the Serenaders of South Willington, who earned $25. Members had to pass a medical examination before initiation and were required to take an oath before being given a password. (Courtesy of Dawn Yedziniak.)

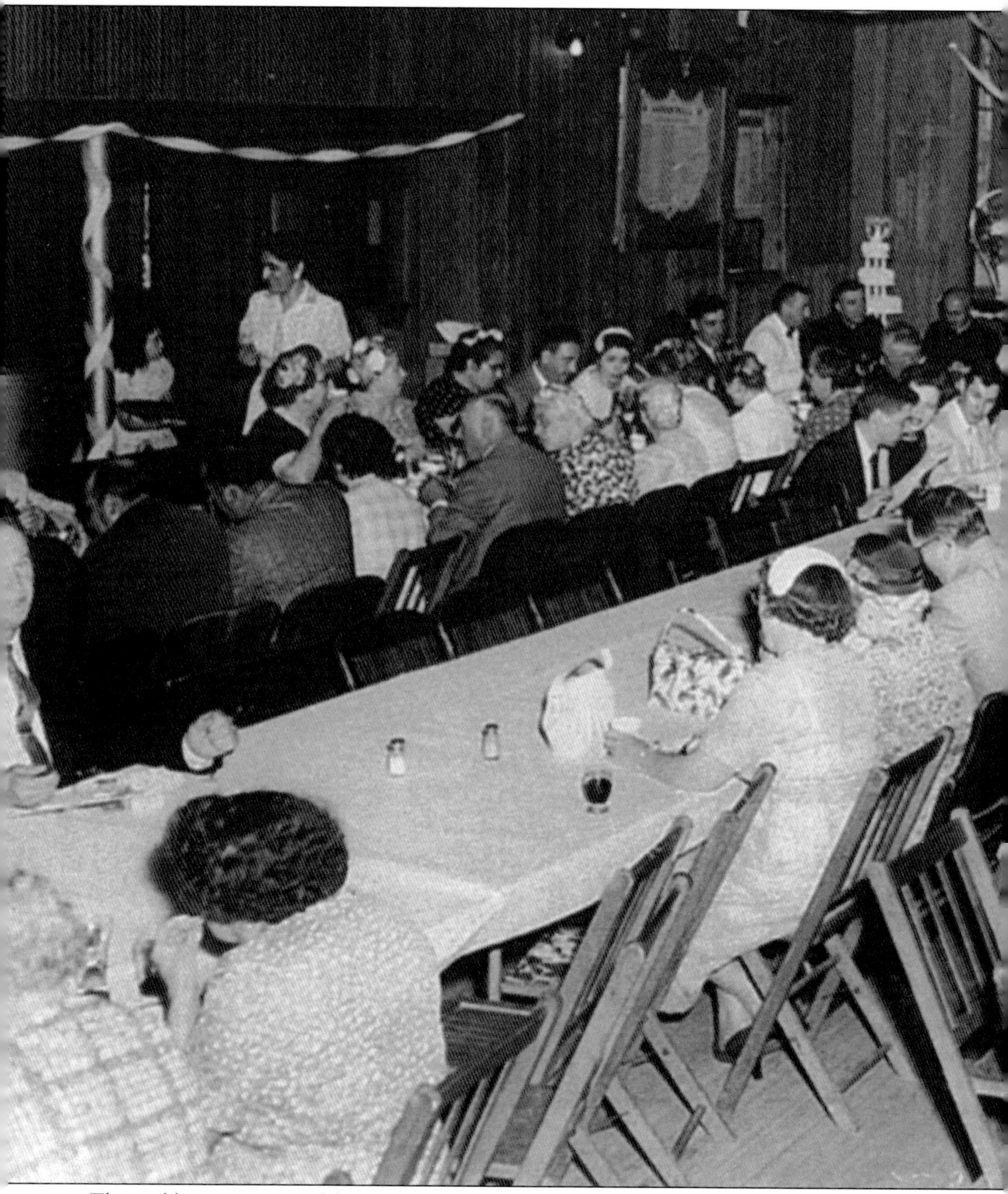

The wedding reception celebrating the marriage of Eliza A. "Betty" Alassi of Mansfield to Joseph Csiki of Willington on June 6, 1959, was held at the Laurel Lodge on Route 32. Members of the Czechoslovak Society of America referred to one another by the familiar title of Brother and Sister. Monthly meetings were conducted formally and in accordance with guidelines provided by the parent organization. Minutes of each meeting were kept, with the secretary fastidiously recording each motion and vote as well as financial data. Members were provided with an annual

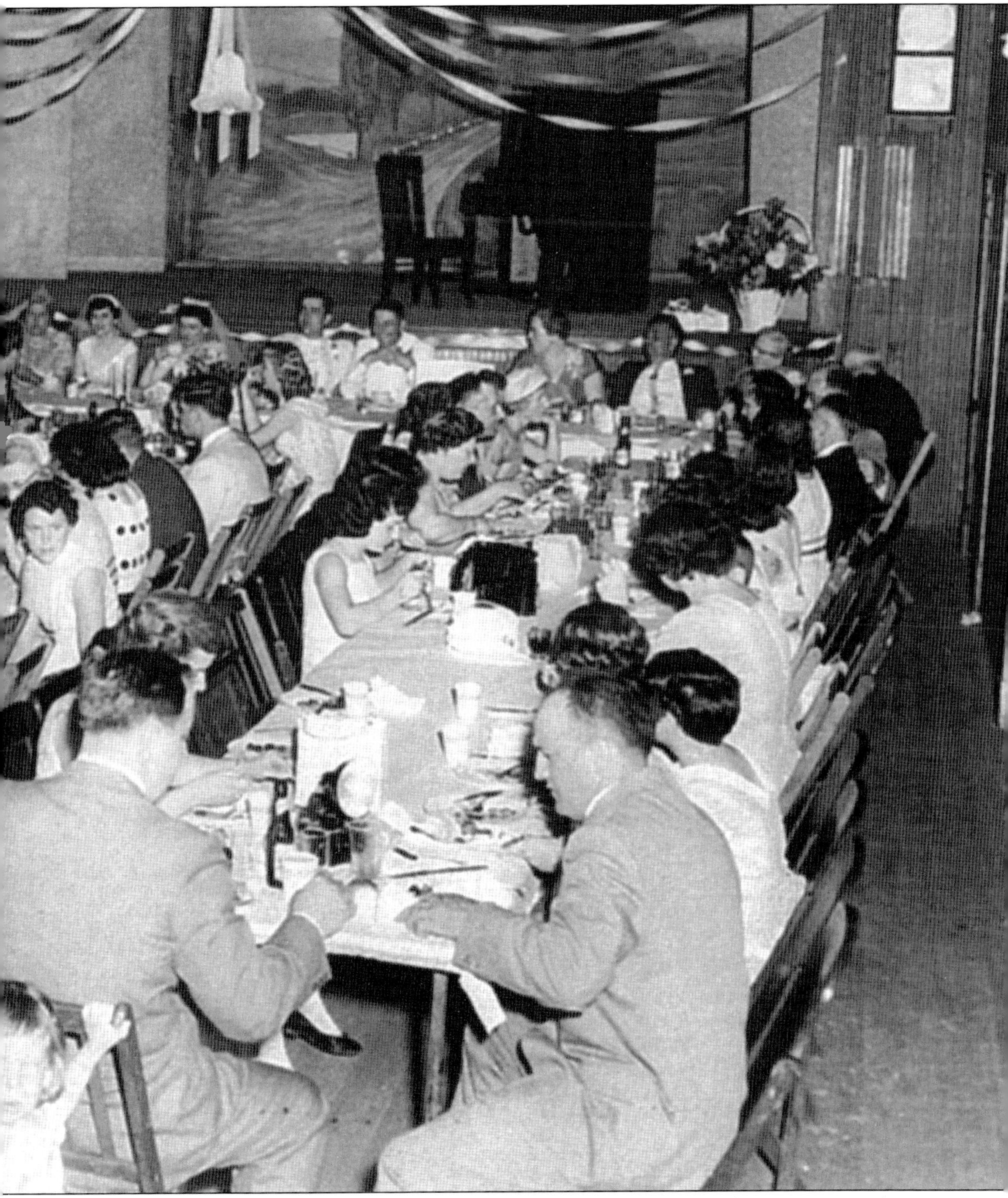

password. Building maintenance expenses eventually exceeded income, and meetings were then held at members' homes instead of at the lodge. Just days before the Csiki wedding, members were making efforts to sell the building. The lodge was rented for a June 13, 1959, wedding and a June 20, 1959, dance recital, as well as for upcoming Christmas and New Year's Eve parties, but members were aware that the eventual outcome would be the sale of the building. (Courtesy of Dawn Yedziniak.)

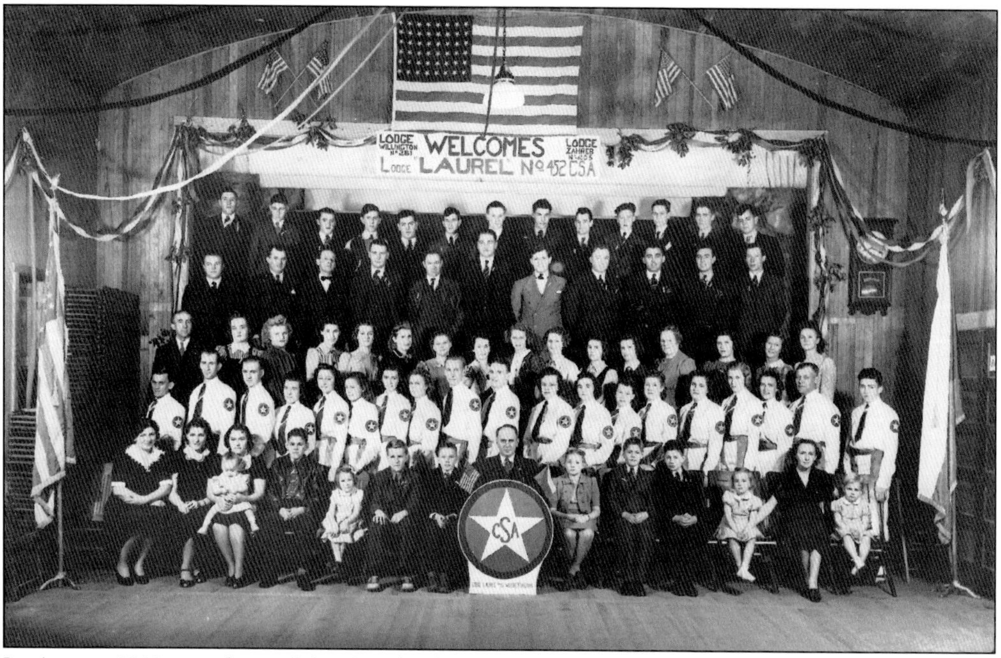

In August 1911, members of the Czechoslovak Society of America built a clubhouse on Kollar Road. In 1940, additional residents formed another chapter, honoring their Czech heritage while embracing their new country, as evidenced by the name Laurel, a tribute to Connecticut's state flower, the mountain laurel. Effective September 1, 1946, the lodges joined together under the name Laurel Lodge and gathered at the lodge on Route 32.

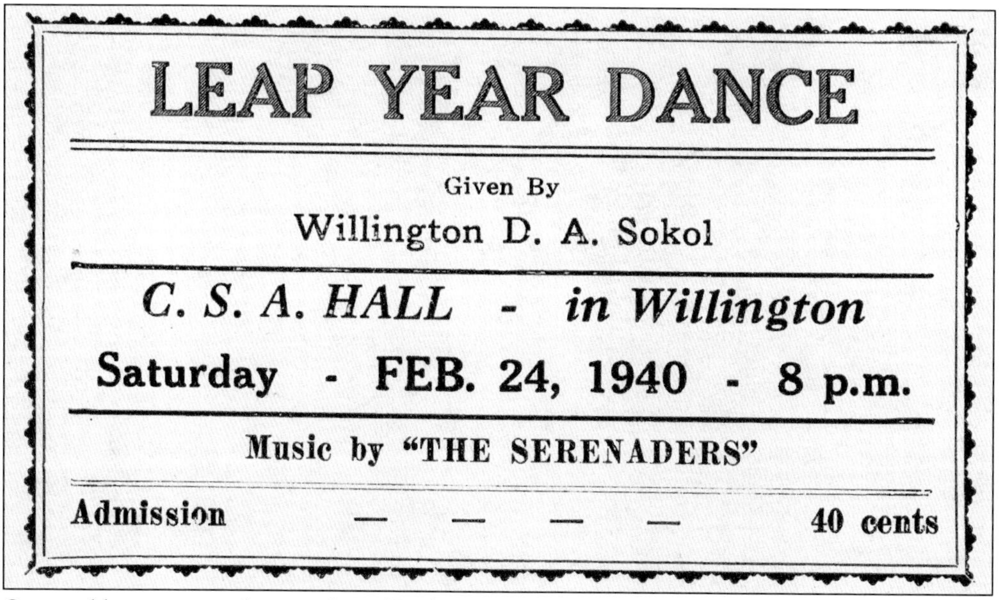

LEAP YEAR DANCE

Given By

Willington D. A. Sokol

C. S. A. HALL - in Willington

Saturday - FEB. 24, 1940 - 8 p.m.

Music by "THE SERENADERS"

Admission — — — — 40 cents

One could expect a good time at Laurel Lodge, as members planned in great detail the refreshments they would serve. The lodge was also known as the bungalow. It is currently a private home that has been lovingly restored by its owners. The wood on the walls and on the barrel ceiling has been thoroughly varnished, and the stage is now the focal point of the home's vast living area. (Courtesy of Dawn Yedziniak.)

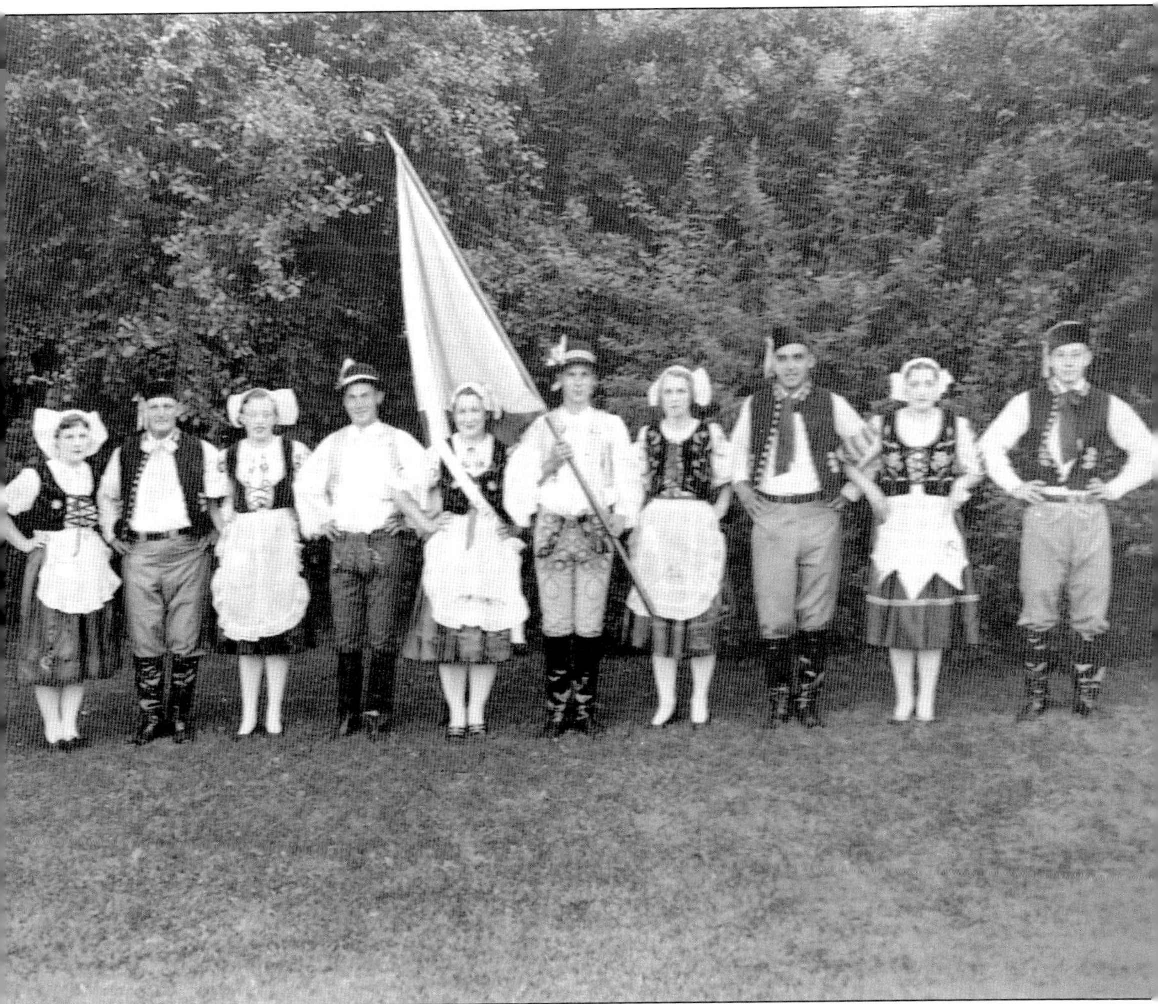

The Beseda is the very formal, regal Czechoslovakian national dance, which originated in the 1860s, when part of what became Czechoslovakia was still known as Bohemia. The male and female dancers have specific roles during the dance and are instructed to focus on their partners, their posture, and the pleasure of the dance. The Beseda tells a story via the movements of the dancers. It can be either a four-part or an eight-part story. The Willington residents seen here in 1933 or 1934 proudly demonstrate their native dance in full costume from the homeland. The dancers are, from left to right, Alice Novotny, Bill Swacha, Elsie Vesely, Louis Zaicek, Bertha Novotny, Emil Pivonka, Geraldine Novotny, Emil Adamec, Helen Swacha, and Frank Placek. Although there have been no performances of the Beseda in Willington in recent years, it is still performed at various events across the United States.

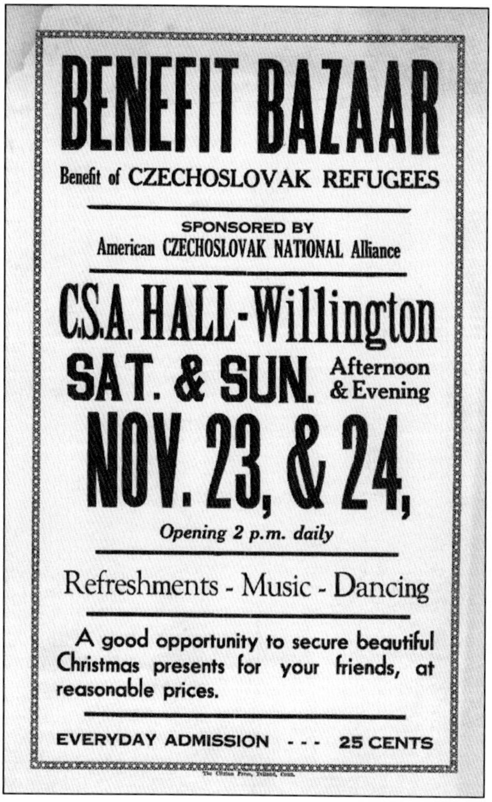

The year in which this particular benefit was held is unknown. However, the Czechoslovak Society of America's Willington lodge actively supported the American Czechoslovak National Alliance throughout its lengthy tenure. From the Willington lodge's formation through the challenges of World War II and the gasoline shortages of the 1970s, the society faced a variety of financial challenges and eventually disbanded in the 1980s.

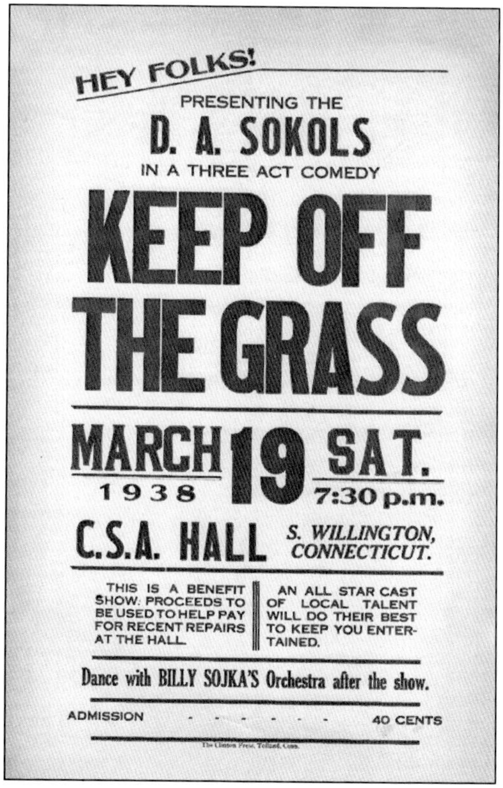

The dedication of the members of the Czechoslovak Society is obvious when one considers the time and energy it must have taken to prepare the lodge for events such as this play, including encouraging members to participate in theatrical performances, finding local orchestras, advertising the event, selling tickets and then collecting them, serving the refreshments, and then cleaning up and preparing the hall for the next event. (Courtesy of Dawn Yedziniak.)

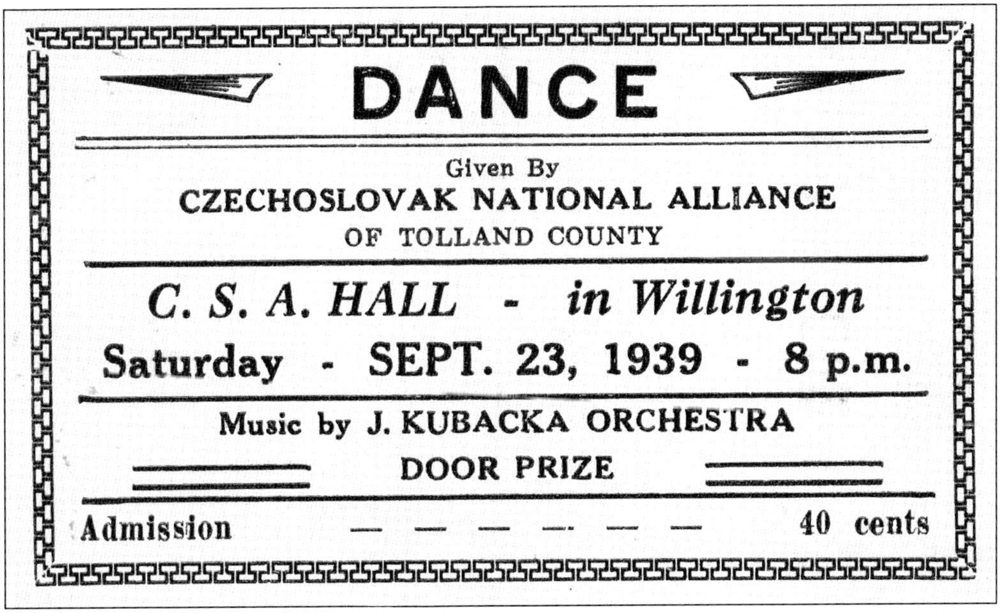

The Czechoslovak Society often held fundraisers in the form of shows, plays, and dances. Some of the proceeds remained with the local lodge; however, at other times, money was sent to the parent organization for the benefit of refugees. In addition, the expenses of insurance, lights, water, heat, and the general maintenance of the lodge were often a source of concern for the members. (Courtesy of Dawn Yedziniak.)

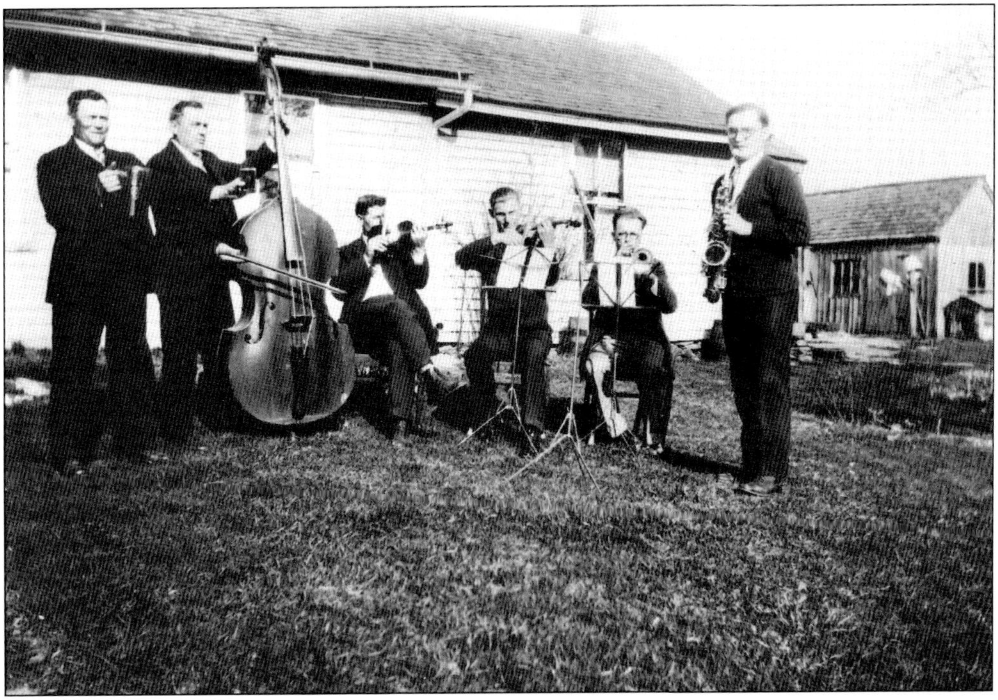

Fiddler John Kubacka (third from left) led the J. Kubacka Orchestra, which was small but so named because of its string instruments. In 1940, the Czechoslovak American Society paid groups such as this one between $25 and $40 for a performance. (Courtesy of Ann M. Kubacka.)

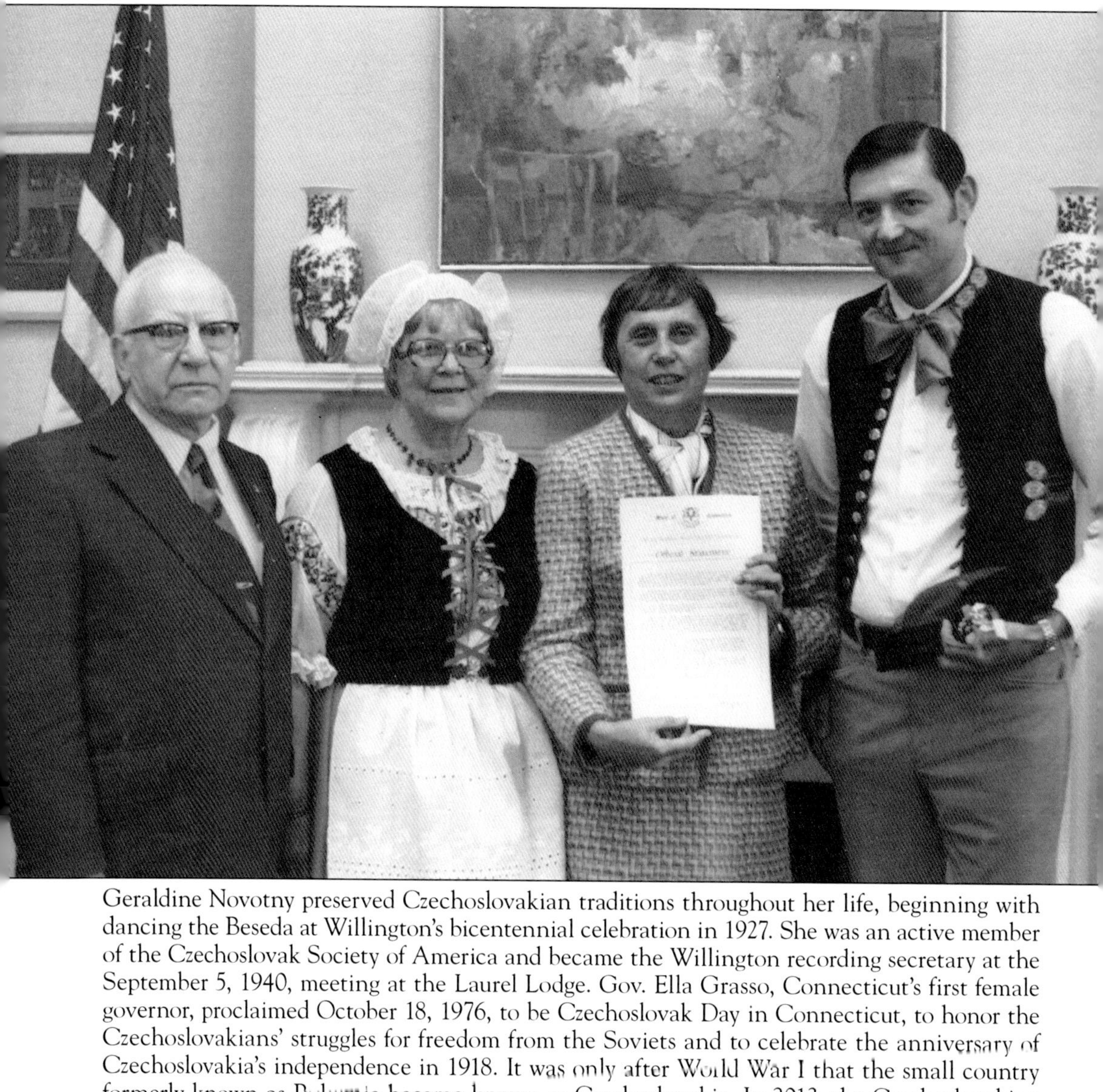

Geraldine Novotny preserved Czechoslovakian traditions throughout her life, beginning with dancing the Beseda at Willington's bicentennial celebration in 1927. She was an active member of the Czechoslovak Society of America and became the Willington recording secretary at the September 5, 1940, meeting at the Laurel Lodge. Gov. Ella Grasso, Connecticut's first female governor, proclaimed October 18, 1976, to be Czechoslovak Day in Connecticut, to honor the Czechoslovakians' struggles for freedom from the Soviets and to celebrate the anniversary of Czechoslovakia's independence in 1918. It was only after World War I that the small country formerly known as Bohemia became known as Czechoslovakia. In 2013, the Czechoslovakian clothing Novotny cherished was donated to the Willington Historical Society. The celebrants in this 1976 photograph are, from left to right, Walter Adams, president of the Connecticut Council for Senior Citizens; Geraldine Novotny; Gov. Ella Grasso; and John Douglas of Mansfield.

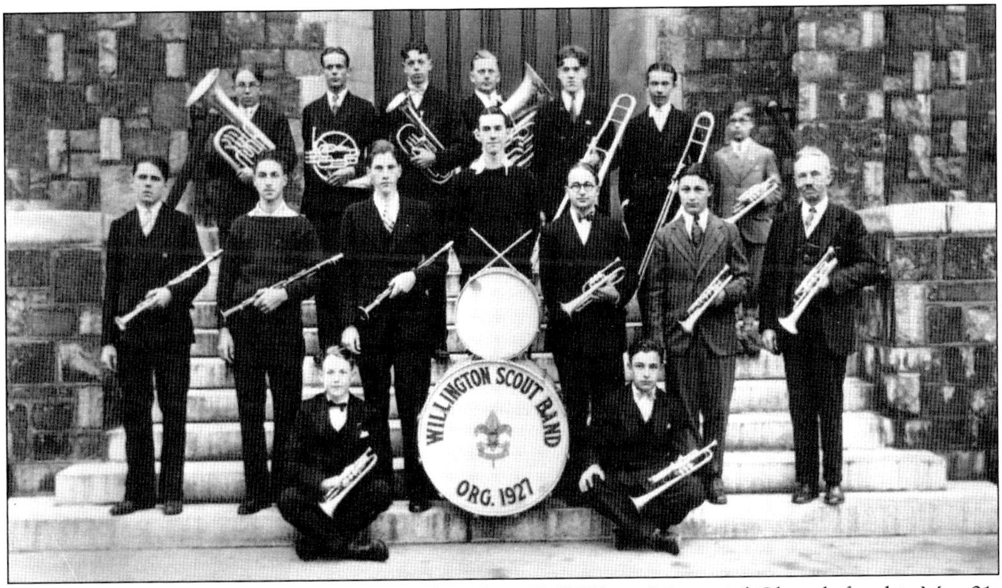

The Willington Scout Band gathered at the Clara Hall Elliott Memorial Church for this May 21, 1929, photograph. The musicians are, from left to right, (first row) Raymond Bruce and Gordon Hanks; (second row) Harry Pospisil, Edward Tomasko, Allen Brownlee, Jack Macleran, Charles Todd, Silvio DeCicco, and director Bert Lyman; (third row) Stanley Todd, Raymond Kormer, Herman Usher, Rev. Edwin Sundt, George Matthews, Frank Kalas, and ? Sundt.

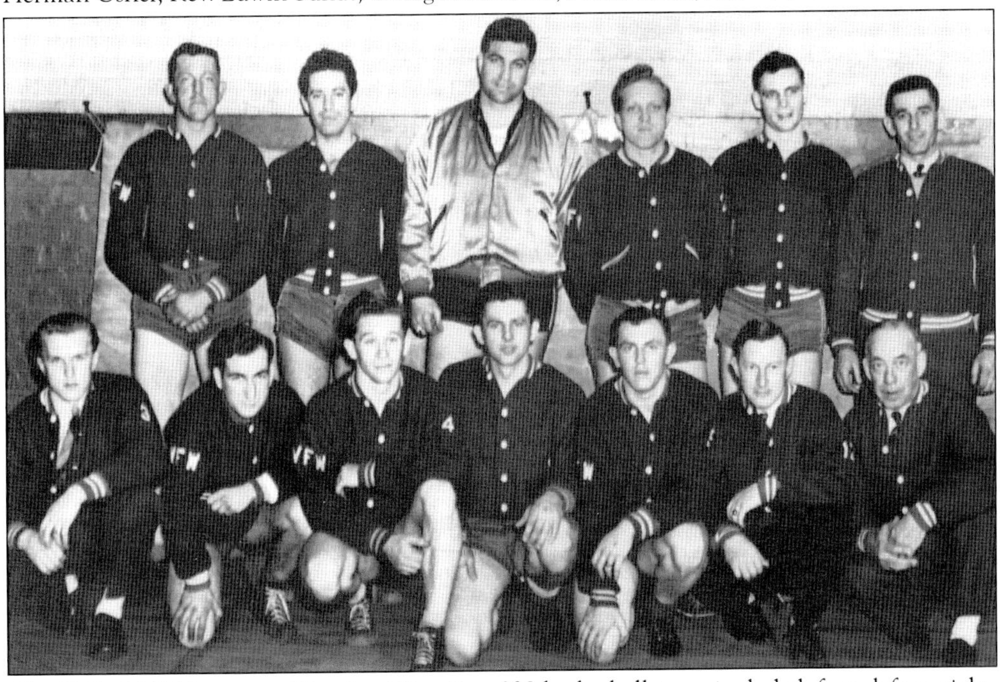

The 1948–1949 Veterans of Foreign Wars Post 938 basketball team included, from left to right, (first row) scorekeeper Jerry Novotny, Philip Zerler, Daniel Stawicki, Frank Navratil, Arnold Keegan, assistant manager William Potter, and post commander Walter Colburn; (second row) Earl Woodworth, Frank Prohaska, John Pringle, Robert Rice, Richard Usher, and manager Joe Rada.

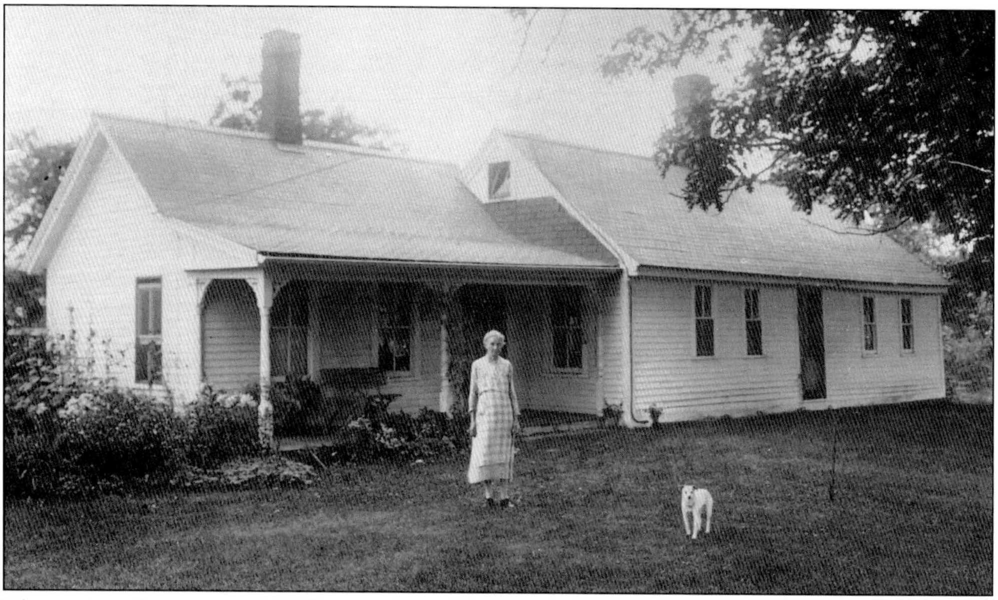

The nationally renowned Willington Pizza House is located in the former home of George and Alice Sterry, also spelled Steery and Stary. The house is now the restaurant's dining room. The surrounding property was George's farm. This undated photograph of Alice and her dog Dolly graces the cover of the Willington Pizza House menu. Alice was 100 years old when she died in July 1970. (Courtesy of Jeff Kelly.)

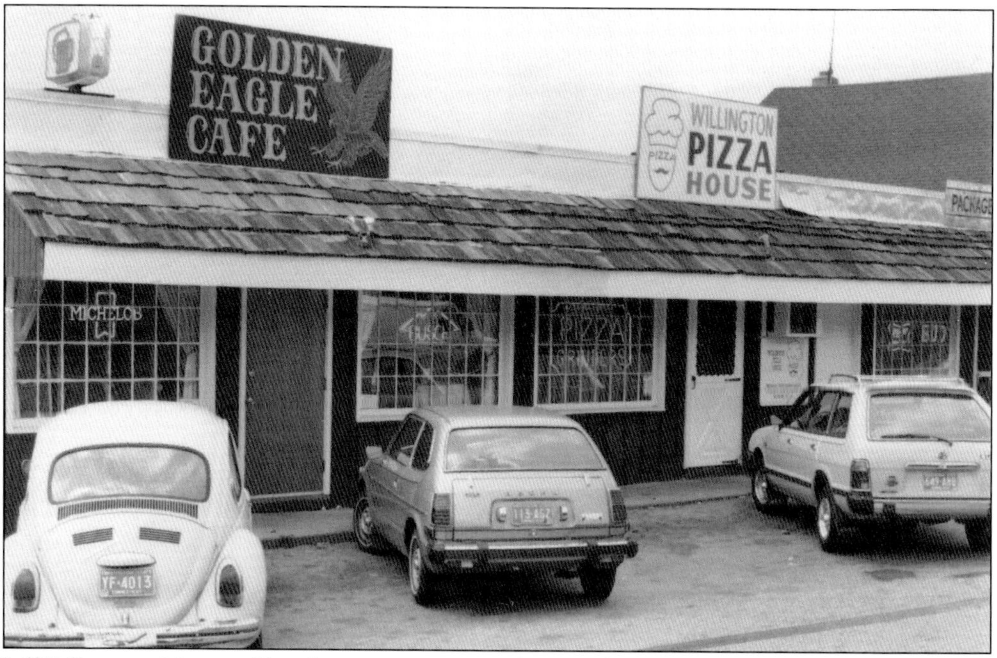

Jeff Kelly was a 24-year-old with no experience in the pizza business when he opened the original Willington Pizza House in 1978. Today's award-winning pizza is famous locally and has been featured on national television. Unlike the original four-table location seen here, Willington Pizza House now has two locations, both of which offer large eating areas, which are necessary at the popular destination. (Courtesy of Jeff Kelly.)

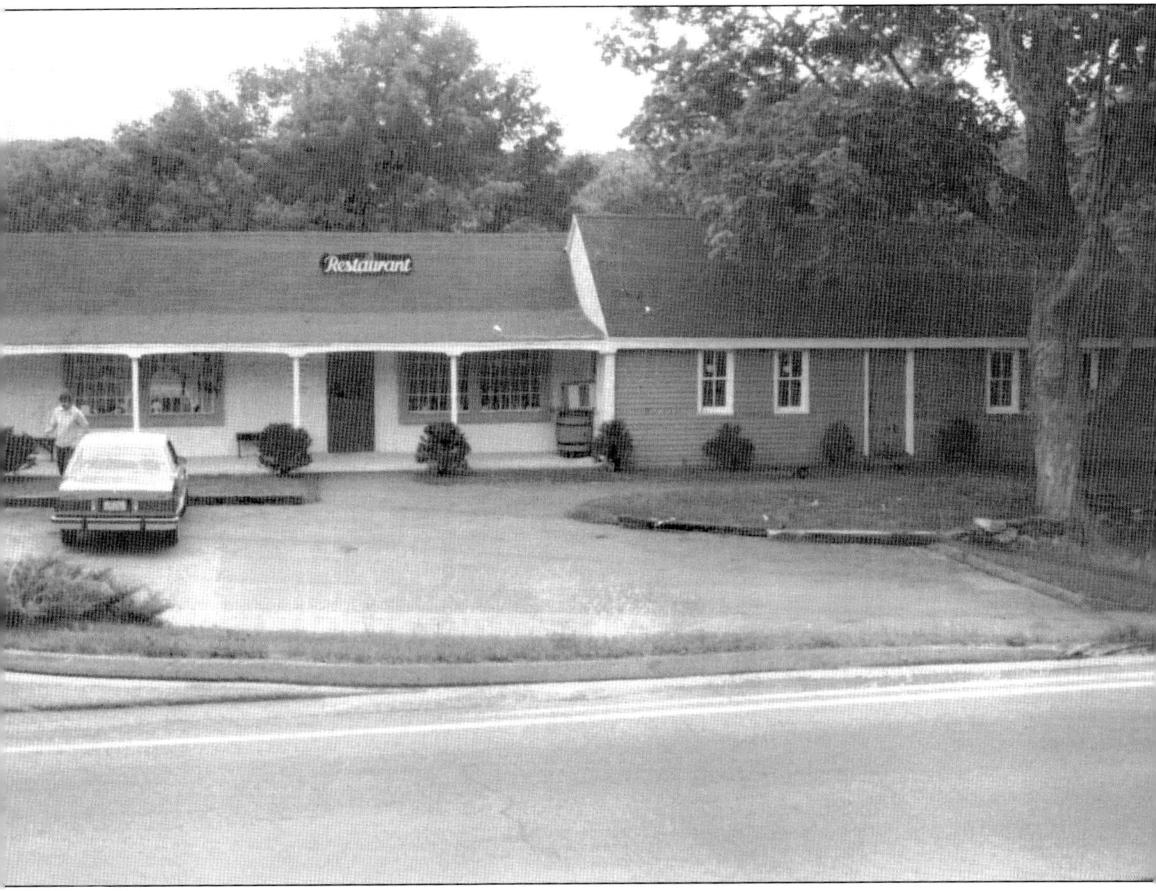

This photograph, taken in 1980 or 1981, shows the first addition (left) to the original Sterry home, which was necessary due to the popularity of the Willington Pizza House. The restaurant has a reputation for serving quality food at reasonable prices and is popular with Willington residents and students from the nearby University of Connecticut. There have been other additions through the years, both to the building itself and to the parking area. The decor in this location and in the newer location in West Willington's Phelps Plaza consists mainly of automobile racing and college sports memorabilia. The original restaurant currently has an outdoor dining area directly in front of the original house, which is shielded from Route 32 by shrubbery. The Willington economy, once boosted during difficult times by the thread industry, has been boosted during more recent difficult times by pizza. (Courtesy of Jeff Kelly.)

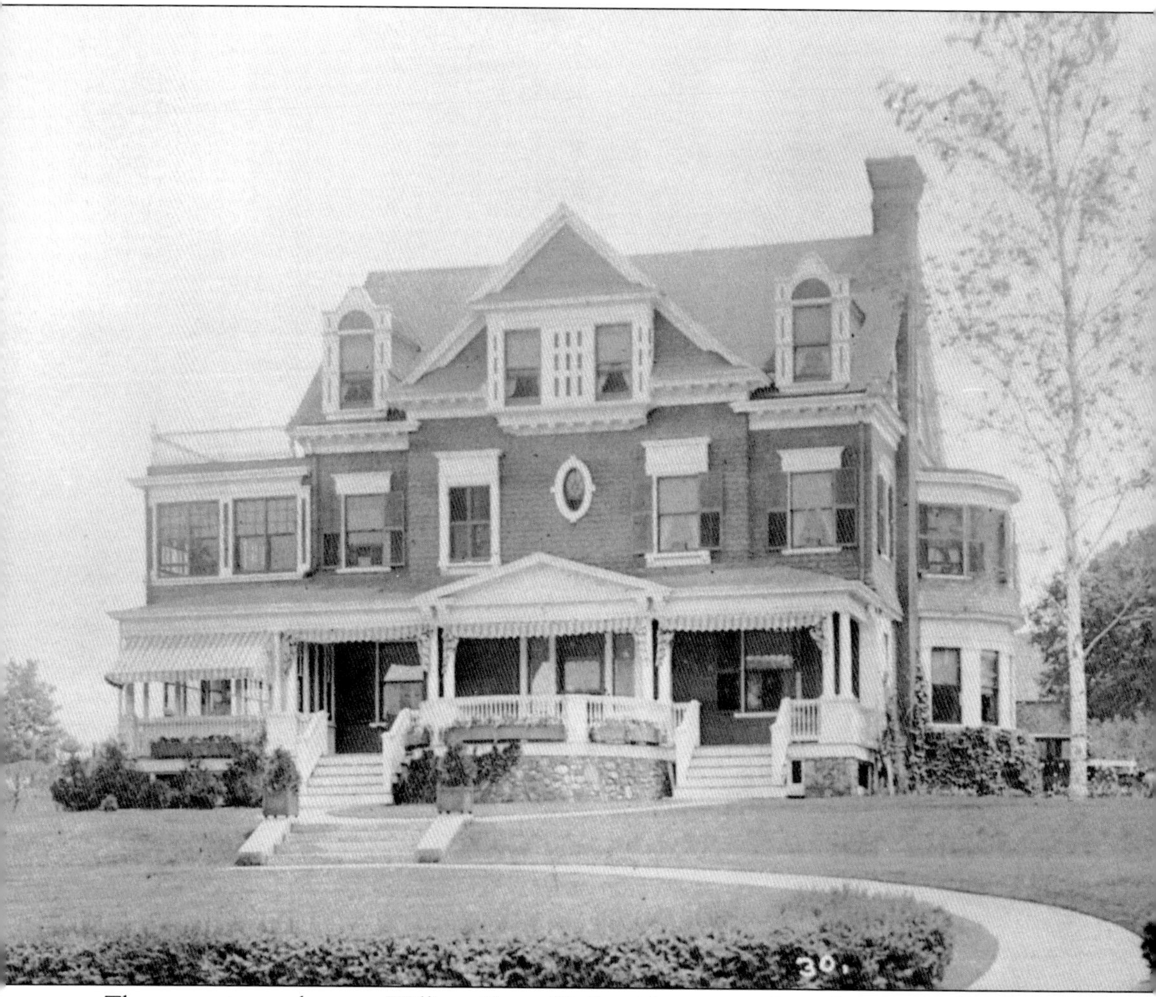

The expansive and ornate William Henry Hall residence must have dominated the rural road that is now Route 32, yet its walkway from the road to the front door is inviting. Hall was born on May 31, 1867, to parents who were already operating the Gardiner Hall Jr. Thread Company. His house was built in 1895, evidencing his success as a young businessman and politician. William Henry was instrumental in encouraging many Czechoslovakian immigrants to settle in Willington, where they could find work in his father's thread mill or in button factories. He, however, was not as interested in the manufacturing industry as he was in politics. His political career included Willington offices such as town treasurer, registrar of voters, and school committee member. He was also elected to the Connecticut House of Representatives nine times and to the Connecticut Senate three times. He was eventually elected by the majority party in the state senate to serve as senate president pro tempore.

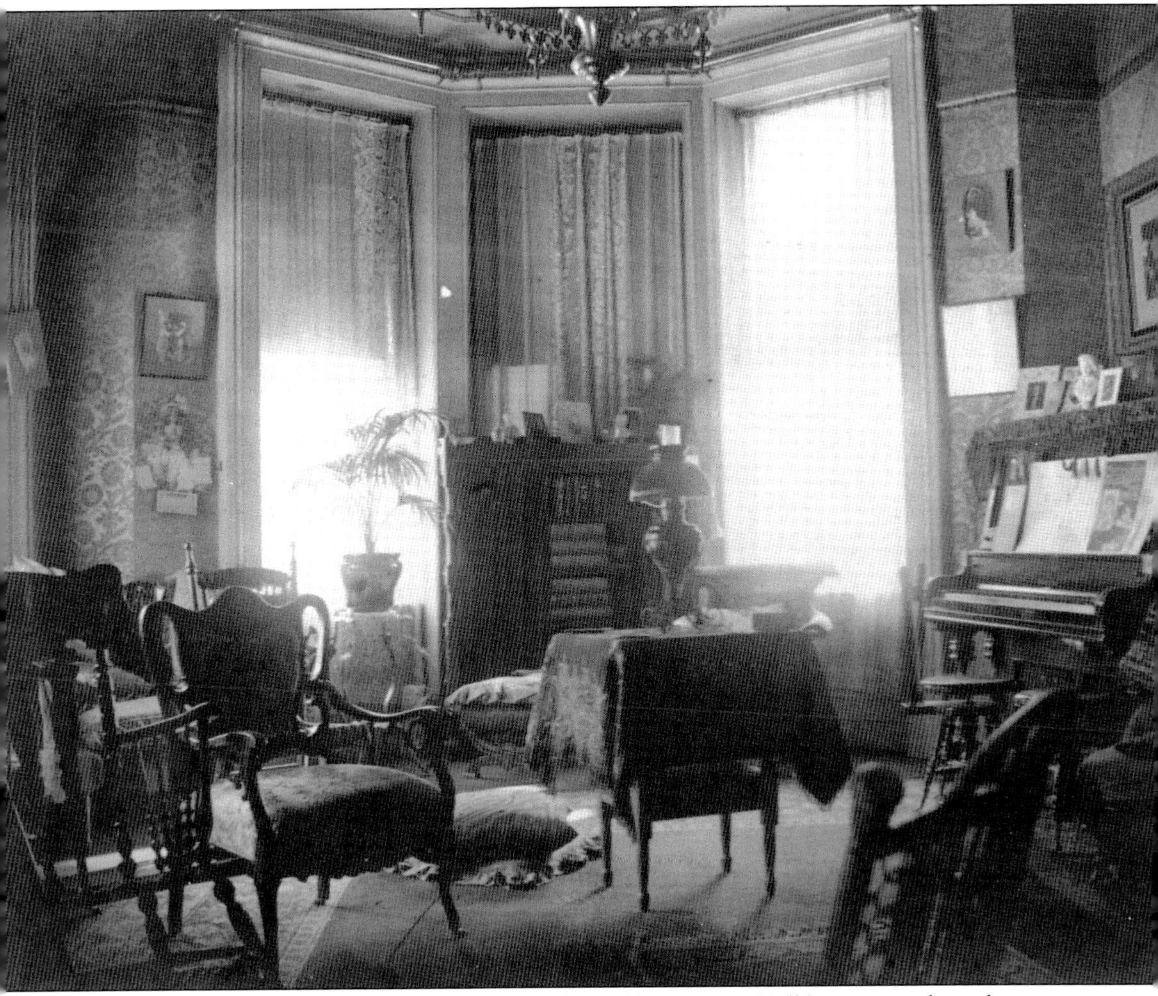

This undated photograph of an interior room at the William Henry Hall home provides a glimpse into the lifestyle of a family whose income afforded them what would be considered unaffordable luxuries by many other residents and especially by the majority of the employees of the Hall family business. The ornate furnishings in what appears to be a music room are indicative of an era of formality, as opposed to the comfortable furnishings one finds today. The lamp on the table in the center appears to be an oil lamp, since there is no electrical cord. The Hall family sold the home in 1957, after which it was converted into a convalescent home. In 1965, an additional 14 rooms were added to the already large home. The home still stands today on River Road; it is currently an adult residential care facility named in honor of Alan Lyon, who owned the home in the 1990s.

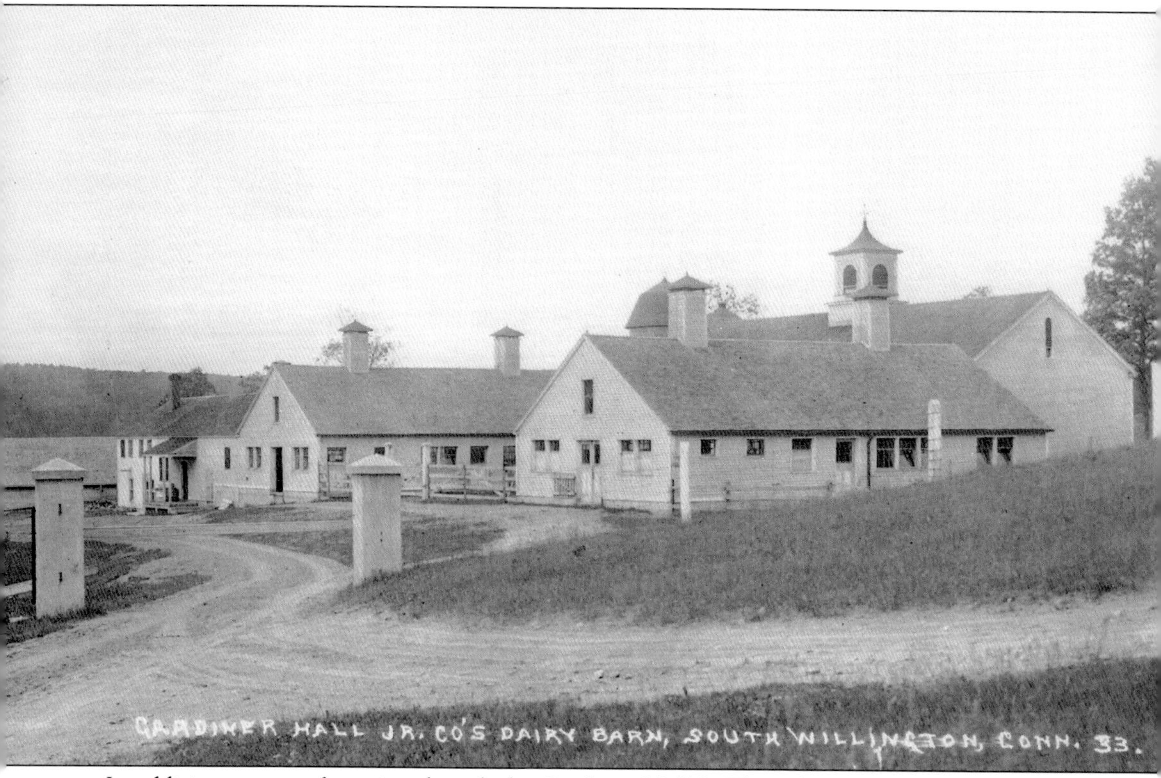

In addition to manufacturing thread, the Gardiner Hall Jr. Thread Company was engaged in a variety of other ventures, including the dairy farm seen in this photographic postcard, which was located within sight of Gardiner Hall Jr.'s home. The cupolas and the design of the buildings reveal the effort that went into creating a farm that blended naturally into its surroundings and was pleasing to the eye. Gardiner Hall Jr.'s son William Henry Hall was as interested in agriculture as his father. William Henry became a trustee of the nearby Connecticut Agricultural College in Storrs, which is now the University of Connecticut. He also received local awards for his Holstein cows. In 1940, the college named a building in William Henry's honor to recognize his efforts as a member of Connecticut's legislature to appropriate funds to the college. (Courtesy of James Buell.)

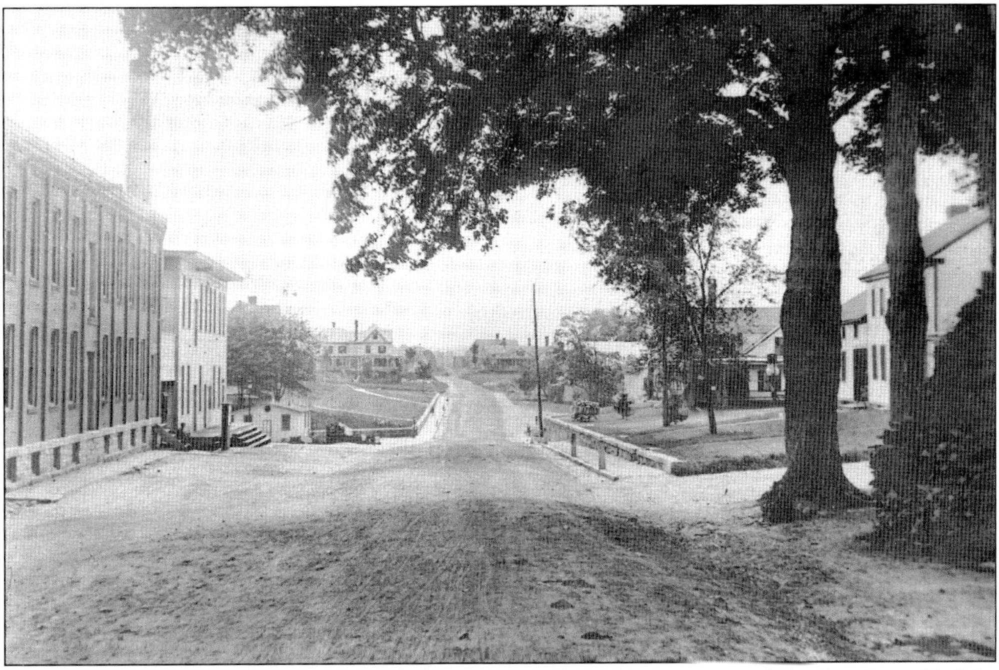

South Willington was known as Hallville in the early 1900s because of the Gardiner Hall Jr. Thread Company and the company housing provided for its employees. This undated photograph shows the mill (left foreground), on what is now Route 32 looking south toward Mansfield. The William Henry Hall home, now called Lyon Manor, is in the left background.

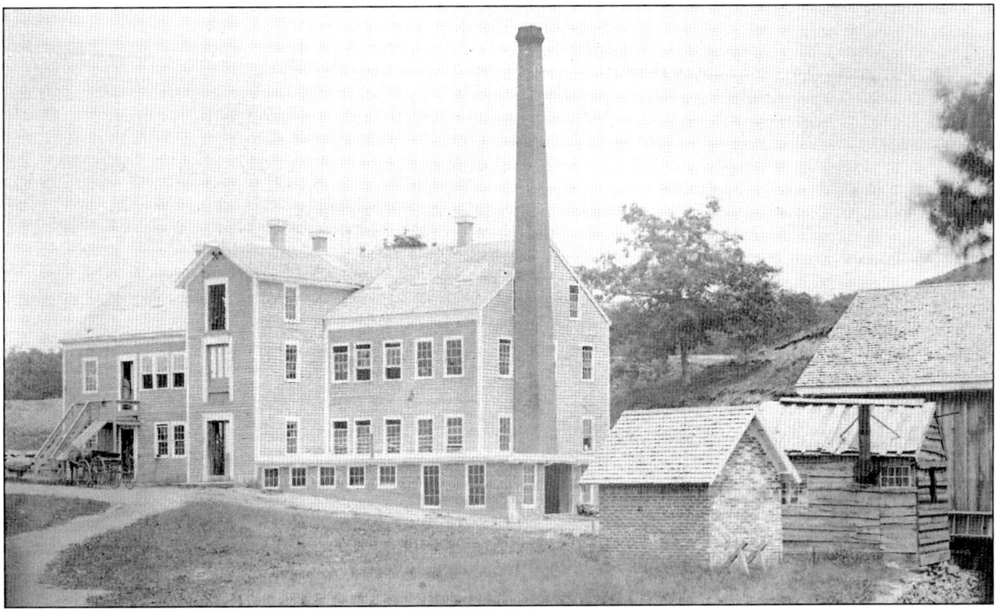

Shortly before the Civil War, Gardiner Hall Jr. founded the Gardiner Hall Jr. Thread Company. Although the Civil War disrupted his manufacturing business, Hall persevered and created what became a thriving manufacturing business. This photograph from around 1870 shows the original building, on what is now Route 32. In 1910, there were 119 people employed at the thread factory.

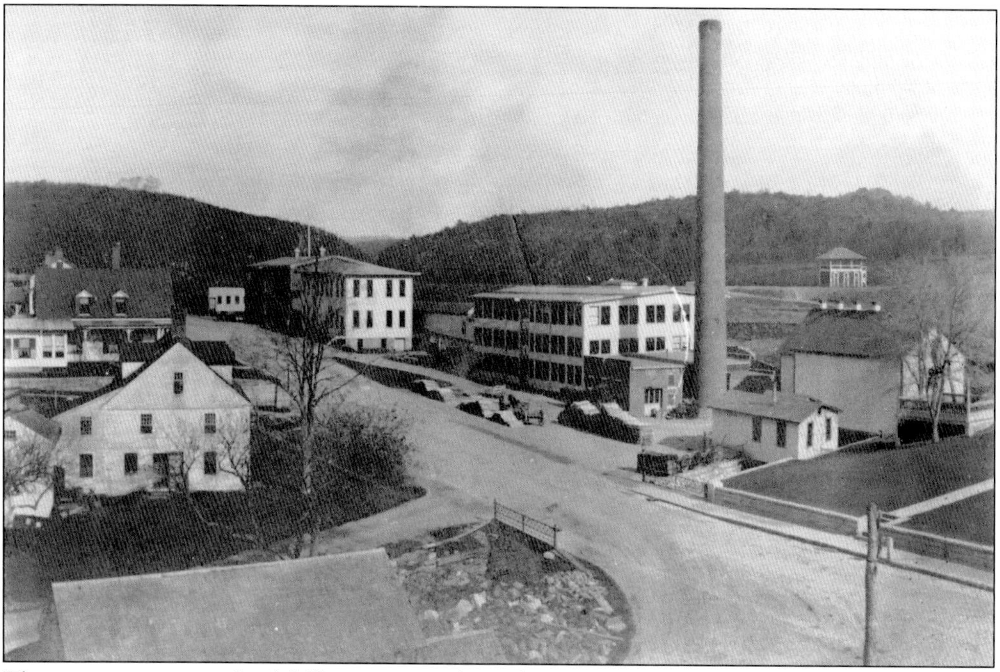

These picture postcards of different areas of South Willington were published by the Gardiner Hall Jr. Thread Company but printed in Germany. On October 3, 1917, a woman named Elsie sent a postcard from South Willington to Lillia Fenton in West Willington. The postcard stamp cost 1¢, and neither the recipient's street name nor a house number were necessary. The sender requested that Fenton remember the sender to "Mr. and Mrs. B," which is likely a reference to the Burdicks, with whom Fenton lived for many years. Today, one can drive from South Willington to West Willington in moments, and there are no longer separate post offices for the various sections of Willington. (Both courtesy of Stuart Cobb.)

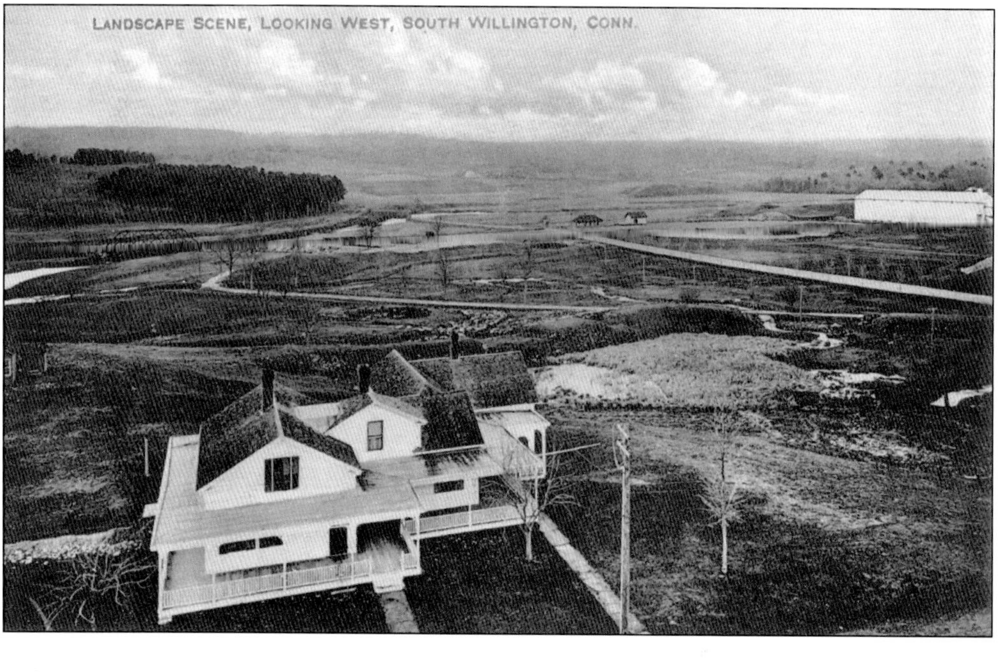

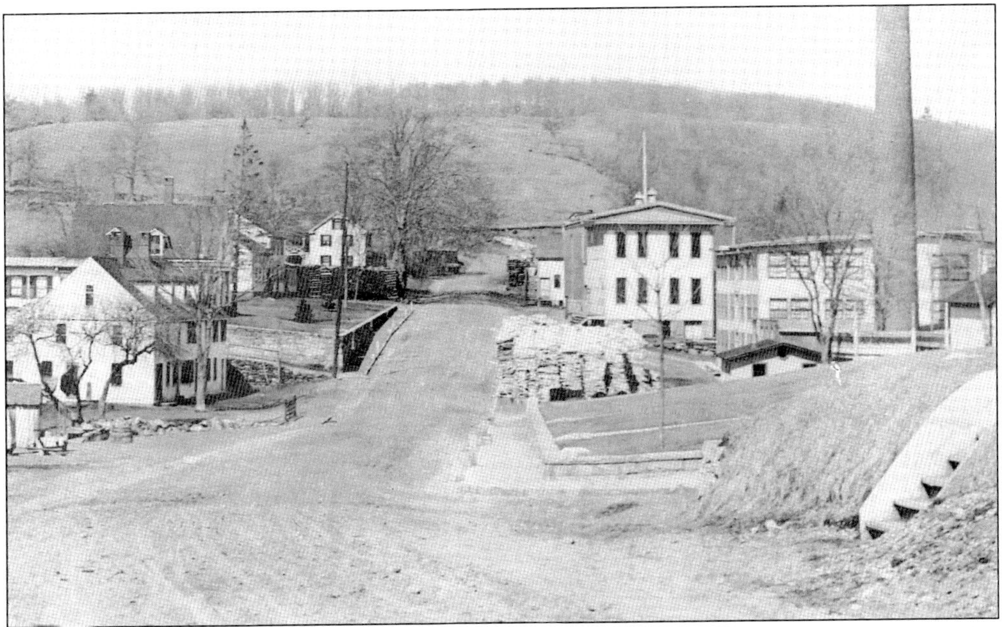

This postcard looks north at what is now Route 32 and shows the Hall mill on the right. On the back, Anna Weigold wrote, "Hoping this will find you better," to her friend Charles Latham while he was at the Backus Hospital, approximately 25 miles away in Norwich. It is not known whether the note, postmarked October 27, 1906, reached Latham before his death on October 31. (Courtesy of Claudia D'Agata.)

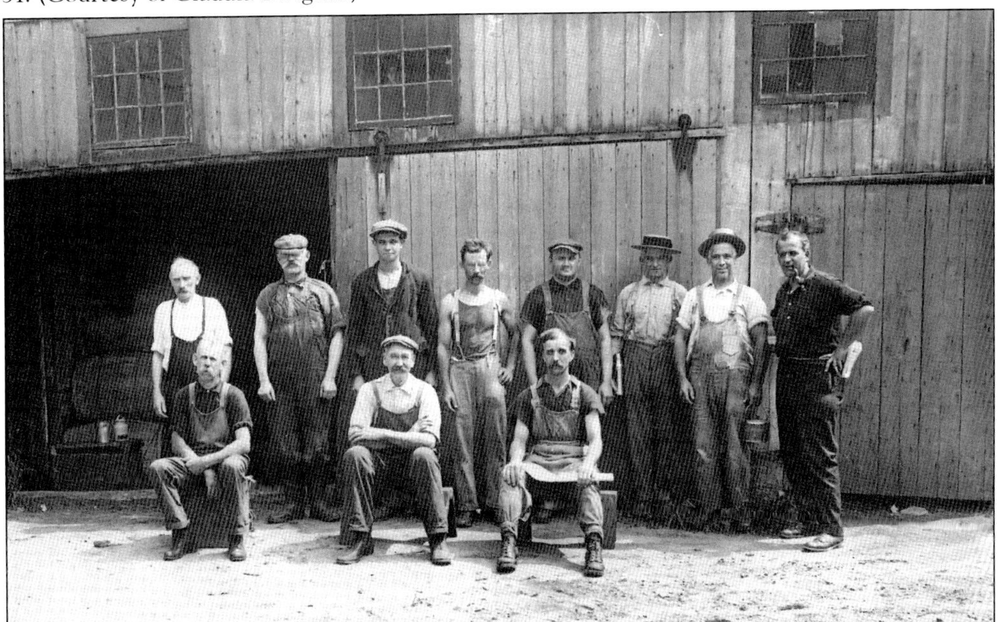

The employees of the bleaching and dyeing department at the Gardiner Hall Jr. Thread Company are seen in this 1916 or 1917 postcard. They are, from left to right, (first row) Carl Curley, Arthur Devereaux Sr., and Frank Novak; (second row) Oldman Klar, John Brownlee, Henry Farra, Joseph DeCicco, Gus Klar, John Edwards, Fred Colburn, and Albert Spicer. The bleach and dye house was built in the early 1900s.

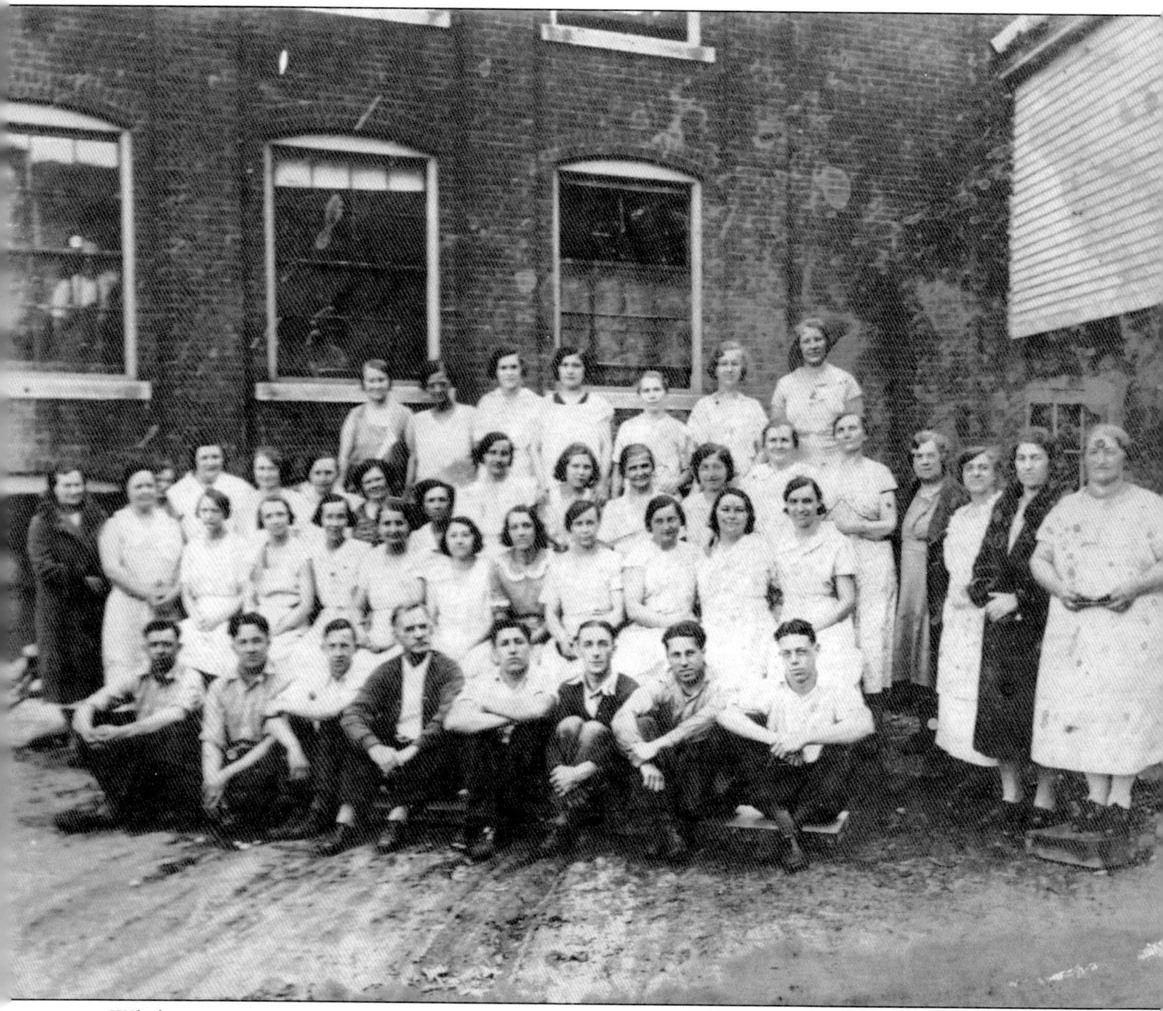

While numerous Americans suffered through the rampant unemployment of the Great Depression, the Gardiner Hall Jr. Thread Company provided employment for many Willington residents. The winding room alone provided employment for the 42 people in this 1930 photograph. They are, from left to right, (first row) Morris Meacham, Steve Luchon, William Potter, John Neil, William Navratil, John Zemek, Edgar Shubler, and Herman Usher; (second row) Annie Knapp Tomasek, Annie Holub, Ruth Masker Coppola, Alice Luchart, Agnes Borovicka Benson, Helen Pardus Church, Jeannette LaBonte Potter, Blanche Vesely Tedford, Lillian Pokorny, Rose Pardus, Annie Farra Haskell, and Emily Vesely Zemek; (third row) Emma Nedwied, Vilma Zydana, unidentified, Louise Wochomurka, Viola Moriarity, Mary Kollar McSavage, Dorothy Tormey, Bertha Hroda, Bertha Pardus Vonasek, Bertha Novotny, and Rose Pospisil; (third row, standing right) Clara Joslin, Lucy Lloyd, ? Crispino, and Angelina DeCicco; (fourth row) Helen Marek Olson, Julia Tomasek, Margie Royce Usher, Mary Kotrba, Louise Vesely, Mildred Hatak Morrison, and Julia Hammer.

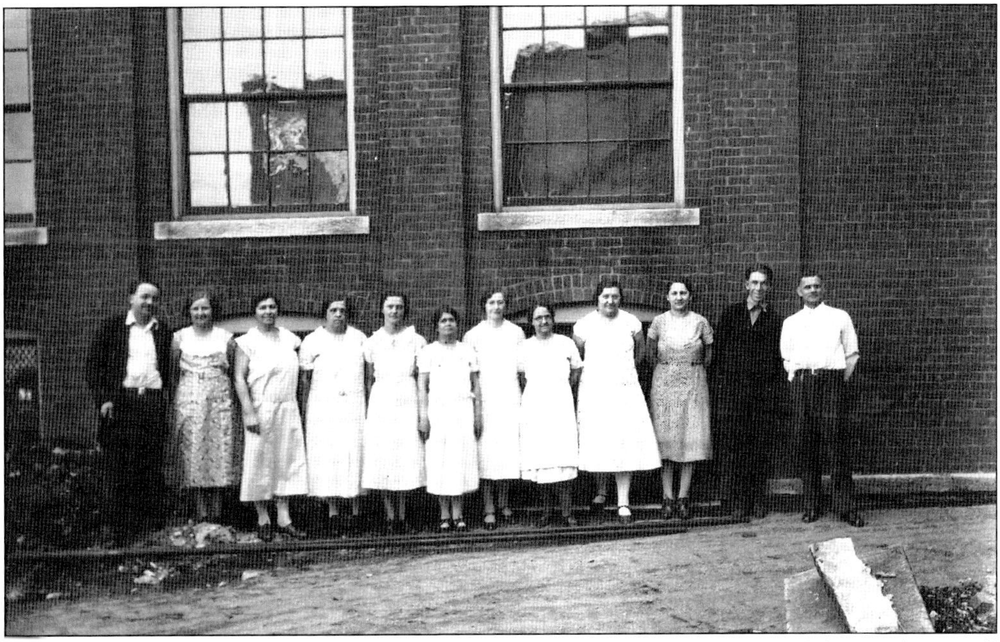

Pictured in this April 4, 1934, photograph of employees of the spooling room of the Gardiner Hall Jr. Thread Company are, from left to right, unidentified, Mabel LaBonte, Gussie Tomasko, Rose LaBonte, Marie Zemek, Frances Safranek, Margaret MacFarlane, Ethel Todd, Carrie Pokorsky, Rose Royce, Merwyn Royce, and Merritt Usher. Many employees of the company were from the same families.

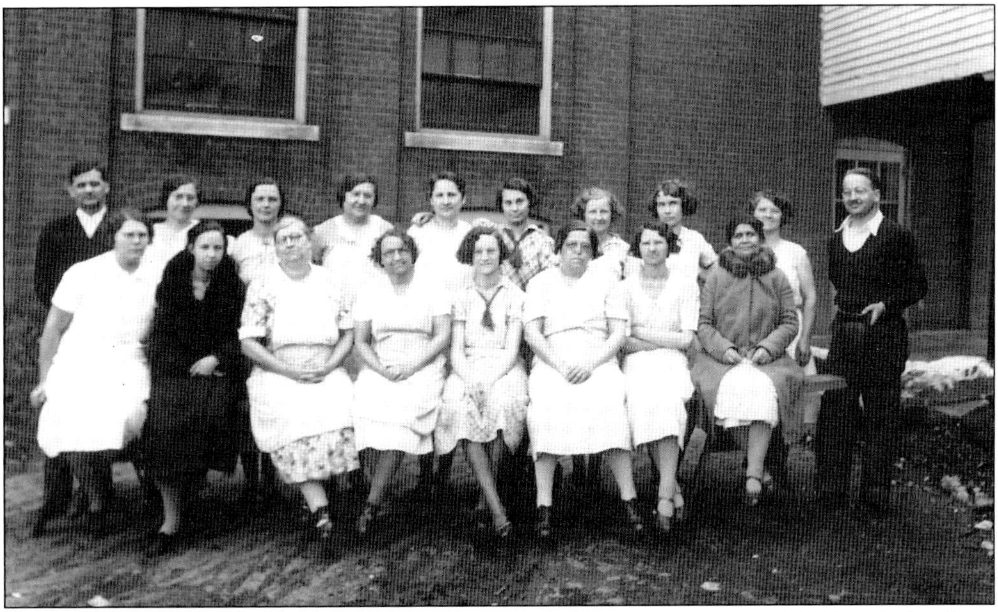

This group of Gardiner Hall Jr. Thread Company employees posing around 1930 includes, from left to right, (first row) Anna Wondrashek, unidentified, Mattie Woodworth, Ethel Todd, Helen Potter, Rose LaBonte, ? Luchon, and ? Safranek; (second row) Merritt Usher, Margaret MacFarlane, ? Zemek, Carrie Nedweid, Rose Royce, unidentified, Mabel Potter, unidentified, Alice Safranek, and Charles Todd.

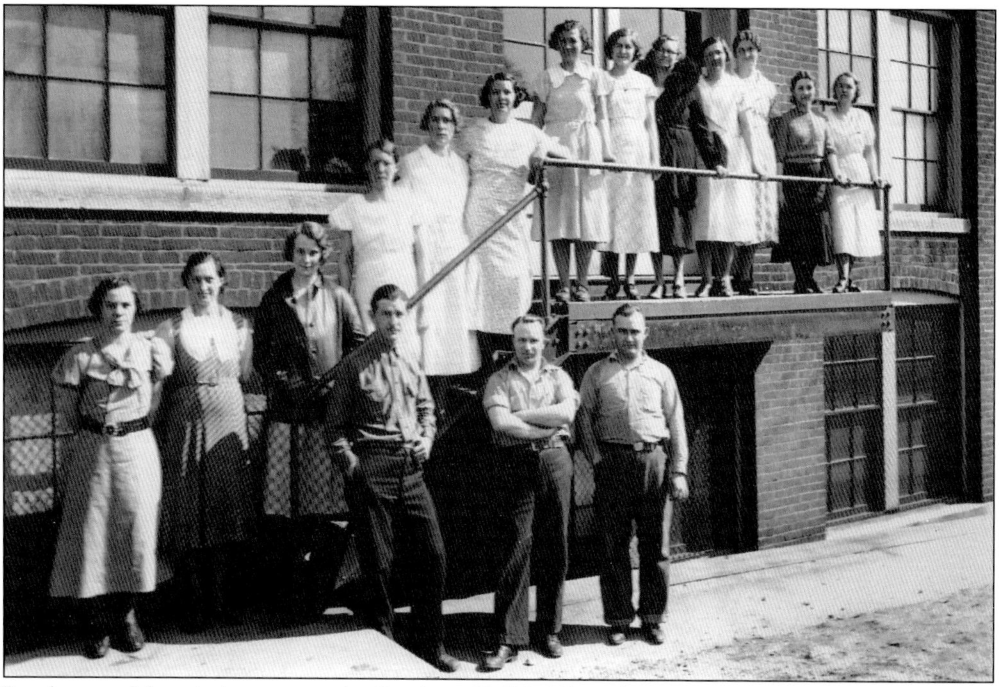

Employees of the winder room at the Gardiner Hall Jr. Thread Company posed for this photograph on April 4, 1934. They are, from left to right, (first row) Charles Farra, Ted Pokorny, and George Toberman; (second row) Helen ?, Josephine Zemek, unidentified, Marion Pardus, Emily Toberman, Teresa Zemek, unidentified, Esther ?, Rose Radla, Marie ?, Antoinette DiCicco, and Amelia ?.

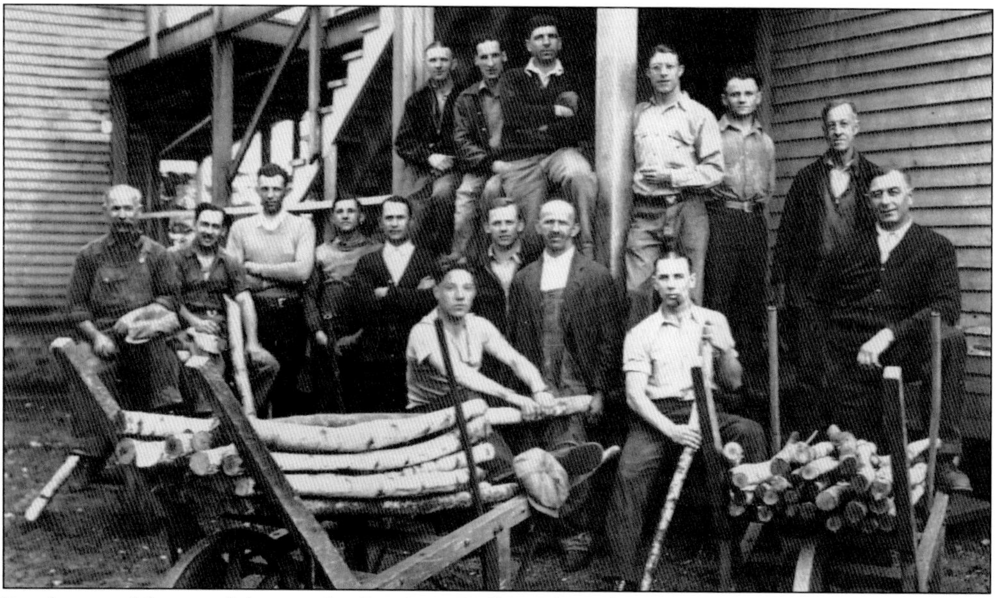

Employees of the spool shop at the Gardiner Hall Jr. Thread Company posed for this photograph in 1933 or 1934. They are, from left to right, (first row) Domilick ?, Sam ?, Louis Vesely, Marty Navratil, Jim Coppola, unidentified, Anton Hatak, Joe Ursin, and unidentified; (second row) Stanley Zemek, Fred Casardi, Carmelo Zanghi, unidentified, Paul Jackapic, unidentified, and Albert Ching.

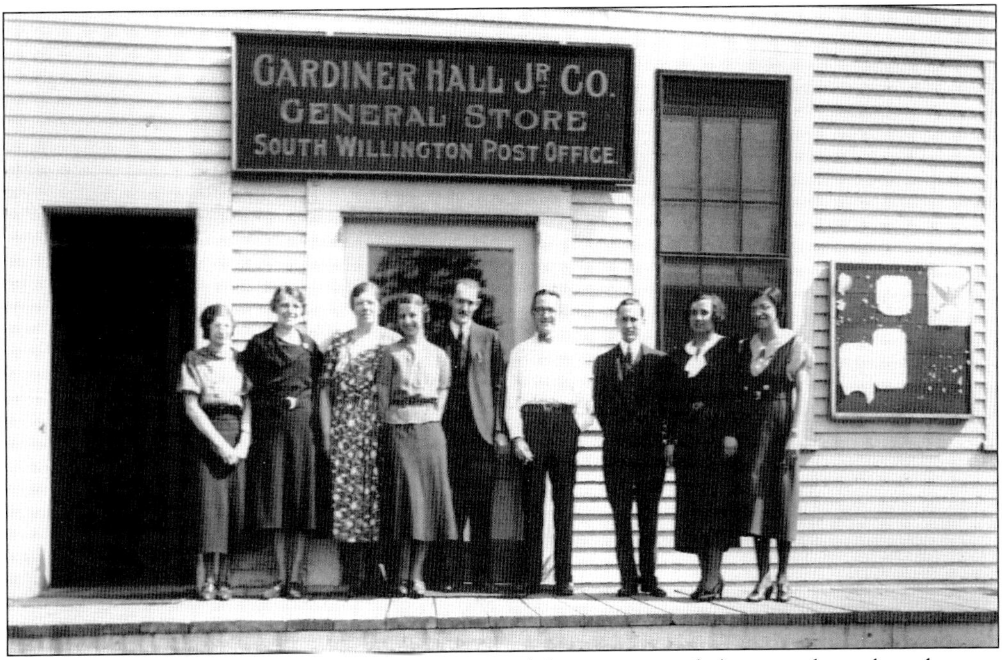

The Gardiner Hall Jr. Thread Company arranged for a variety of photographs to be taken on April 4, 1934. The employees posing in front of the company store here are, from left to right, (first row) Barbara ?, Helen Nedham, Ruth Colburn, Elsie ?, Louis Service, Jack Norwood, J.G. Service, Doris ?, and Betty Voboril. The South Willington post office no longer exists.

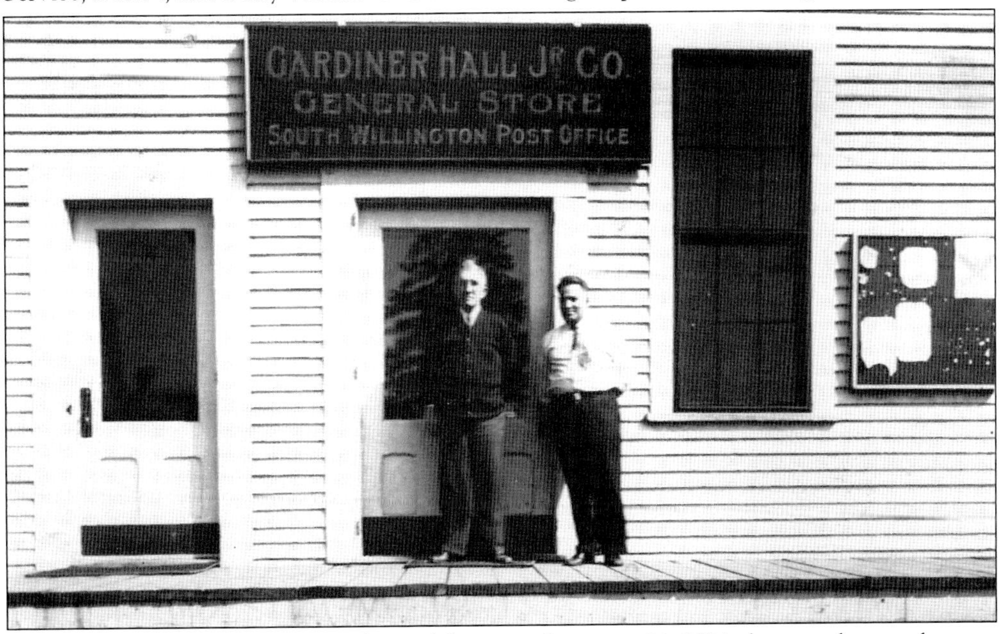

The names of the men standing in front of the general store in this 1934 photograph are unknown. The South Willington post office was established on May 13, 1889. James Service Jr. served as postmaster from 1905 to 1934, when Arthur J. Caisse became postmaster. Elmer Macfarlane was later postmaster from 1958 to 1967, and Eleanor Elton was South Willington's final postmaster, serving from 1967 to 1980.

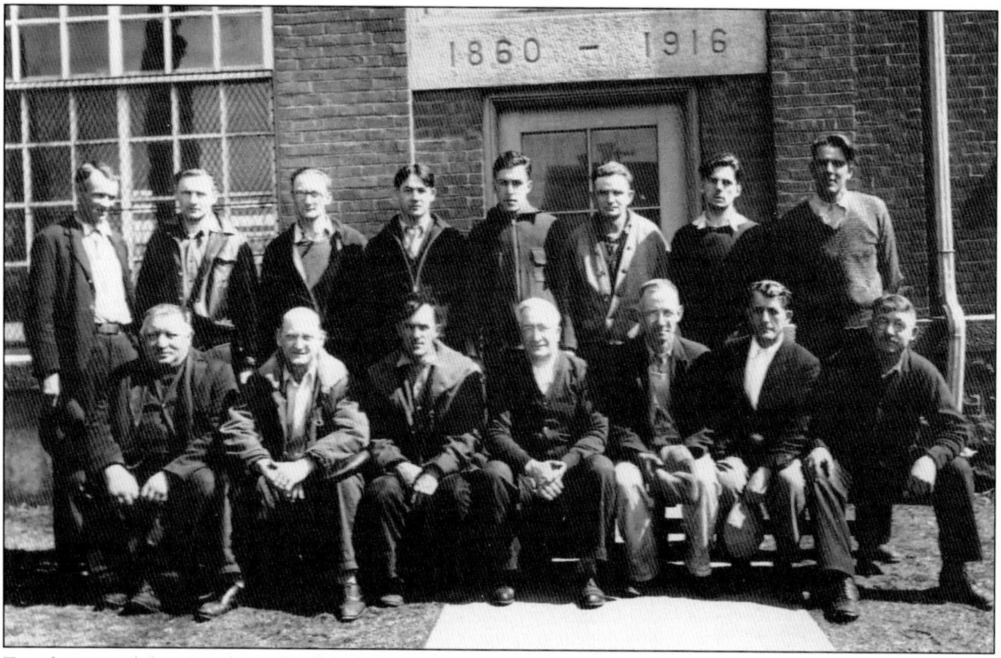

Employees of the Gardiner Hall Jr. Thread Company's bleach house posed for this photograph on April 9, 1934. They are, from left to right, (first row) Frank Zemek, Joseph ?, Steve ?, Roy Walker, John DeCicco, Charles Safranek, and Fred Luchon; (second row) Tom Moriarty, Frank Zemek, Charles Zemek, John Luchon, Fred Tomasko, Roy Waldo, Harry Pospisil, and Walter Mather.

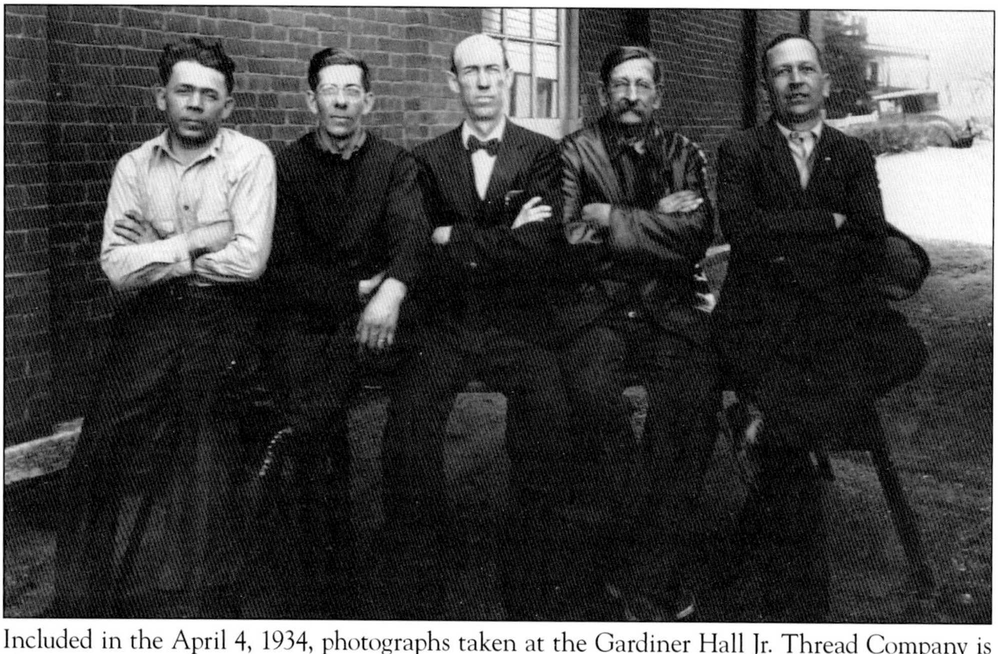

Included in the April 4, 1934, photographs taken at the Gardiner Hall Jr. Thread Company is this one of machine shop workers (from left to right) Henry ?, Ernest Smith, Walter Malo, Lee Royce, and Elmer Macfarlane. The thread company had been in business for approximately 75 years when the April 1934 photographs were taken. It was the major industry in South Willington, providing employment and housing opportunities for residents.

In 1923–1924, long before the advent of electric freezers and ice makers in most homes, the unidentified men in this photograph harvested ice from Hall's Pond. In 1869, the inventive Gardiner Hall Jr. created a process in which ice from the pond was transported via chutes across the road, down the hill, and onto conveyor belts to trains, which then took it miles away to New London.

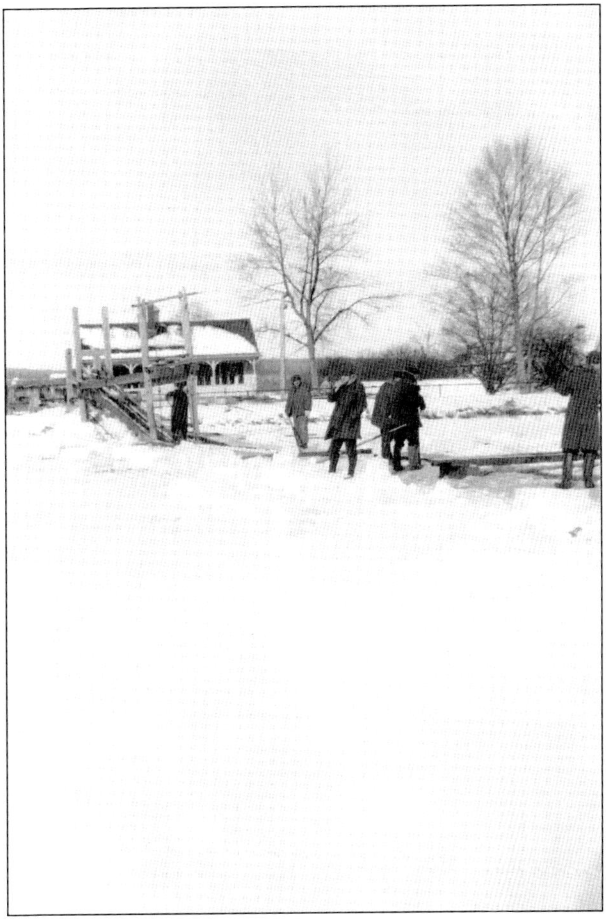

This postcard shows an artist's rendering of the Gardiner Hall Jr. Thread Company employee housing (right). These buildings remain on Village Street today, and many of the apartments are still occupied. (Courtesy of James Buell.)

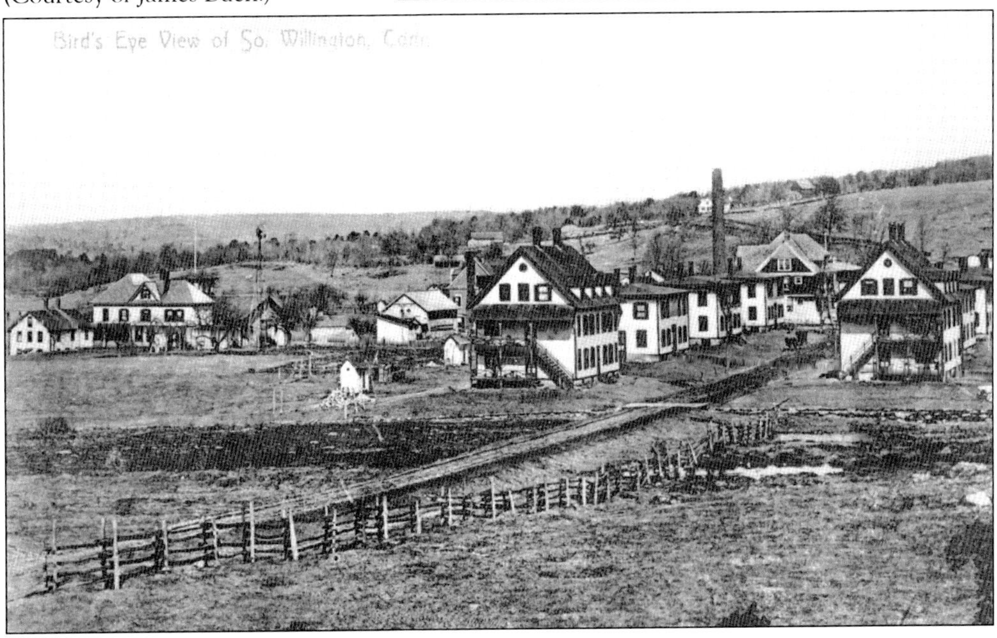

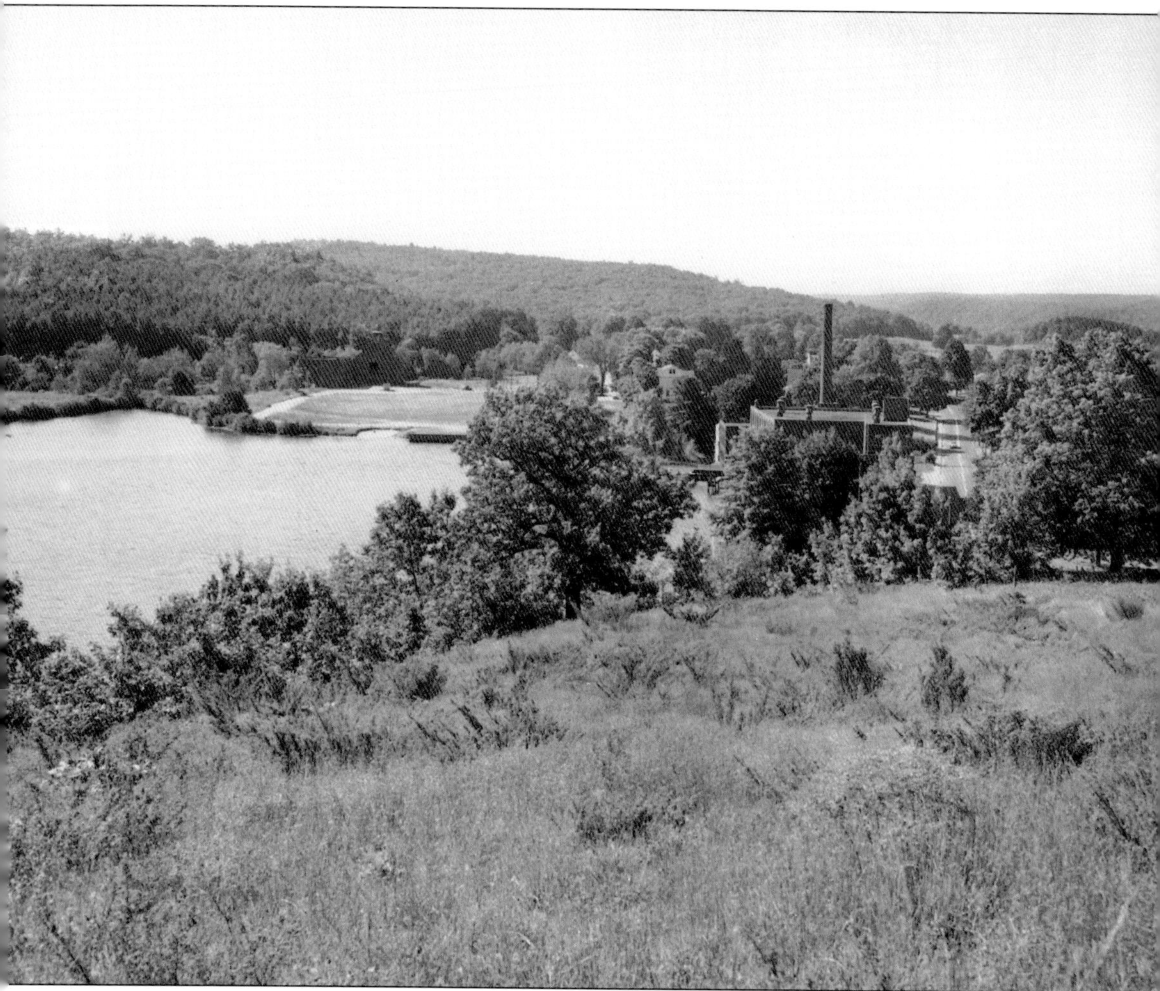

This 1960 photograph shows Hall's Pond, a 20-acre body of water created when a dam was built. In Willington's early days, it was known as Lake Beauty. It was later named Lake Congerhale. The Hall family owned the land surrounding the pond. Talented Hall Thread Company employees built a steamboat that crossed the lake on summer evenings as a recreational activity. Employees were also able to swim in the lake during the summer, and the Hall family held ice-skating parties on the frozen lake in the winter. There is currently a town-owned beach area at one end of the lake that is available to Willington residents. The use of the lake became the subject of a lengthy lawsuit that was brought in 2000 and reached the Connecticut Supreme Court in 2005.

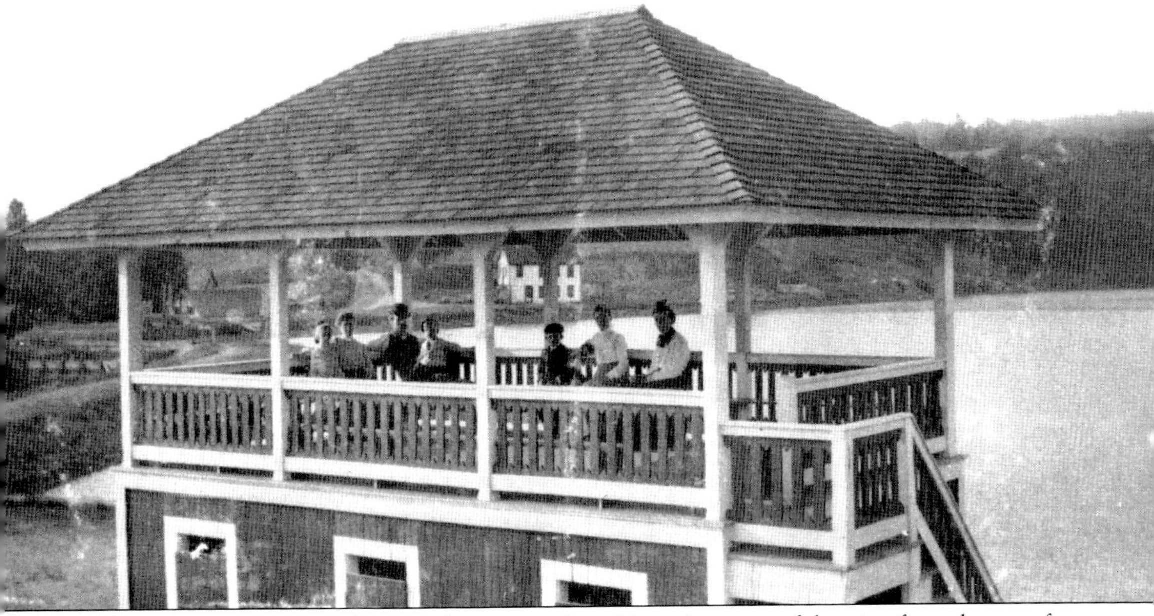

The people in this undated photograph appear to be taking advantage of the view from the top of the bandstand at the south end of Hall's Pond. In the summer of 1875, the Hall Thread Company steamboat made excursions every hour after 6:00 p.m. during the week and after 3:00 p.m. on Saturdays. Since many Willington residents opposed the drinking of alcoholic beverages long before the entire country did so, it is fairly certain that there were no intoxicating beverages either sold or allowed at the bandstand or in the surrounding area. There is no longer a bandstand at Hall's Pond, although current residents who purchase a beach pass from the town are welcome to enjoy swimming at the south end of Hall's Pond from late June through mid-August each year.

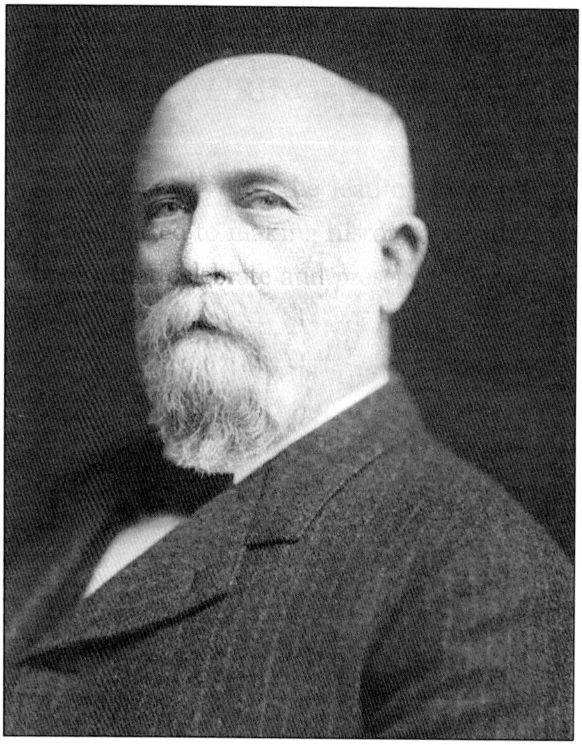

Gardiner Hall Jr. was born in Rhode Island in 1839 and started Willington's most enduring industry as a young man in 1860, when he built his thread factory. The timing was not good, however, and the venture failed due to the Civil War. It was his second attempt, in 1862, that became the profitable Gardiner Hall Jr. Thread Company. Hall was a talented man who, with his wife, Fannie Parker Hall, envisioned and made possible the majority of the village of South Willington, including the boardinghouses they made available for employees, the church they had built in memory of their daughter Clara Hall Elliott, and the school constructed in honor of three generations of the Hall family. Gardiner Hall Jr. died on April 17, 1915. Fannie, born on November 26, 1839, died on November 13, 1923. They each left a lasting mark on the Willington community.

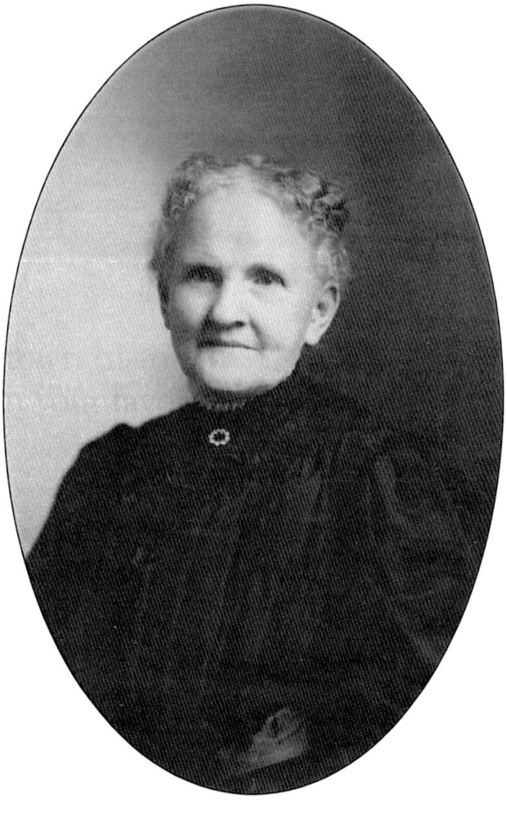

About the Willington Historical Society

Willington Historical Society
Est. 1968

The Willington Historical Society was initially created in 1968 but not incorporated until 1977. It is a nonprofit organization whose purpose is to promote, preserve, and celebrate Willington's history. The society works to identify, acquire, display, and maintain a wide variety of documents, artifacts, and materials of historical significance. The society's interests extend beyond Willington to the surrounding region. Members of the society have conducted extensive research into the history of many early Willington families.

The society publishes a quarterly newsletter, which is distributed not only to members but also to other local historical societies. In addition, it hosts programs four times a year on a variety of topics. Recent programs have discussed the impact of the Civil War on Willington and surrounding towns. Each year, the society reserves a booth at the Federated Church of Willington flea market, where attendees can purchase maps, postcards, and books, as well as view some of the society's artifacts.

As part of her effort to acquire a permanent home for the society's acquisitions, Isabel Weigold, Willington's former town historian, initiated discussions with Edward and Martha Williams regarding their property on what is now Route 74, at the west end of the town common. In 2009, Edward donated the Daniel Glazier Tavern and the surrounding three-acre property to the society. It is estimated that the two-story, hip-roofed building dates to 1815.

The society is in the process of stabilizing and restoring the tavern to function as an interactive museum. The restoration process is supported in part by a matching grant from the Connecticut State Historic Preservation Office. Pictures of the interior and exterior restoration are available on the society's website, at www.willingtonhistoricalsocietyct.org, where visitors may also find information about membership and programs.

All of the authors' proceeds from the sale of this book will be donated to the Willington Historical Society.